I0810322

IMAGES
of America

OAK HARBOR

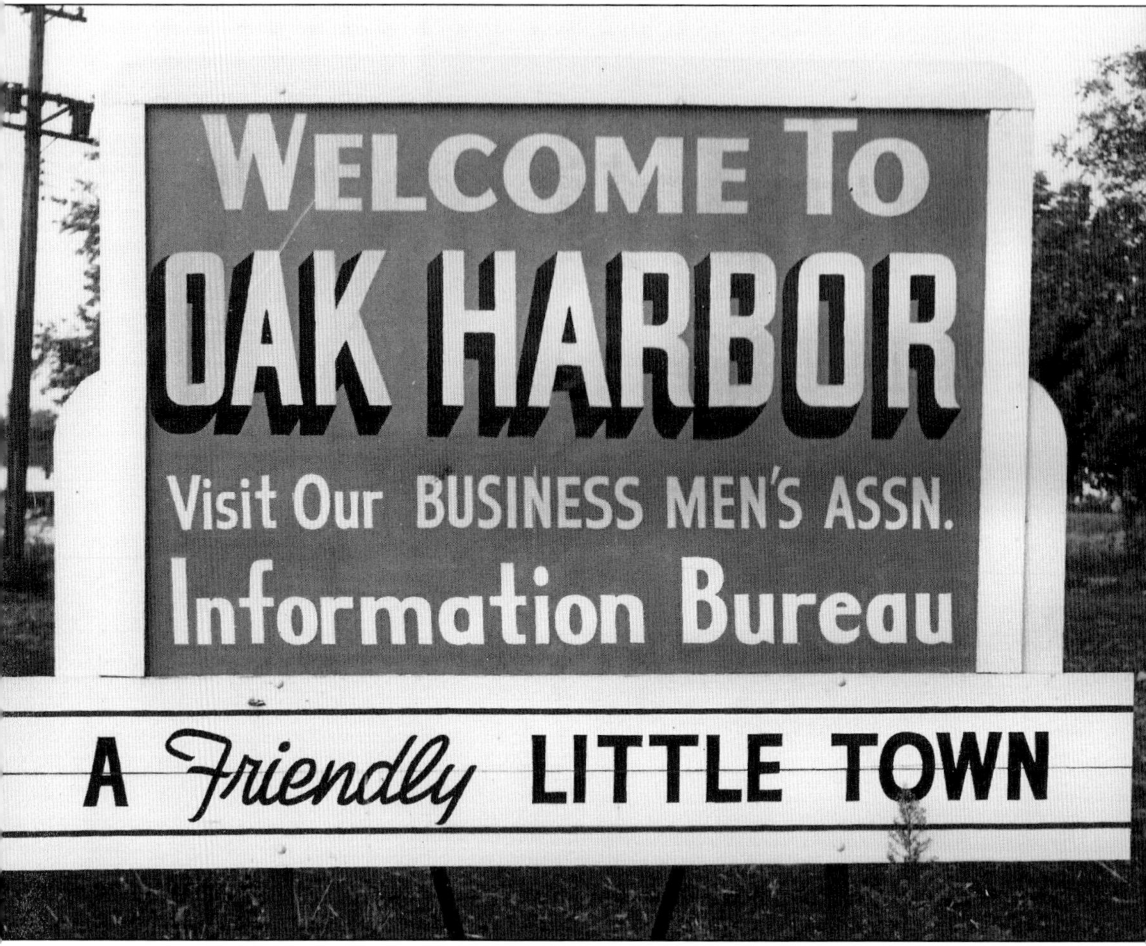

Welcome signs greeted residents and visitors alike as they entered the friendly village of Oak Harbor in the 1950s. (Oak Harbor Public Library.)

ON THE COVER: The Grand Parade of the Oak Harbor Fall Fair was a major event in the community from the 1930s through the early 1960s. Here, local Girl Scouts march before a capacity crowd in a mid-1950s parade. (Bernita Hiles and Sharon Sweeney.)

IMAGES
of America

OAK HARBOR

Frank Gluth, John Liske,
and Richard Martin

ARCADIA
PUBLISHING

ISBN 978-0-7385-9879-6

Published by Arcadia Publishing
Charleston, South Carolina

Printed in the United States of America

Library of Congress Control Number: 2012949828

For all general information, please contact Arcadia Publishing:
Telephone 843-853-2070
Fax 843-853-0044
E-mail sales@arcadiapublishing.com
For customer service and orders:
Toll-Free 1-888-313-2665

Visit us on the Internet at www.arcadiapublishing.com

We dedicate this book to the past, present, and future residents of Oak Harbor. May our hometown's history always be preserved.

Contents

Acknowledgments

After several years of saying that someone ought to write a pictorial history of Oak Harbor, the three of us—Frank Gluth, John Liske, and Richard Martin—decided to do it. Inspired by Jennifer Fording, of the Harris-Elmore Public Library, who had just completed an Images of America book on neighboring Elmore and Genoa, the three of us got busy and began our quest for photographs. We sincerely thank Jennifer for her advice and support.

We were also very thankful to have the support of Lina Hall, head librarian, along with the employees and trustees of the Oak Harbor Public Library (OHPL). Without their support in allowing us access to pictures, to meeting room facilities, and to museum resources, this book would not have been possible. All author royalties from this book will be donated to the Oak Harbor Public Library to use as staff sees fit in preserving our local history.

We were very pleased with the support we received from present and past Oak Harbor residents who searched through their attics to find photographs we might use. We wish we had room to print every image we scanned.

We would like to thank Peggy Dieben and Kevin Winters of the Ottawa County Historical Museum (OCHM) and Dorothy Waterhouse and Donna Gyde of the Carroll Township History Committee (CTHC) for their respective museum's contributions. We also thank the *Ottawa County Exponent* for its help in promoting our search for photographs.

We have tried to acknowledge the source of each image printed in this book, either by OHPL, OCHM, CTHC, or the name of the individual contributor. Photographs contributed by each of the three authors are listed by his last name only. We sincerely thank each and every one of you who submitted images. All photographs that were scanned, whether published in this book or not, are available for viewing on CD at the Local History Room and Museum Center on the lower level of the Oak Harbor Public Library.

Finally, the three authors would like to thank our wives—Deanna Gluth, Sharon Liske, and Judy Martin—for their tolerance and support as we took on this project.

Introduction

Oak Harbor has a long and colorful history, originating with a man named Adolphus Kraemer, a Toledo, Ohio, merchant who, in the mid-1830s, dreamed of developing a town near the headwaters of the Portage River that would rival the likes of Cleveland and Detroit. Although the village was first platted under the name of Hartford by Joseph Wardlow in 1835, it was Adolphus Kraemer and his family who settled in the Black Swamp wilderness and developed the village that was to become Oak Harbor.

The name Hartford was likely selected because the town was located just west of the Firelands, an area set aside for residents of Connecticut whose homes had been destroyed by fire during the Revolutionary War. The village's name created some problems for the Post Office Department, however, as there were several other Hartfords in Ohio. So, in 1845, Adolphus Kraemer suggested that the name of the post office be changed to Oak Harbor, since the town was located on a river harbor and there was an abundance of oak trees in the area. Interestingly, there must have been an error in communication when the name was selected, because the postal service officially listed the village's post office as Oakharbor—one word instead of two. In addition, while the post office became Oakharbor in 1845, the town did not officially change its name from Hartford to Oak Harbor until 1863.

While the town was known as Oak Harbor, the post office was Oakharbor. This created some interesting confusion. Believe it or not, it took the postal office 120 years to finally get it straight. In 1965, the Post Office Department officially revised the spelling of the Oak Harbor post office to its correct name. However, if one looks at the name carved in the front of the 1939-era post office, one will still see "OAKHARBOR."

With the abundance of oak and other hardwood trees in the area, Oak Harbor was initially a lumber town with many sawmills and stave, barrel, and basket factories. Many logs were floated up the Portage River to the sawmills in Oak Harbor. In the early years, hundreds of men were employed by these mills and factories. These were often hardworking and hard-drinking men. In fact, in 1894 Oak Harbor boasted 16 saloons, far exceeding its number of churches.

As the timber industry began to wane in the middle to late 1800s, the area began to see an influx of German immigrants, many from the lowlands of northern Germany, who understood how to drain and farm this swampy land. So, by the turn of the century, Oak Harbor's economy had transferred to a mostly agricultural base of traditional crops such as corn, hay, oats, and wheat, but also tomatoes, sugar beets, peaches, and apples. The town continued to grow alongside the businesses and industries supporting this agrarian economy.

Oak Harbor showed significant growth from the mid-1870s through the early 1900s, when two rail lines and one interurban line came through the village. In 1872, the Lake Shore & Michigan Southern Railway crossed the northern edge of the village, and in 1882, the Wheeling & Lake Erie rail line came through the center of Oak Harbor. With the advent of rail service, the river became much less important for shipping and transportation. Then, in 1903–1904, the Toledo, Port Clinton and Lakeside interurban electric streetcar line passed through Oak Harbor. This gave Oak Harbor residents quick and easy access to Toledo and points beyond.

The period from the 1870s through the late 1920s could be considered the golden age of Oak Harbor. As you reads through this book, you will note many of Oak Harbor's downtown business blocks were built between 1885 and 1915. Although somewhat modified, most of these buildings remain in place today.

Likewise, many churches and homes were also built in the early part of the 20th century. In many cases, the current churches of Oak Harbor are the second or third building constructed by the congregation, the first being a wood-frame structure, followed by a smaller brick structure, and then a large brick or stone structure.

Much of Oak Harbor's growth can be credited to the Kraemer family, including the aforementioned Adolphus Kraemer, his son James H. (J.H.) Kraemer, and grandson DeWilton A. Kraemer. Adolphus and J.H. wore many hats, including serving as county prosecuting attorneys and county probate judges. They also owned the local newspaper, the *Ottawa County Exponent*, which was established in 1871 and has been in continuous publication ever since. In fact, the Kraemers were credited with convincing the owners of both the Lake Shore & Michigan Southern (LS&MS) and the Wheeling & Lake Erie (W&LE) rail lines to route their planned tracks through Oak Harbor even though it required laying a number of extra miles of track. DeWilton followed his father's role as editor of the *Ottawa County Exponent*, serving in that capacity from 1897 to 1946. In 1946, the *Ottawa County Exponent* was sold to a group of investors and is still published as a weekly newspaper.

One thing the Kraemers did not achieve, however, was the establishment of Oak Harbor as the county seat. When Ottawa County was formed in 1840, just a few years after Hartford was platted, Adolphus Kraemer campaigned to have the county seat situated in Hartford. However, Port Clinton, established a number of years earlier, and significantly larger, was selected. When a new courthouse was needed in 1898, J.H. and DeWilton Kraemer also campaigned vigorously but unsuccessfully to have the county seat moved to Oak Harbor.

As the 20th century progressed, Oak Harbor has gone the way of many small towns across the nation. Trains no longer stop there. The interurban electric rail line fell victim to the automobile. Farms became larger and less diversified. Families became smaller. Many family-owned retail stores could not compete with the big-box stores in neighboring communities. Employment was no longer found in small machine shops but rather in large industries, such as the Davis-Besse Nuclear Power Station, located just north of the village. While Oak Harbor still has a viable business district, the village has largely become a bedroom community.

Like many small communities, Oak Harbor's strength is in its people. Many families have lived in the area for generations. The spirit that Adolphus Kraemer and the early pioneers possessed remains in the people of today's Oak Harbor. Through photographs and stories, the three authors have tried to capture and preserve the essence of Oak Harbor's history and spirit.

One

In the Beginning, It Was Hartford

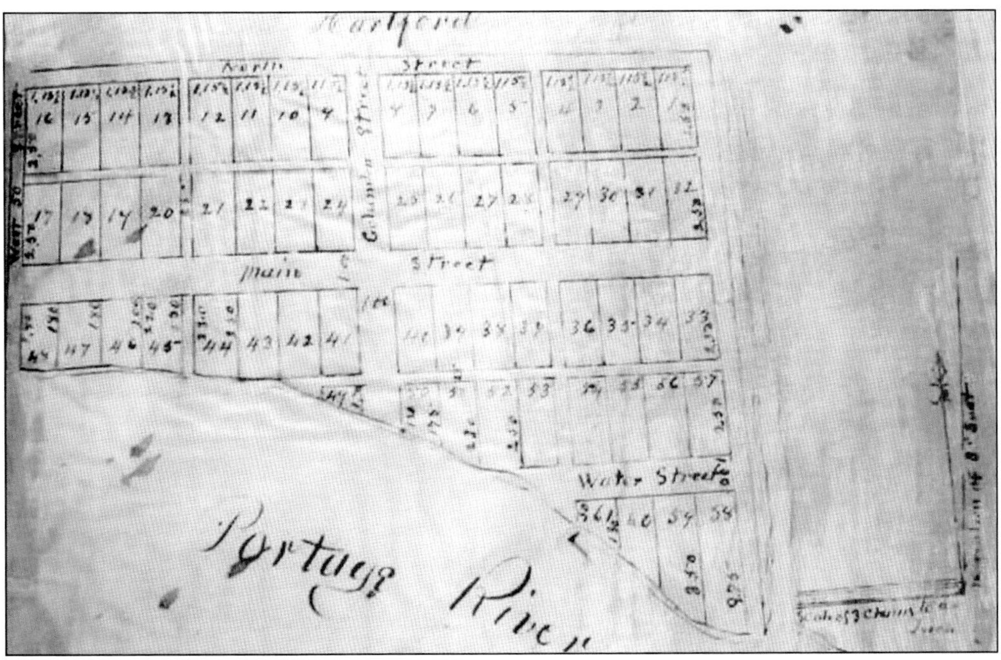

The original plat map for the village of Hartford was surveyed for Joseph Wardlow, a land speculator. It was filed at the Sandusky County Court House on April 7, 1835, since Ottawa County had not yet been established. From this humble beginning, Adolphus Kraemer began to fulfill his dream of establishing the town that was to become Oak Harbor. (Martin.)

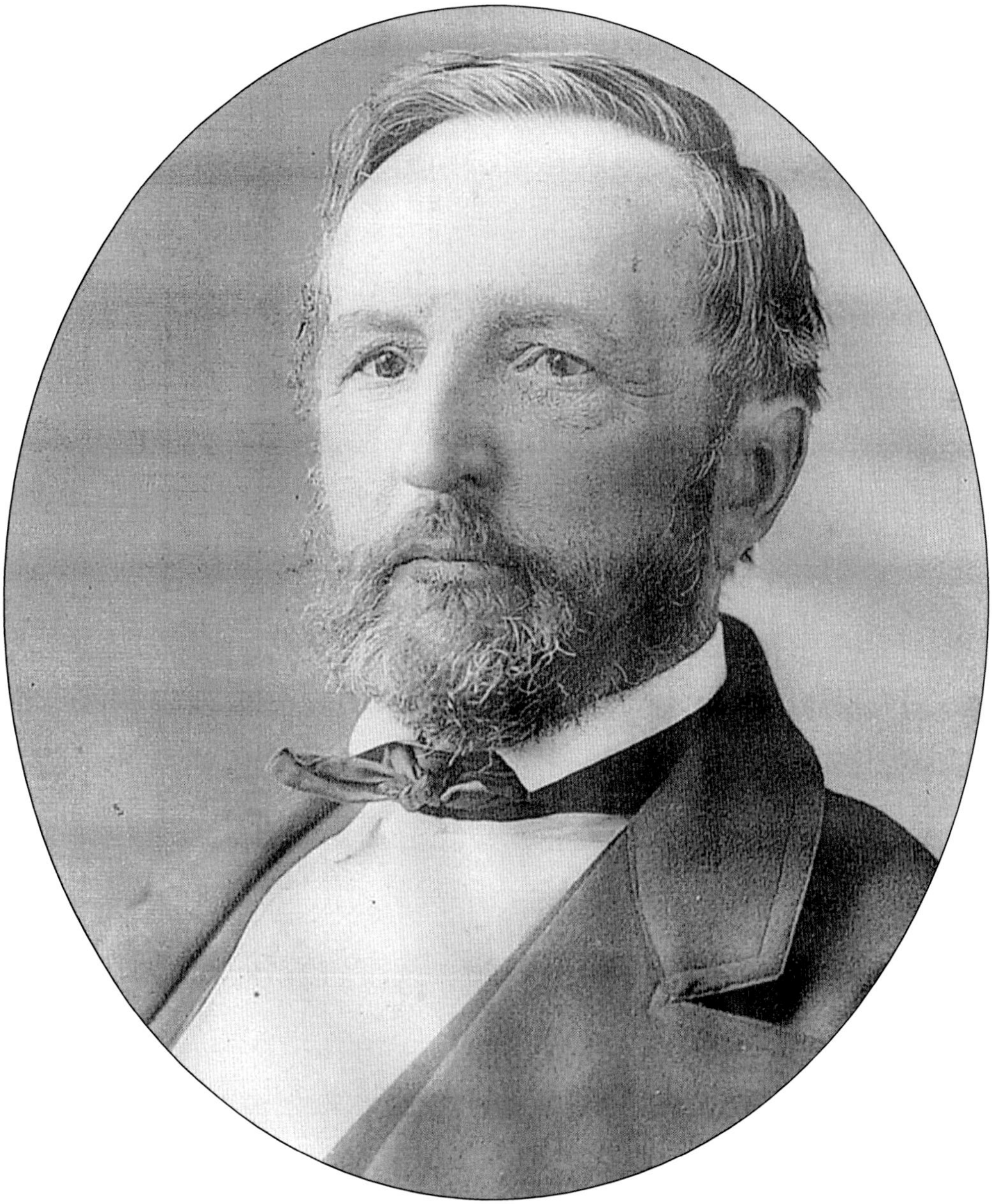

Adolphus Kraemer (1810–1885) was born, raised, and educated in Germany. After immigrating to the United States, he settled in Toledo, where he was a local merchant and attorney. In 1836, he purchased much of the land originally platted as Hartford by Joseph Wardlow and expanded the plat to encompass much of today's Oak Harbor. After settling his family in this heavily forested land along the Portage River, he established a sawmill and general store. He later served as a probate judge, county surveyor, and prosecuting attorney. He also farmed and practiced medicine. A loyal Democrat, he was a delegate to the State of Ohio Constitutional Convention in 1873 and 1874. Kraemer was also given credit for suggesting the name Oak Harbor when the Post Office Department asked for Hartford's name to be changed. Adolphus and Eliza Kraemer had eleven children—eight boys and three girls. The Kraemer family and their descendants continued to be political and business leaders in Ottawa County well into the 20th century. (Gluth.)

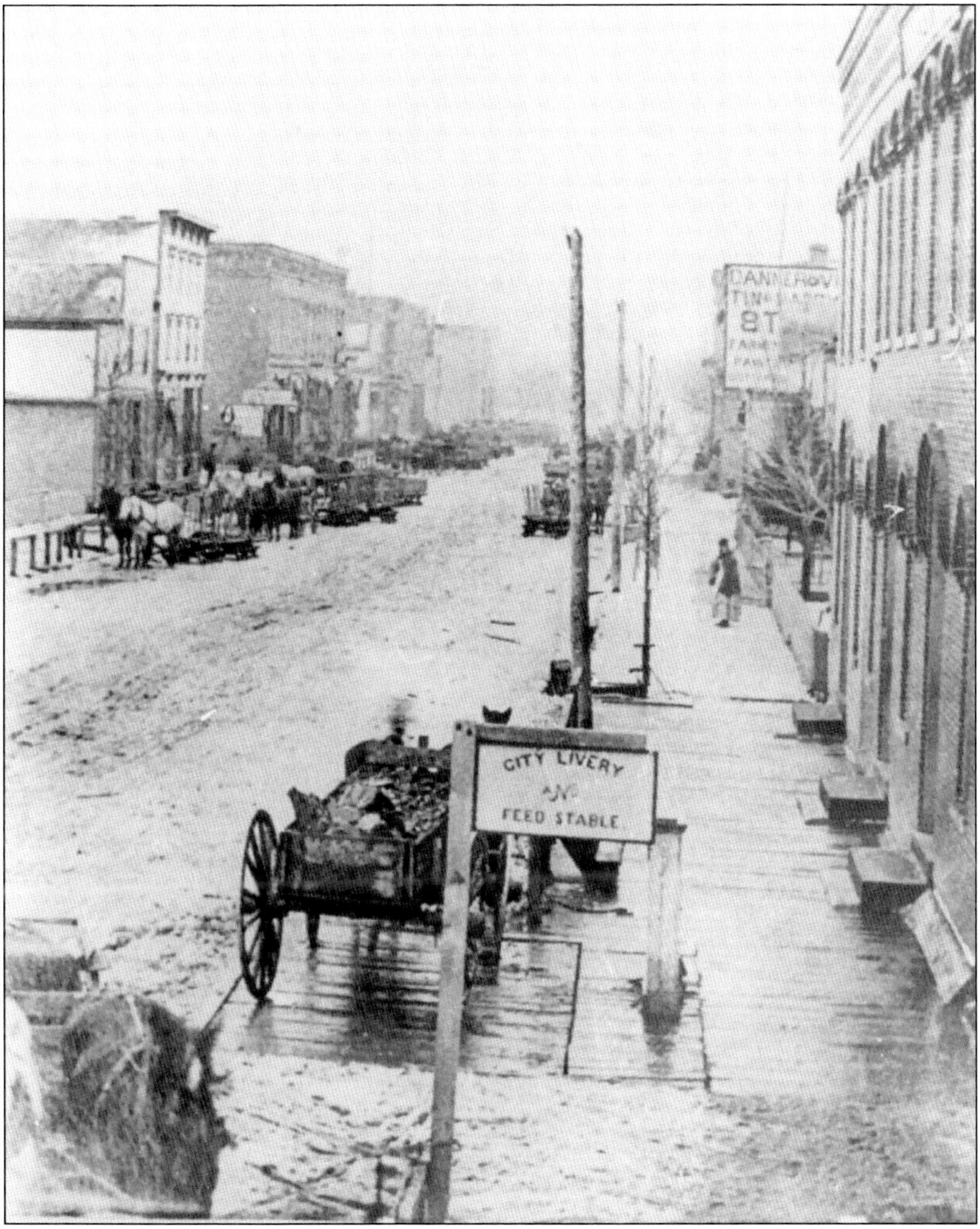

Taken by Jacob Hoover on Christmas Eve in 1883, this is the earliest photograph known to exist of Oak Harbor. Hoover was one of three early photographers, along with J. Windisch and George D. Smith, who visually recorded many of Oak Harbor's early scenes. This particular photograph was taken looking to the east from the south side of Water Street (across from the present fire station) . The brick building on the right was a hotel known as the Portage House. It was built about 1878, replacing the Vogel House hotel, which was destroyed by fire. The Portage House was destroyed in the great fire of 1894, which burned everything on the south side of Water Street from Church Street to the railroad. The three-story wooden building on the left side of the photograph was the original Fought grocery store, located on the northwest corner of Church and Water Streets, the site of the present hotel. (OCHM.)

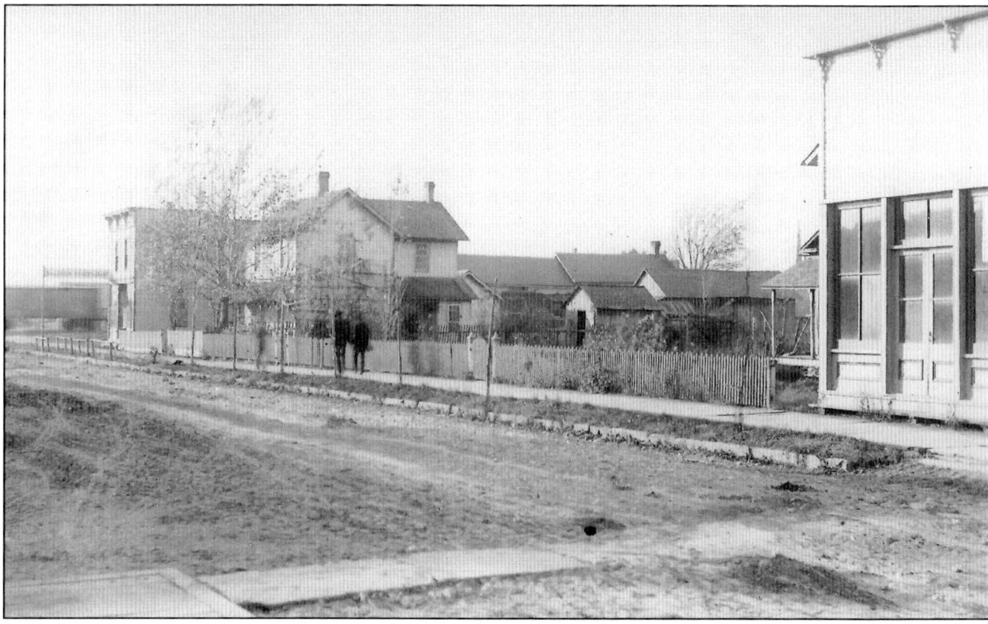

This photograph, taken between 1885 and 1892, is looking west on Water Street, midway between Church Street and the railroad. None of the buildings in the photograph remain today. On the left is a train crossing Water Street on the Wheeling & Lake Erie tracks. The building on the right is the site now occupied by the fire department, and the building near the railroad was a saloon. (OHPL.)

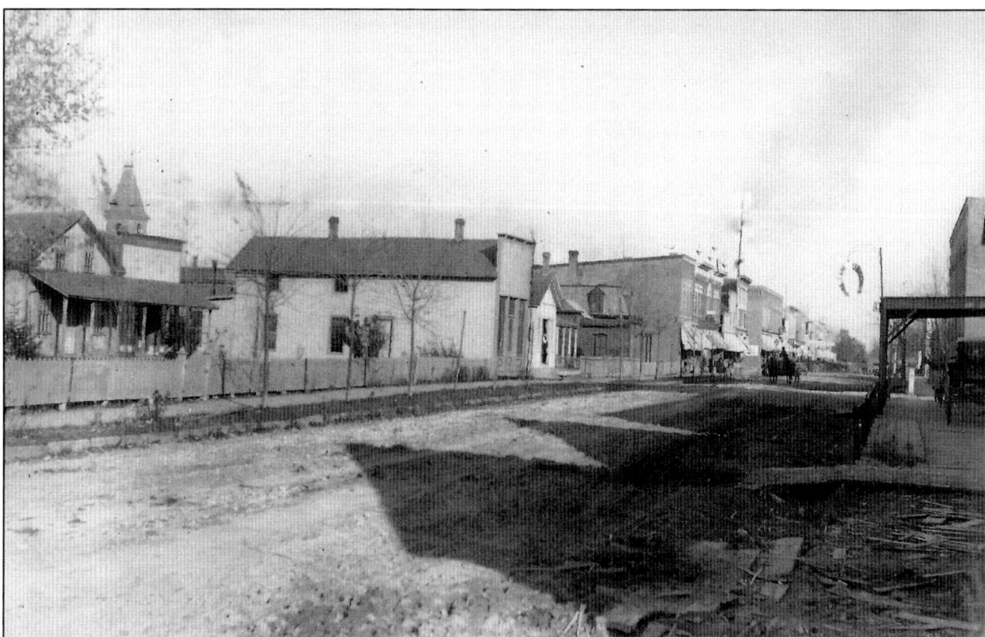

Most likely from the same time period as the one at top, this photograph of Water Street was taken looking east from the railroad. The store at center is the same building found on the right in this photograph. On the extreme right is the Leow Blacksmith Shop and the Portage House hotel. Although wooden curbs were in place, streets were largely unimproved. (OHPL.)

The Schell Saloon was located on the southwest corner of Water and Church Streets. It was owned by Gottlieb Schell, and early advertisements indicate it was a place for groceries and provisions as well as a saloon and boardinghouse. This photograph was taken sometime prior to the 1894 fire. (Liske.)

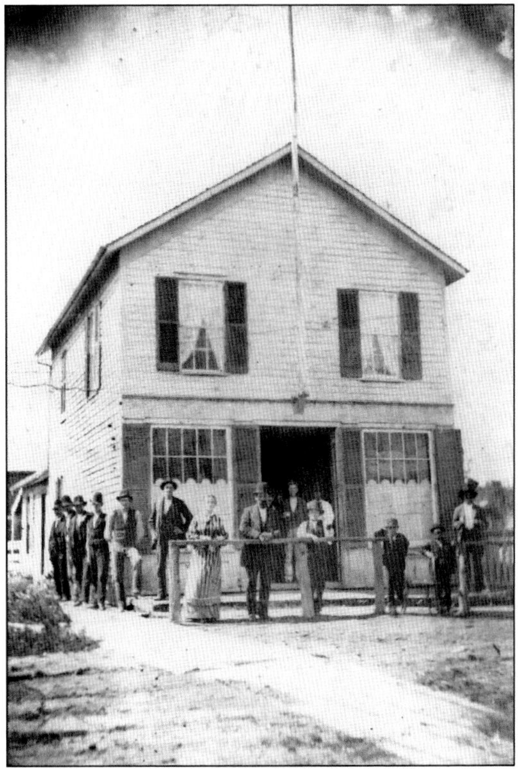

This c. 1900 photograph shows the Pomerenke saloon and house, on the southwest corner of South Railroad and Church Streets. The saloon provided food and drink for travelers on the Lake Shore railway in northern Oak Harbor. The house and saloon were later separated, with the house remaining at the South Railroad site and the saloon now a house at 601 Church Street. (Becky Lewis.)

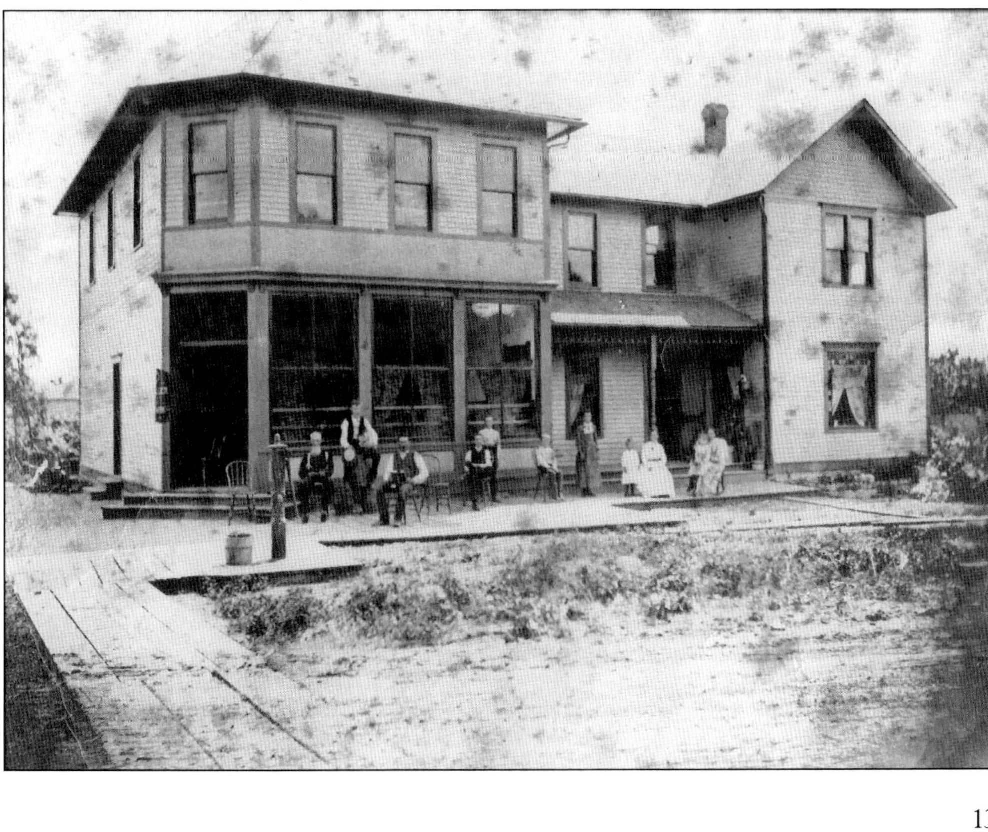

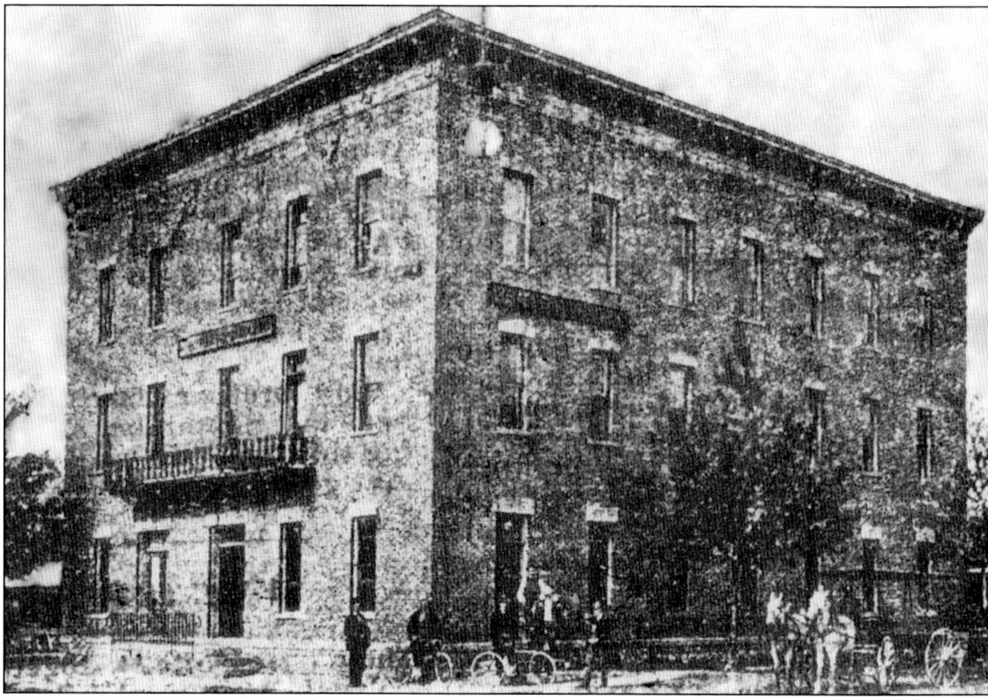

This is the only photograph known to exist of the three-story Central Hotel, located on the northeast corner of Church and Main Streets. Although appearing to be a substantial brick building, the hotel lasted less than 20 years, from 1887 until the early 1900s, when it was converted into a one-story mitten factory. This is the site of the present municipal building. (Martin.)

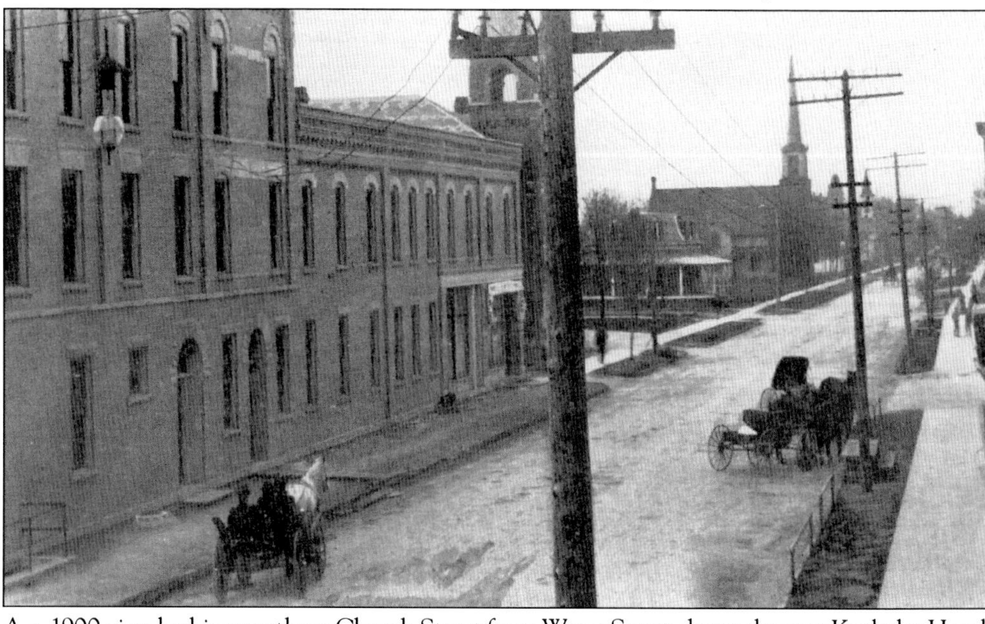

A c. 1900 view looking north on Church Street from Water Street shows the new Kuebeler Hotel, with the original 1883 Town Hall immediately behind it. Farther down the street can be seen the Methodist church and its steeple, at the corner of Church and Ottawa Streets. The steeple was removed in 1902. On the right is the cornice of the three-story Central Hotel. (Liske.)

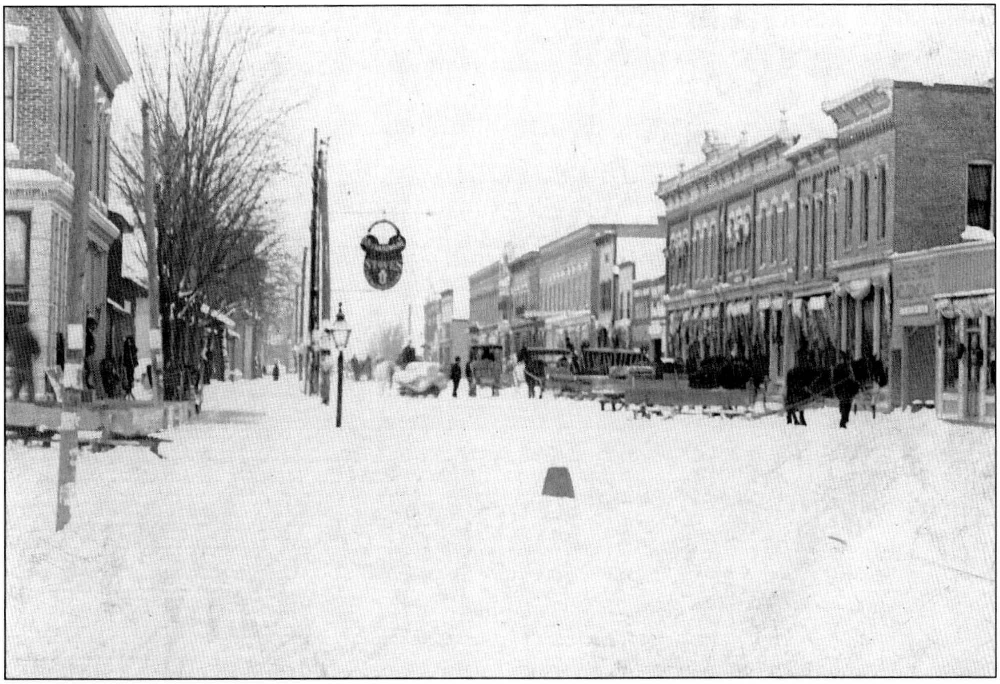

Looking west from the Locust Street intersection, this snowy view of Water Street was likely captured between 1894 and 1898. Horses and sleighs are the form of transportation on this busy winter day. Note the gas streetlights and the unusual key lock sign of City Hardware's sign. (OHPL.)

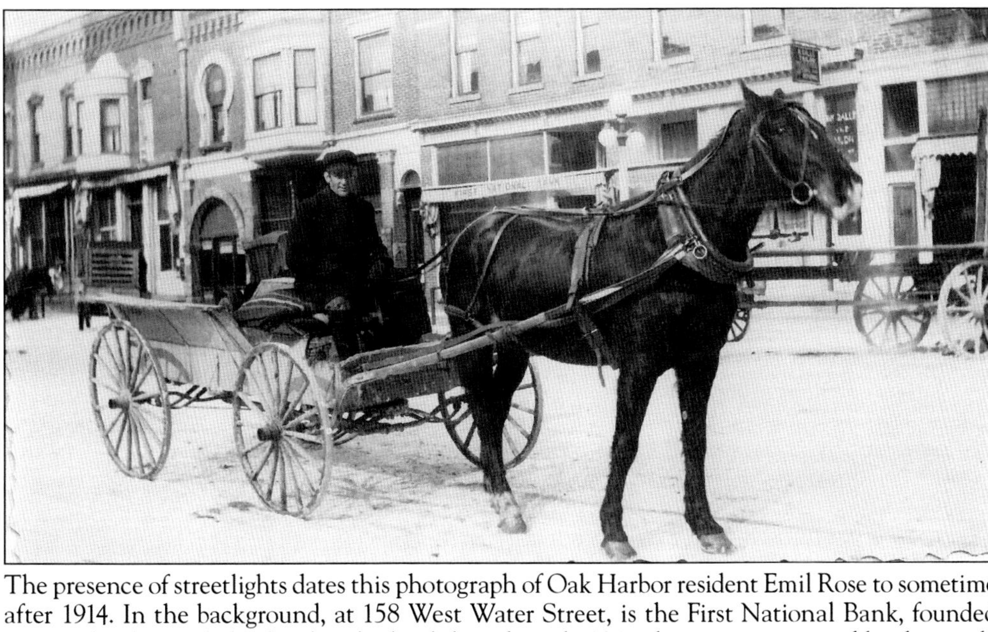

The presence of streetlights dates this photograph of Oak Harbor resident Emil Rose to sometime after 1914. In the background, at 158 West Water Street, is the First National Bank, founded in 1903 by the Kuebeler family. The bank lasted until 1934, when it was acquired by the newly formed National Bank of Oak Harbor. (Mary Paulsen.)

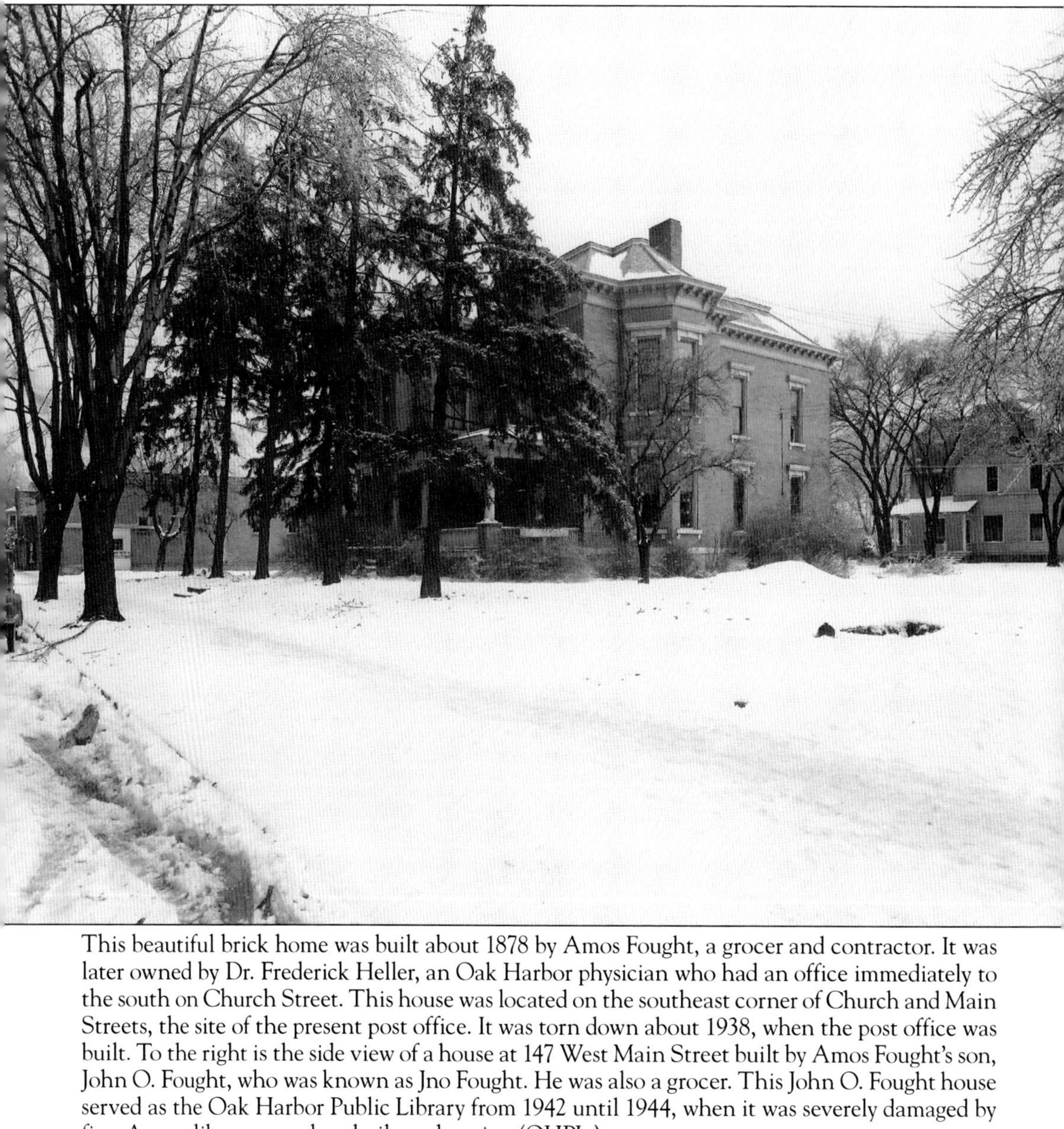

This beautiful brick home was built about 1878 by Amos Fought, a grocer and contractor. It was later owned by Dr. Frederick Heller, an Oak Harbor physician who had an office immediately to the south on Church Street. This house was located on the southeast corner of Church and Main Streets, the site of the present post office. It was torn down about 1938, when the post office was built. To the right is the side view of a house at 147 West Main Street built by Amos Fought's son, John O. Fought, who was known as Jno Fought. He was also a grocer. This John O. Fought house served as the Oak Harbor Public Library from 1942 until 1944, when it was severely damaged by fire. A new library was then built at that site. (OHPL.)

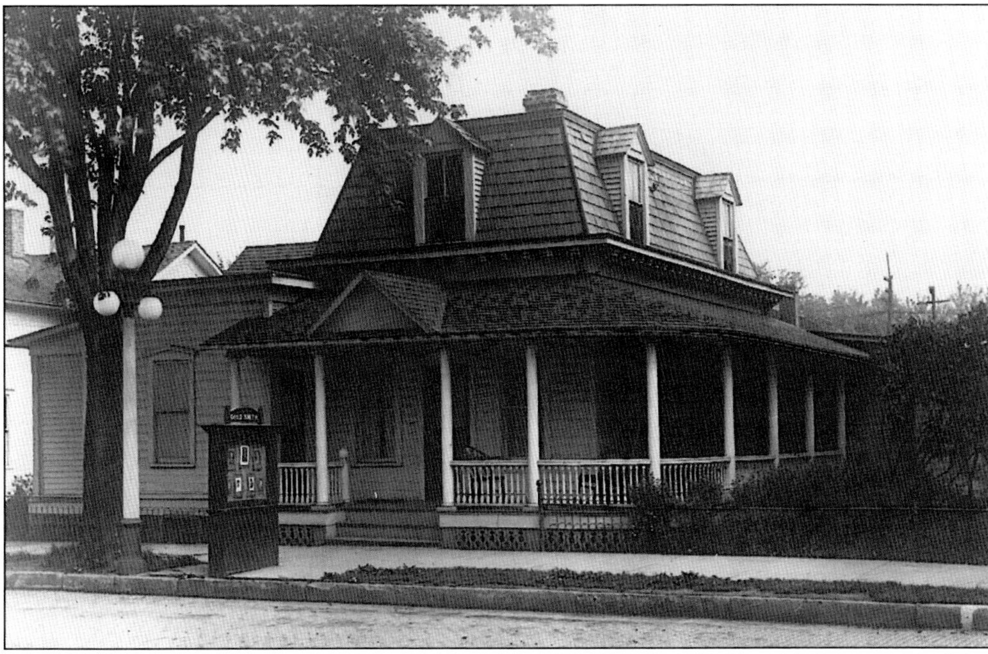

This home at 224 West Water Street was built about 1864 and owned by Jacob Hoover, one of Oak Harbor's early photographers. It was purchased around 1898 by another photographer, George D. Smith, who also used it as a residence and studio. Several generations of Oak Harbor residents likely have photographs taken by Smith or Hoover in their attics. (OHPL.)

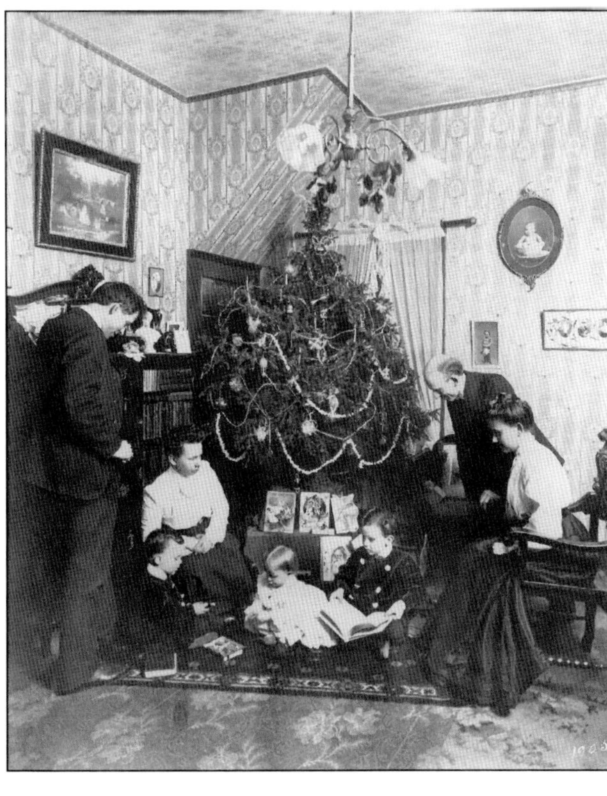

With three boys, Christmas morning at the George D. Smith home must have been an exciting time. Smith graduated from Oak Harbor High School in 1893 before entering the photography profession. He is seen here (far left) at his West Water Street home with his wife, Celena Smith (far right), their three sons, and most likely one set of grandparents. (OHPL.)

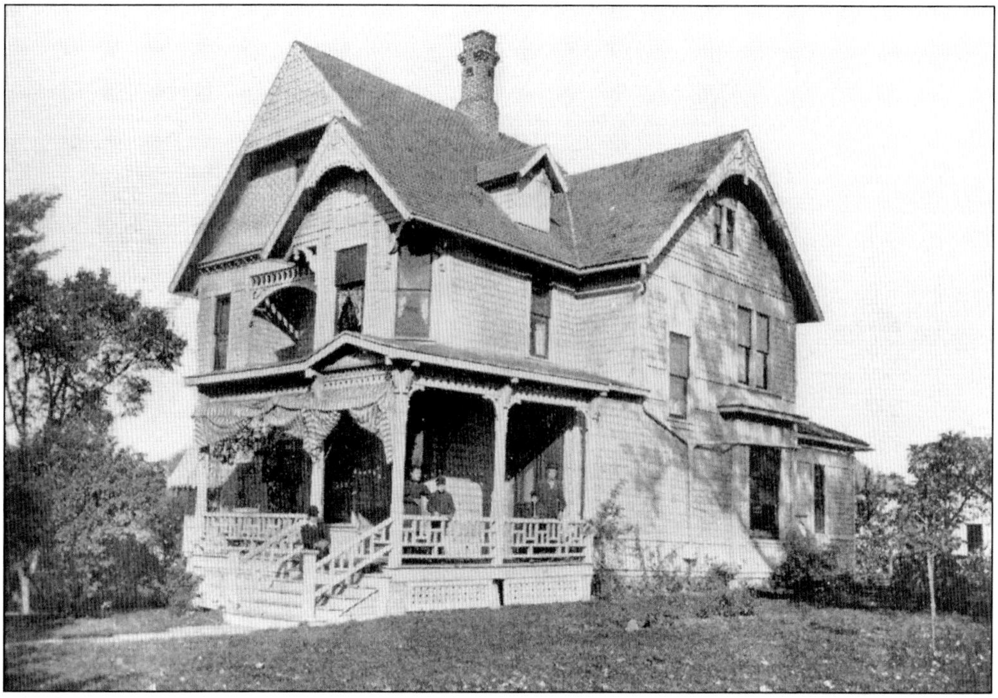

This home, at 120 East Water Street, was built in 1910 by J.H. Kraemer, one of Adolphus Kraemer's sons. J.H., an accomplished businessman and political figure, followed in his father's footsteps, serving as editor and publisher of the local newspaper, the *Ottawa County Exponent*. He was also elected Ottawa County probate judge in 1896. After his election, J.H. turned the editorship of the *Exponent* over to his son, DeWilton A. Kraemer, who served as editor for the next 50 years, retiring in 1946. In the early 1950s, the Kraemer home fell into disrepair and was greatly modified into the apartment building seen below. That structure was removed, along with another home, in 1995 when a McDonald's restaurant was built at the site. (Both, OHPL.)

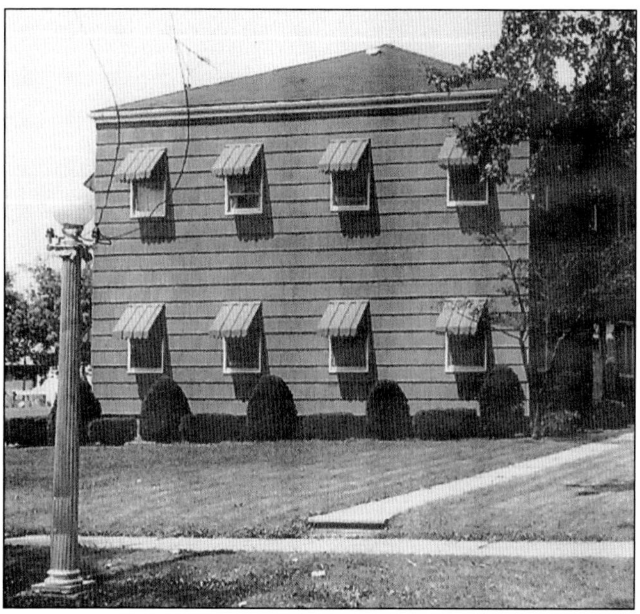

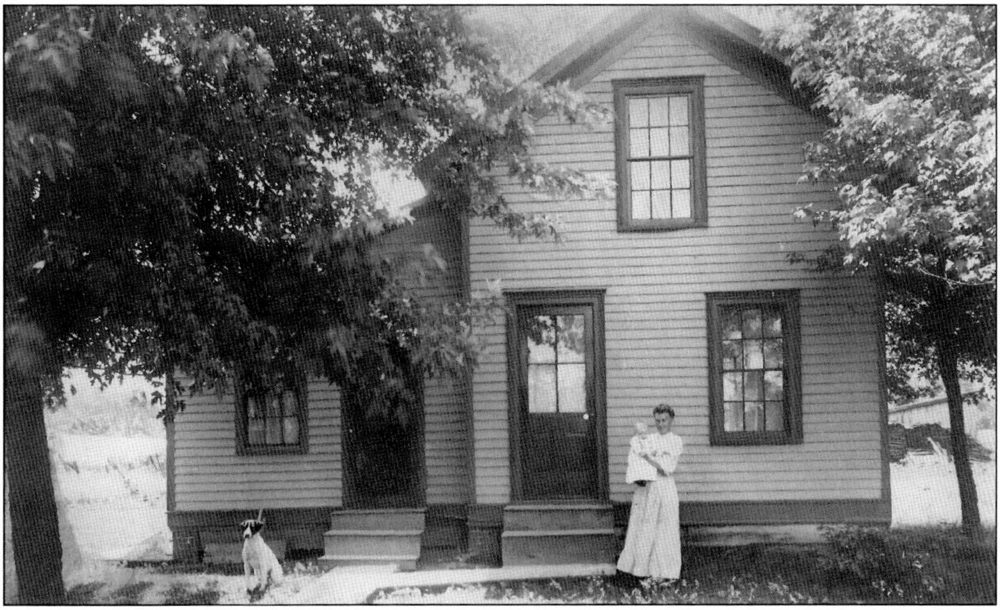

Home construction boomed in Oak Harbor in the late 1800s and early 1900s. The above photograph, taken prior to 1912, shows one of the earlier homes constructed in the northern part of town, at 121 Houghton Street. The nicely kept residence was owned by Albert and Agnes (Schelhase) Rose. Shown here are Agnes and her baby daughter, Luella. The home, although greatly modified, still stands today. In the below photograph, workmen take a break as they construct a new brick home at 227 Church Street, which still stands at that site today. The workmen are wearing nail aprons from the Graves & Meyer Hardware store, which operated from about 1902 through the mid-1920s. (Above, Mary Paulsen; below, OHPL.)

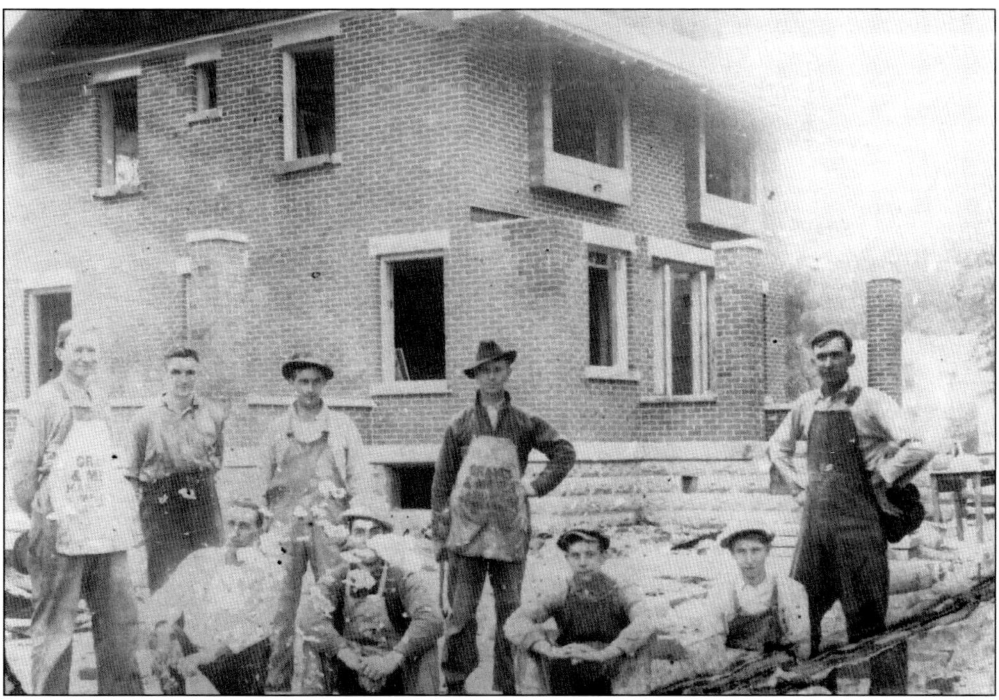

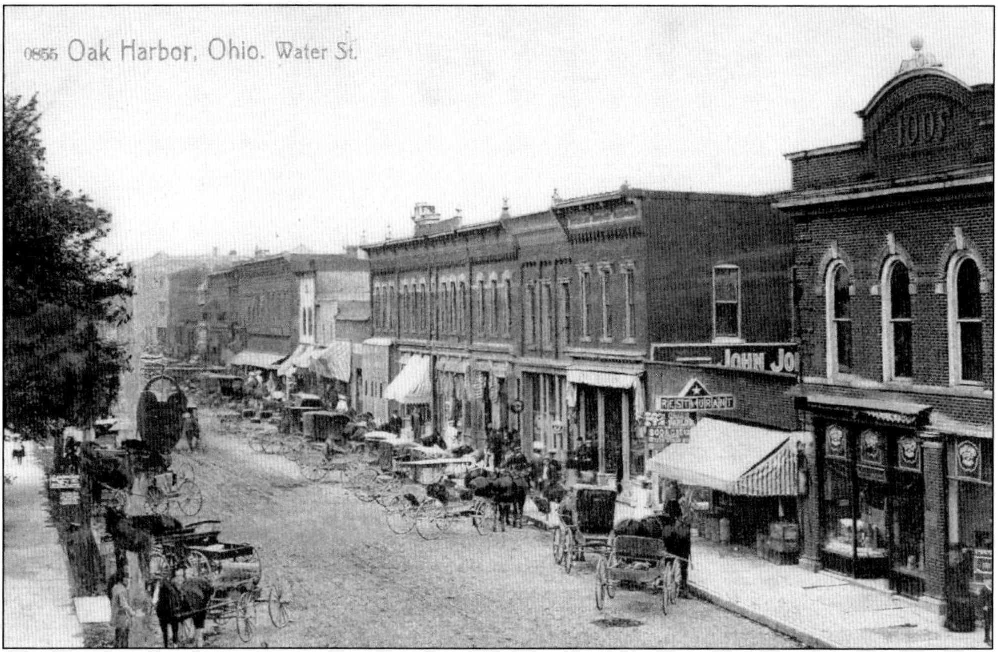

These two photographs of Water Street, one looking east and the other looking west, were taken between 1900 and 1914. The above scene looks west from near the corner of Locust and Water Streets. Most likely, the photographer was standing on the balcony of the Kramb Company building, erected in 1900, located at the southeast corner of Locust and Water Streets. The IOOF lodge building is visible on the right. The below photograph was taken looking east from the intersection of Church and Water Streets. Note the sign for Jno O. Fought, grocer, on the left. Most of the buildings depicted in these two scenes are still present over a century later. (Both, Liske.)

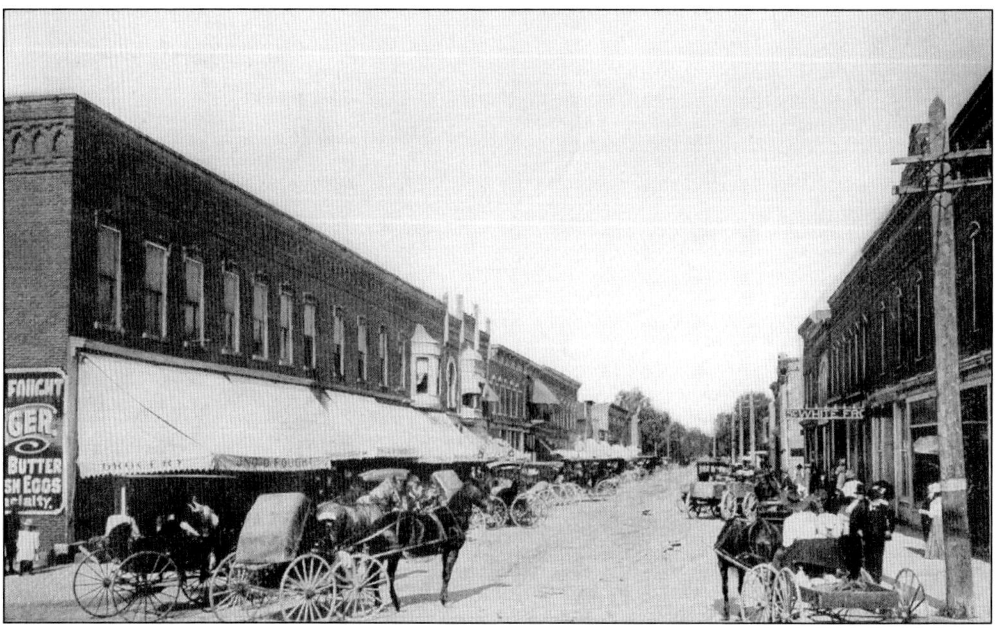

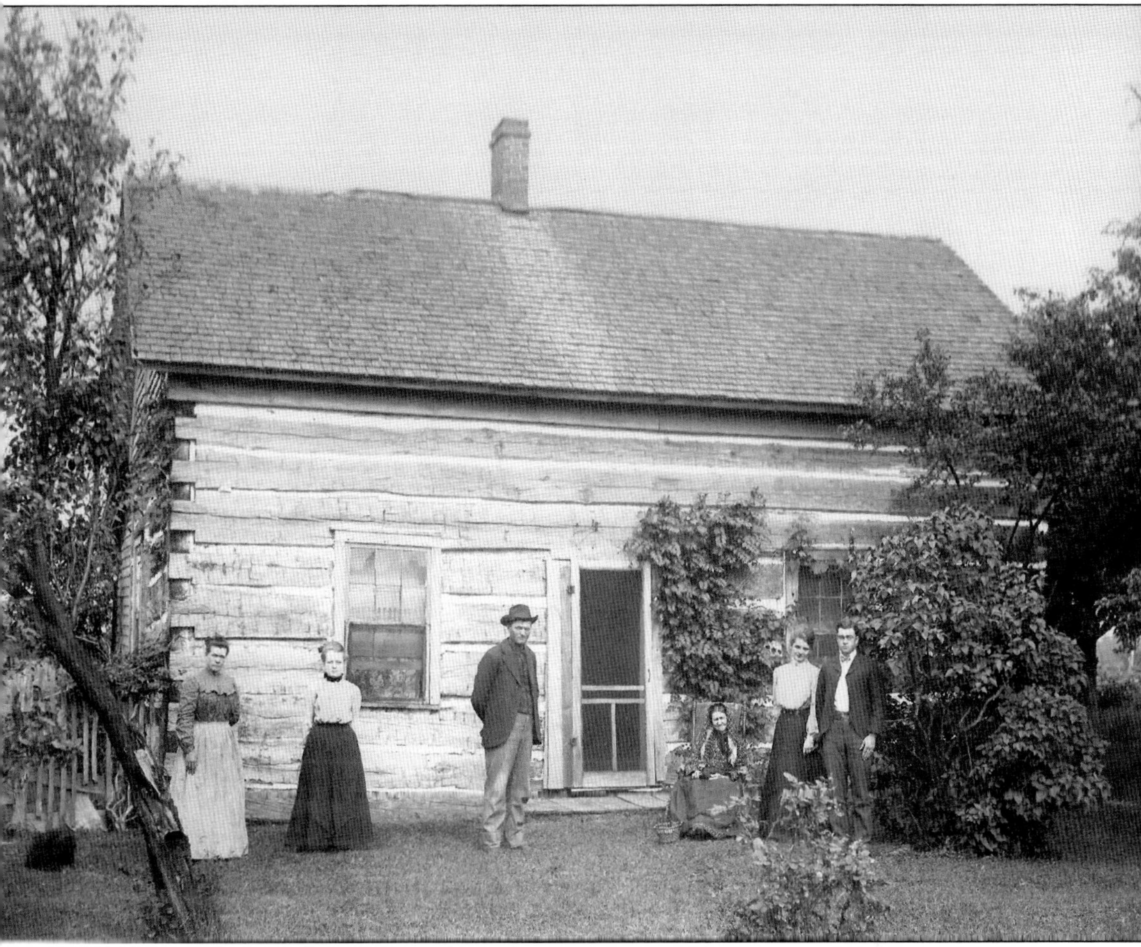

Log houses were very common in the surrounding rural area and within Oak Harbor prior to 1900. This log structure, typical of many built from the mid-1800s, was erected by Henry Nehlig around 1863. It was located near the northeast corner of State Route 105 and Benton-Carroll Road, west of Oak Harbor. By the time this photograph was taken in 1904, the house was owned by the Link family, who purchased it, along with an adjoining 40 acres, in 1871. John Link, wearing a hat by the front door, was head of the household. He lived with his sister Mary (Link) Smith (far left) and their mother, Mary Link, who is seated in the rocking chair. Mary Link was 81 years old when this photograph was taken. Amazingly, she lived to be almost 99 years old. The photograph was taken following the wedding ceremony of their niece, Cora Stewart Leeders (second from right), who had just married Lawrence Leeders (far right). Also pictured is Myrt Stewart Leow (second from left). (OCHM.)

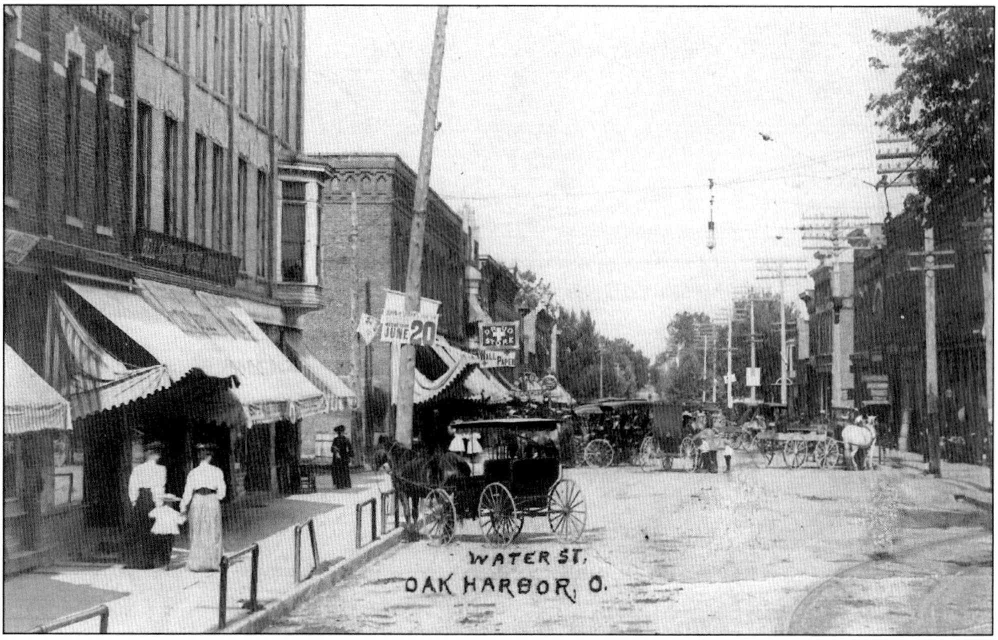

Here are two Water Street scenes from different years. The above photograph was taken in 1906, based on the Wednesday, June 20 sign advertising the Sparks Circus. One has to wonder why the two ladies and young child on the left are dressed so nicely. Were they on their way to the circus? The bottom photograph, taken from a similar position, shows the Toledo, Port Clinton and Lakeside interurban car as it makes its turn from Water Street on to South Church Street. The sign on the back of the streetcar is advertising the Bowling Green Fair. The sign at left is from George Smith's photography studio, displaying some of his recent works. (Both, Liske.)

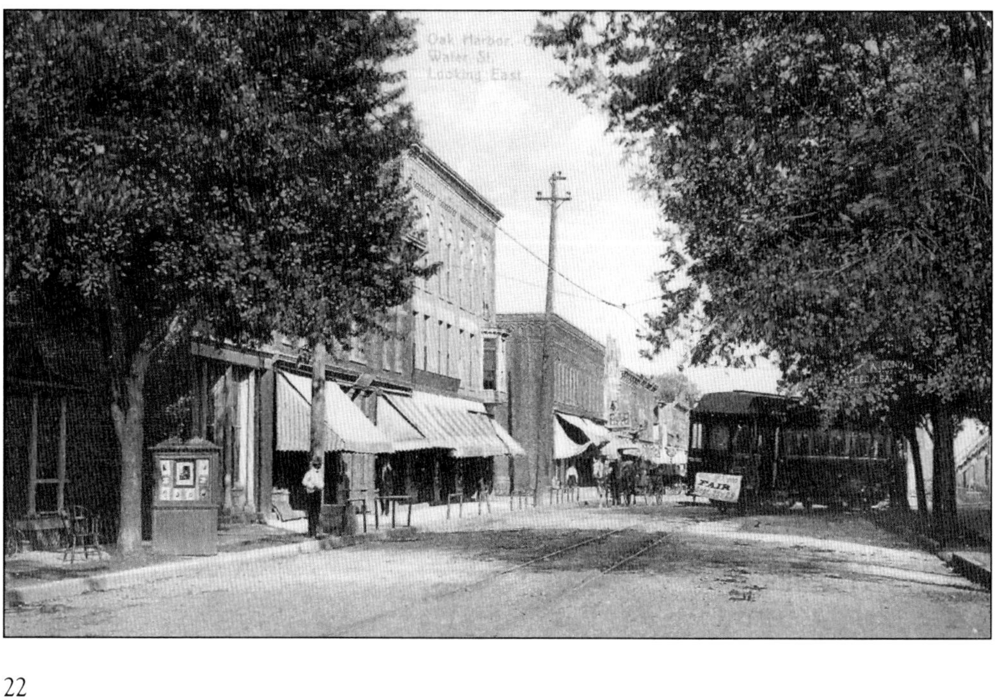

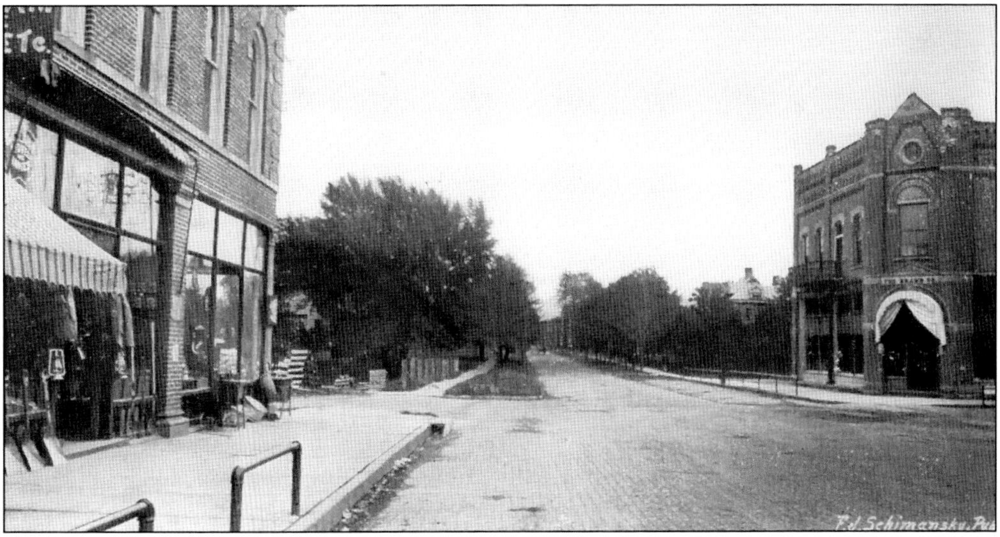

Above, shovels are displayed in front of Bredbeck Hardware in an early-1900s photograph looking east on Water Street toward the Locust Street intersection. On the right is the Kramb Company building, constructed in 1900 on the site of the Sherman House Hotel. This was the site of the 1879 murder of Edward Welsh by Cornelius Hennessey. Continuing east on Water Street into an upscale residential area, the below photograph, taken after 1914, shows the new single-globe streetlights used until the late 1960s. In addition to these lights, Oak Harbor is well known for its three-globe lights in the downtown area, also installed in 1914. Updated versions of the three-globe lights still adorn Water Street in the business district today. (Both, Liske.)

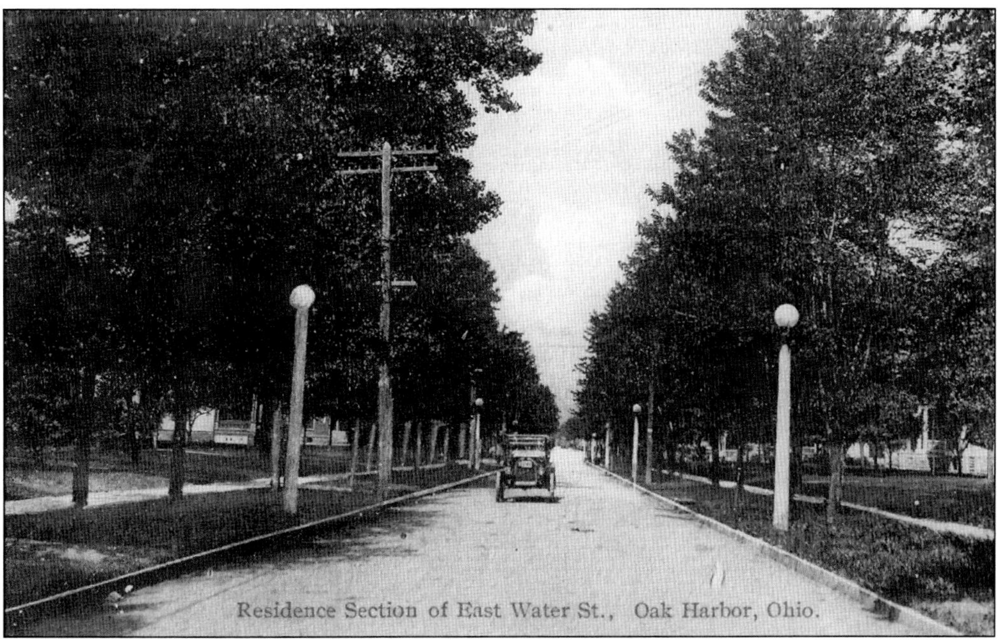

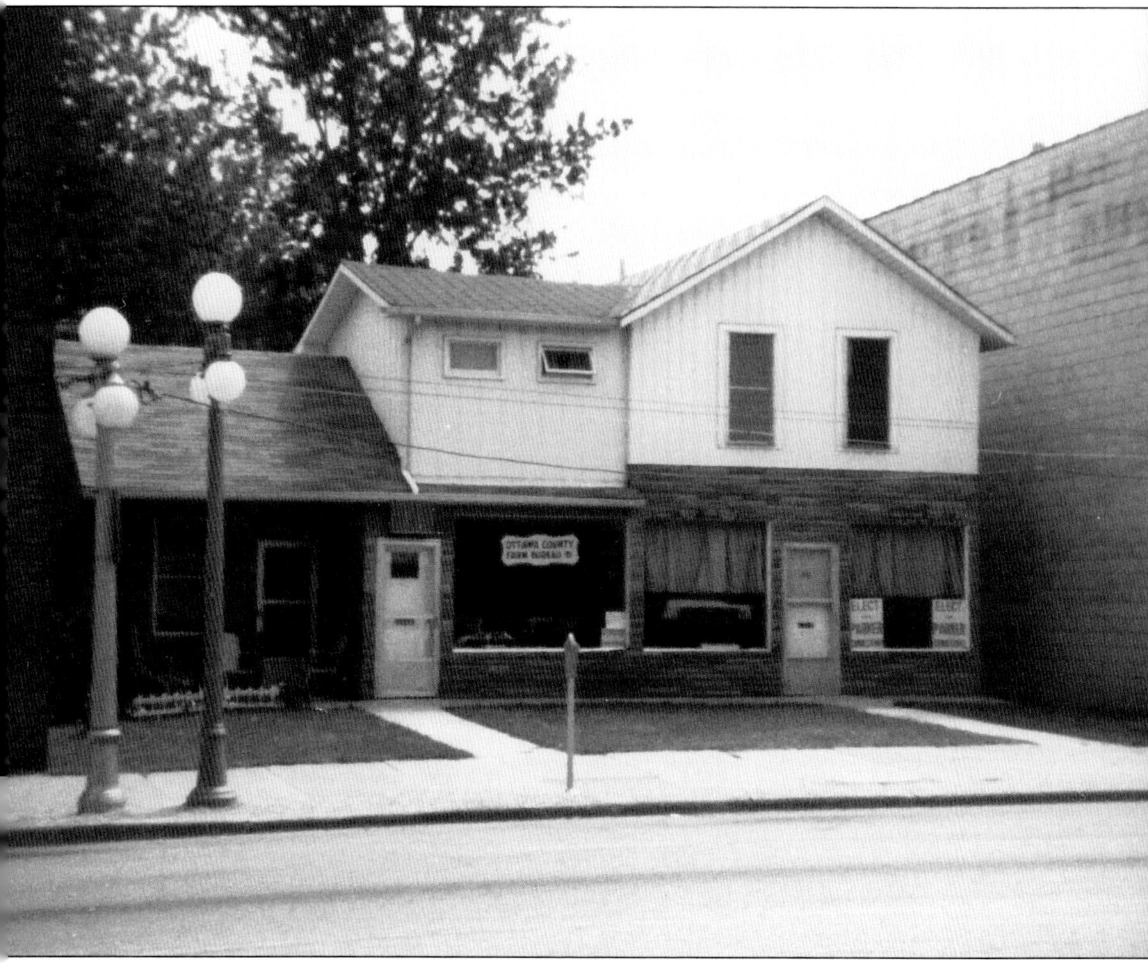

Many people wonder why there is a house located in the middle of the business district. Few realize, however, that this may be one of the oldest structures in Oak Harbor. The home, on the south side of Water Street, was built in 1861 by Herman H. Mylander, more commonly known as H.H. Mylander or Dutch Hank. Mylander first clerked for J.H. Blinn in a general store west of the present railroad tracks along the river. In 1858, he bought out Blinn. Then, in 1861, Mylander built this house, along with a small frame store just to the west. Finally, in 1872–1873, he built the brick Mylander building (page 51). It is not known when Mylander moved out of this house, but it has remained ever since and has seen many uses. This photograph, taken in 1984, when the old streetlights were replaced, shows the differences between the old and the new lights (Liske.)

Two

The Portage River

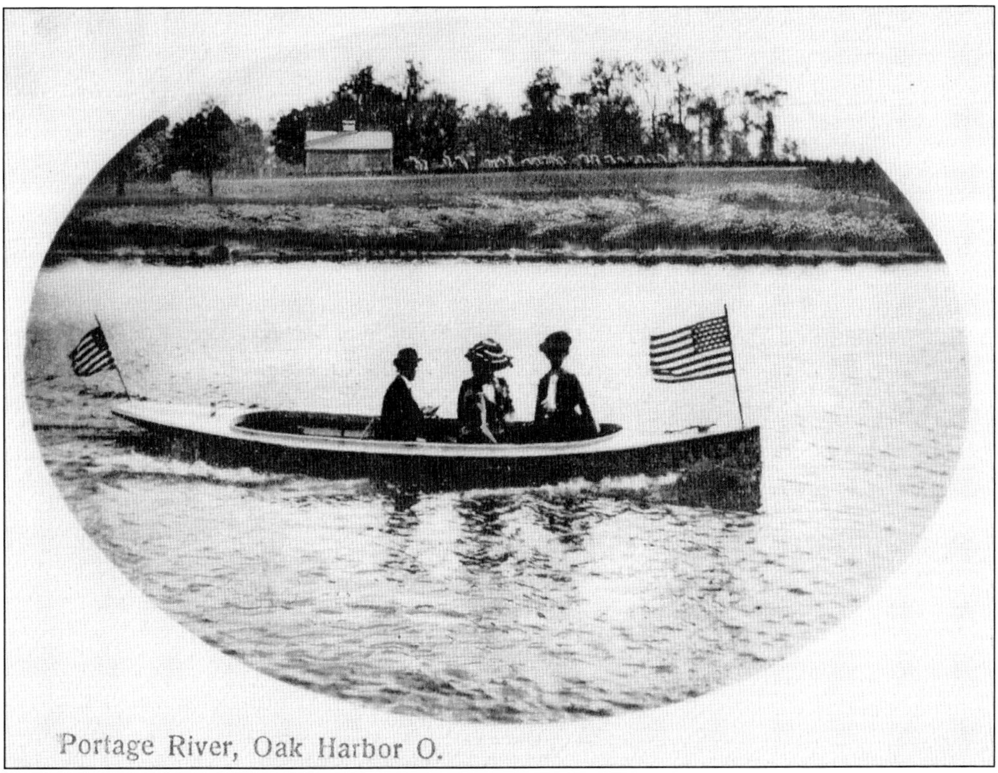

The Portage River has always been an integral part of Oak Harbor's history. Over the years, the river has been a source of recreation, transportation, and even tragedy. This boat was likely owned by the Kraemer family. (Liske.)

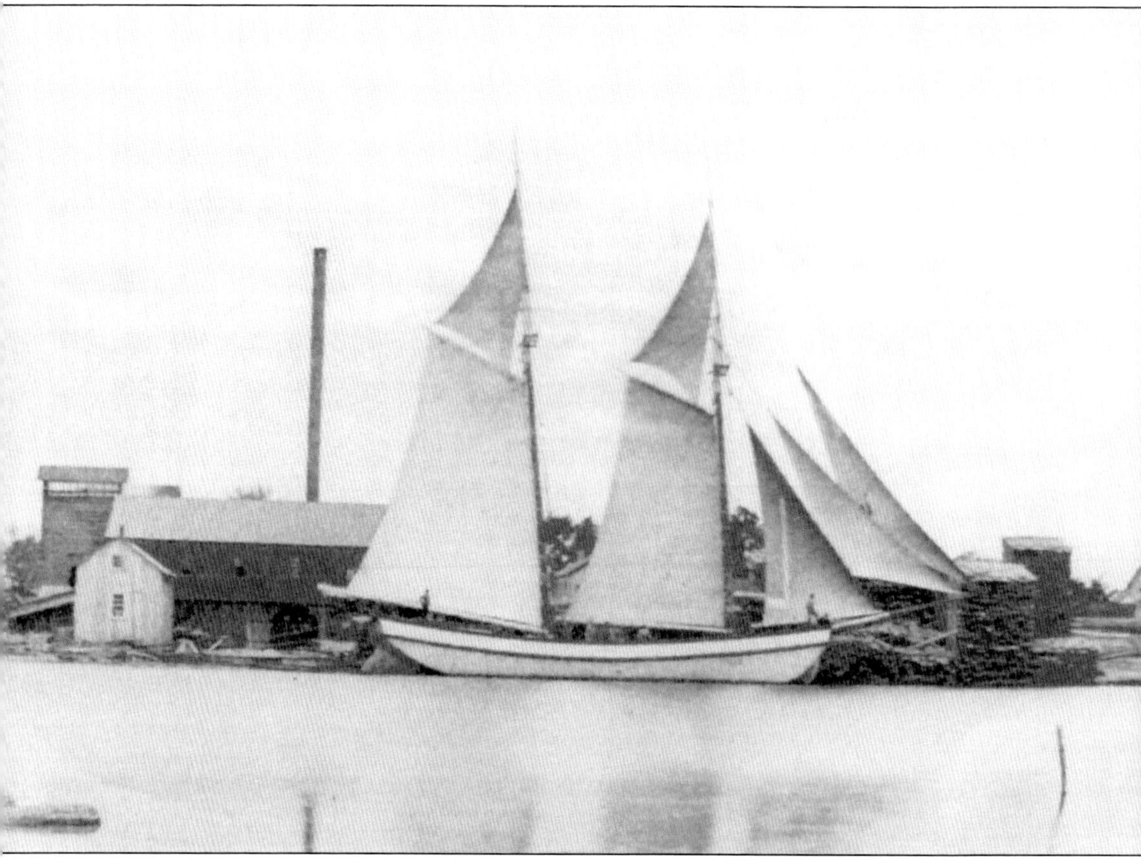

In the latter part of the 1800s, the Portage River was much deeper than it is today. This two-masted ship, christened the *Faugh-a-Bella*, is shown docked in Oak Harbor at the Anspach Lumber & Hoop factory, located on the north bank of the river, on West Water Street between Benton and Toussaint Streets. John P. and Allen Anspach milled lumber at this site for various commercial and residential uses, and manufactured coiled barrel and keg hoops. This photograph was taken prior to the factory burning down on September 1, 1895. The small house on the right side of the factory still exists at the southeast corner of Main and Toussaint Streets. An 1898 newspaper article reported that the *Faugh-a-Bella* was to take a load of ties for the Hotel Victory at Put-in-Bay. Local lore also states that the ship brought the stone trim for the Hotel Kuebeler up the Portage River in 1899. (OHPL.)

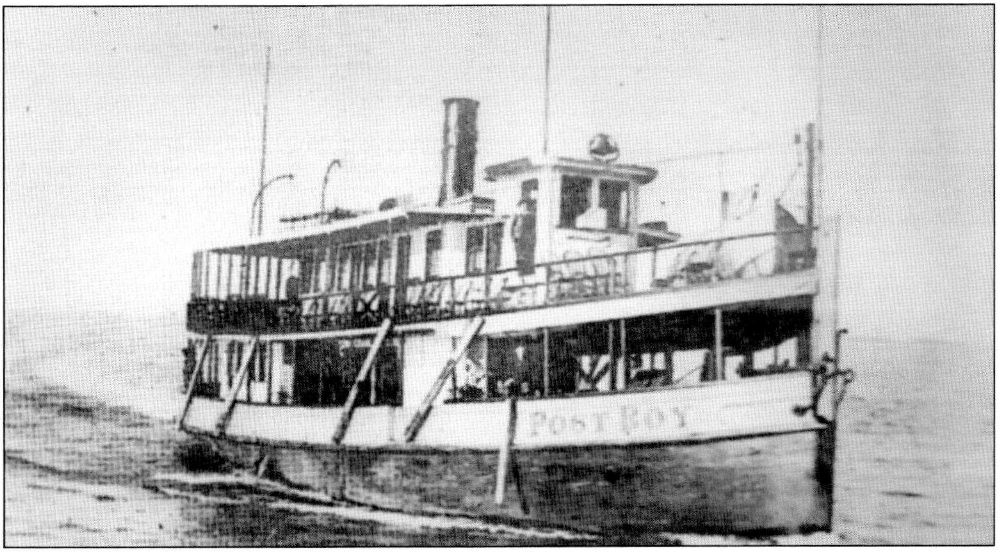

Not only did the river transport freight, but passenger ships also docked regularly in Oak Harbor. Seen here is the *Post Boy*, a two-decked steamer that made regular excursions from the foot of Church Street to the Lake Erie islands. A July 1898 advertisement reads, "A cool ride down the Portage on the *Post Boy* and a visit to Middle Bass will do you good. Round trip—50 cents." (OHPL.)

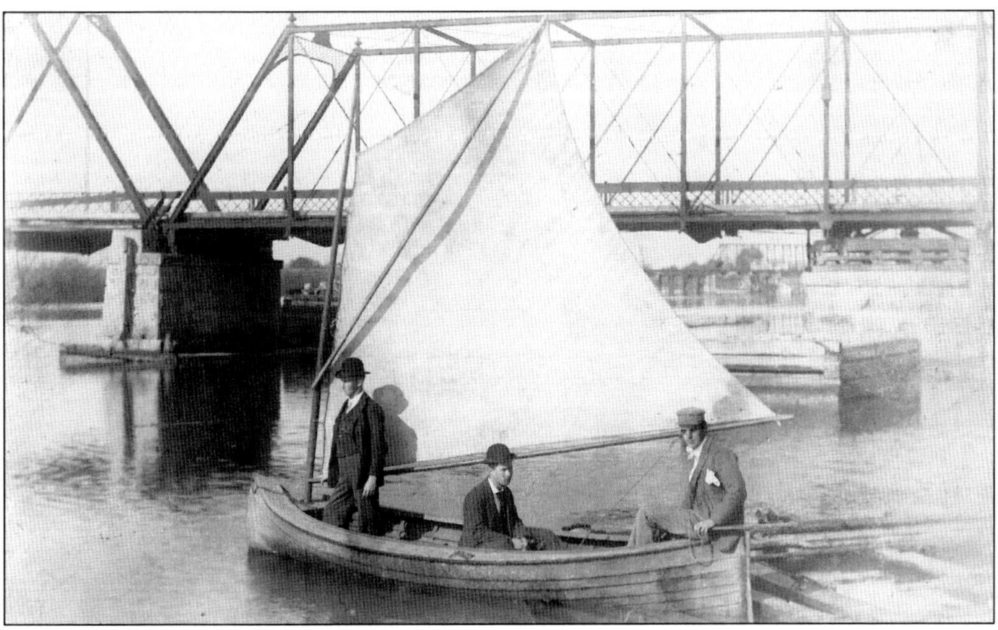

Three well-dressed young men enjoy a sailboat ride on the Portage River just east of the wagon bridge, now State Route 19. Note that the center section of the bridge is a swing span, allowing the bridge to be opened for larger boats. At that time, all Oak Harbor bridges were built to open for river traffic. The bridge in the background is the Wheeling & Lake Erie Railway bridge. (OHPL.)

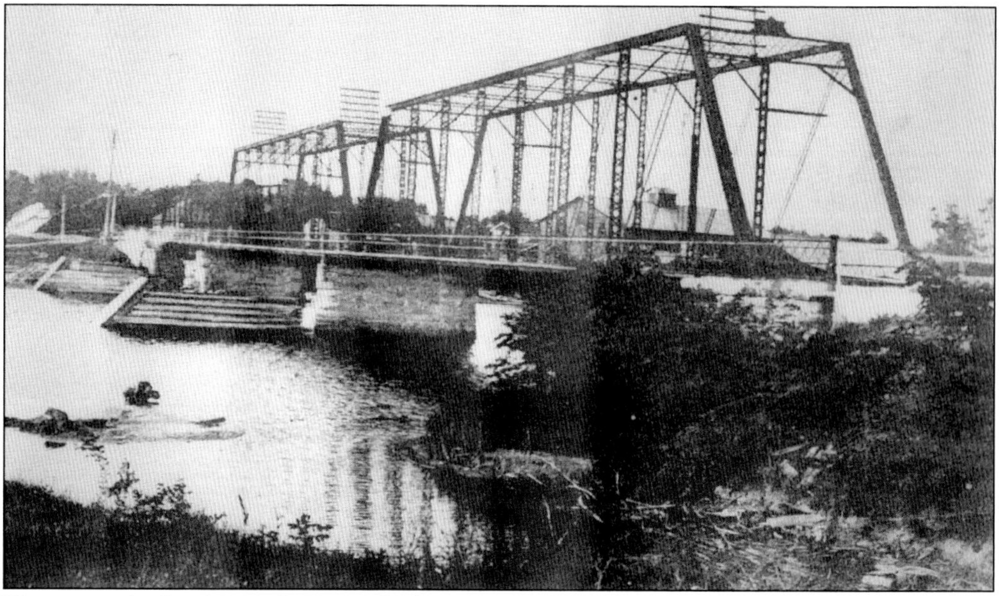

The wagon bridge shown above was built in 1870–1871 and was the fourth or fifth span at that location, dating from the first bridge in the 1850s. Earlier, less substantial bridges were taken out by ice jams. The northern section of the bridge was a swing span. The bridge lasted over 60 years and was replaced in 1932. (Bernita Hiles and Sharon Sweeney.)

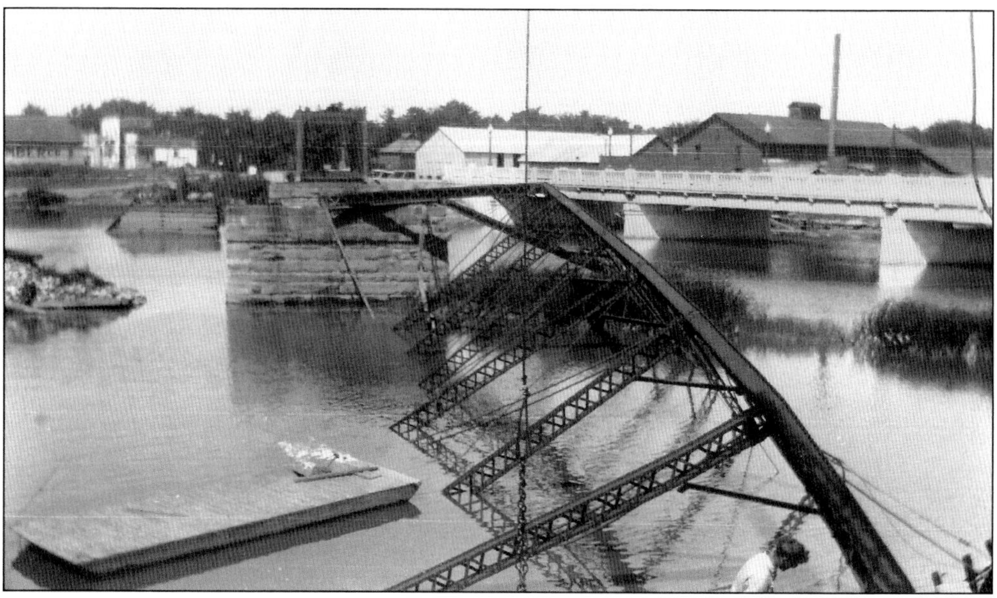

In 1932, a new, concrete bridge was built across the river, replacing the 1870–1871 wagon bridge, shown being demolished in this photograph. The new State Route 19 bridge can be seen in the background. Note how the wagon bridge approached the south riverbank slightly to the west of the new bridge. (Liske.)

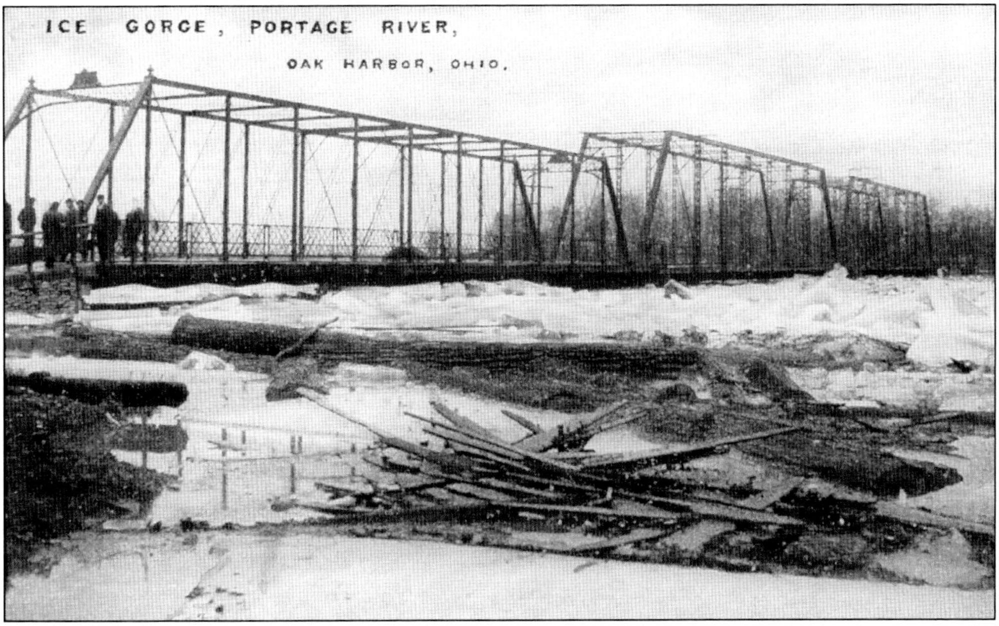

A cold winter followed by an early thaw and heavy rain can create tremendous ice jams, as the river ice breaks up and moves toward the lake. In this January 1904 photograph, a huge ice jam is threatening to take out the wagon bridge. Dynamite was often used to break up the ice gorges before they could do any damage. (Liske.)

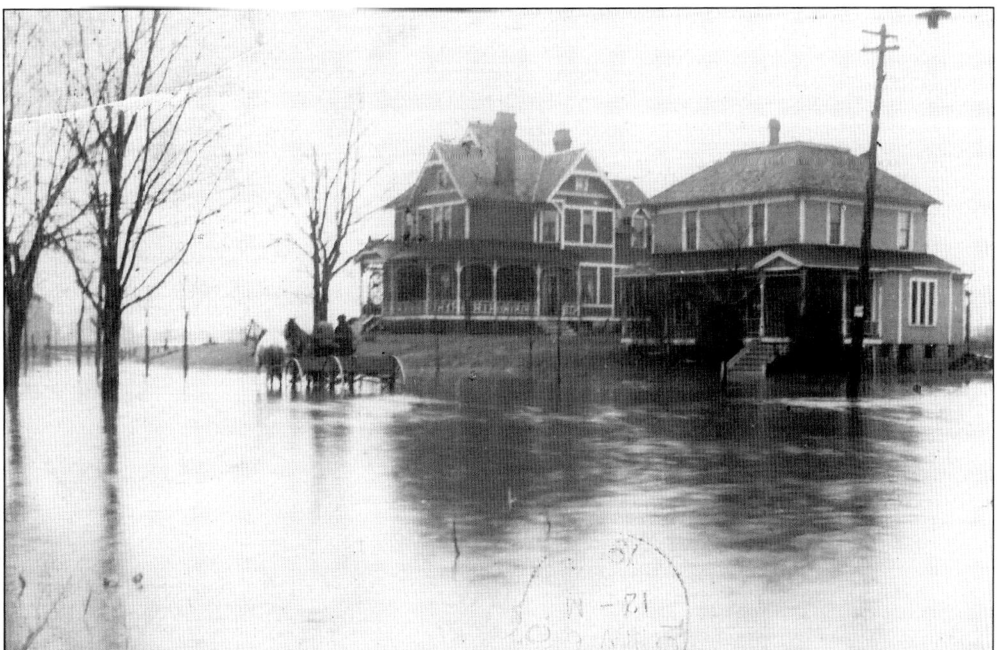

These two houses on the northeast corner of Locust and Main Streets are completely surrounded by ice and water in the 1904 flood. The home on the left was owned by Henry Kilmer, and the one on the right by Peter Kramb. The homes still stand today. (Liske.)

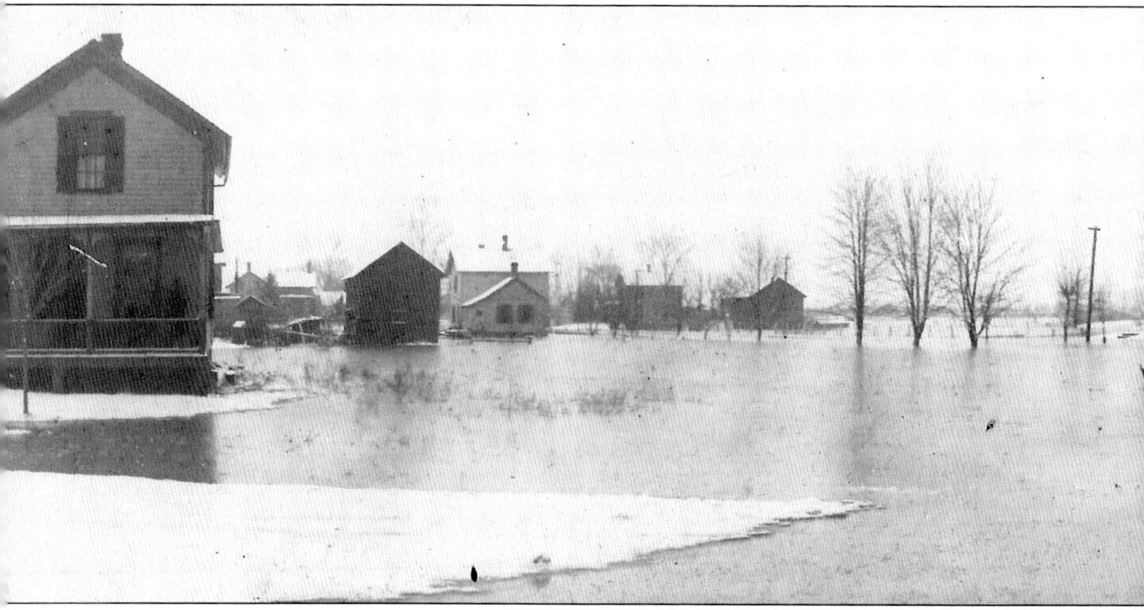

The Portage River has not always been kind to Oak Harbor. Ice jams and torrential rains sometimes cause the Portage to overflow its banks, resulting in damage to homes and businesses. One of the worst floods, in 1904, is shown in this panoramic photograph, looking east toward the corner of Main and Locust Streets. That area of town is part of the old "East Bayou," also known as the

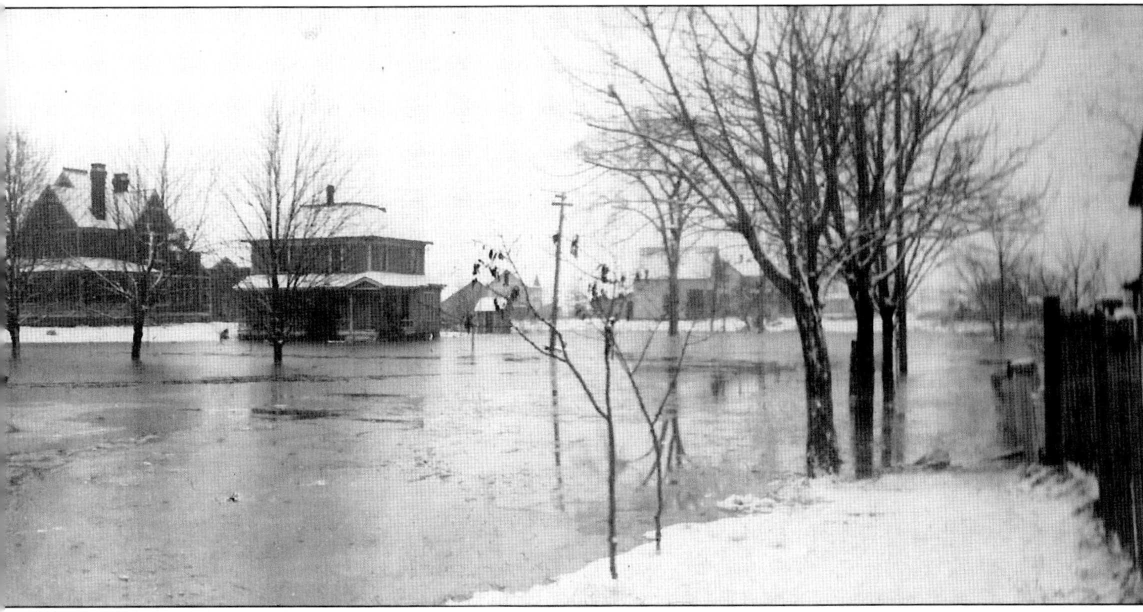

Hartford Bayou, and has always been prone to flooding. The 1904 flood was particularly bad, extending north on Locust Street for several blocks and damaging a number of Water Street businesses. Other major floods occurred in 1913 and 1929. The last serious flood in Oak Harbor occurred on July 4, 1969, when 10 to 12 inches of rain fell in just a few hours. (OHPL.)

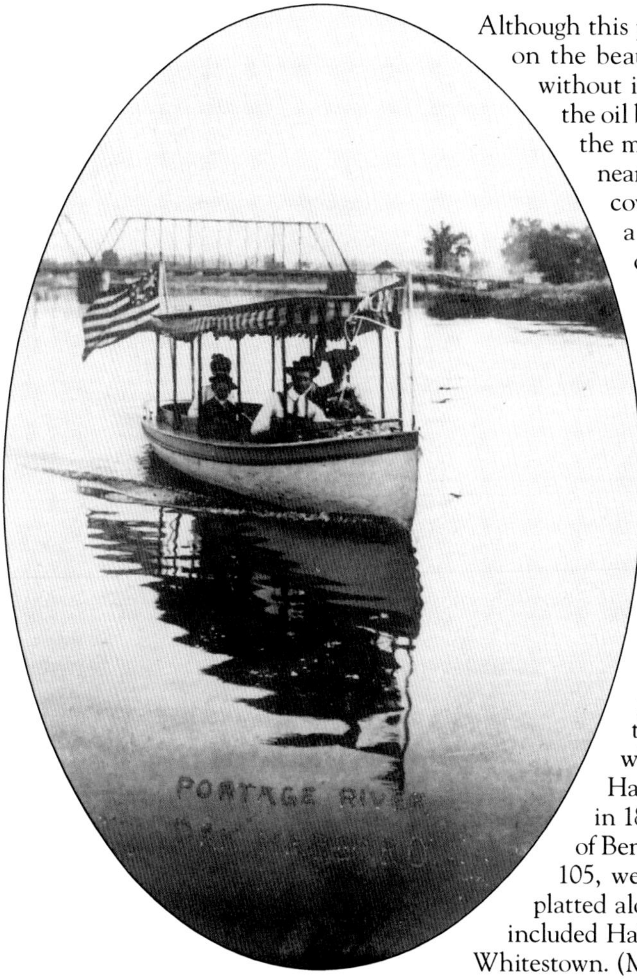

Although this photograph depicts a peaceful ride on the beautiful Portage, the river was not without its problems and pollution. When the oil boom occurred in Wood County in the mid-1880s, runoff from the oil fields near Cygnet came through Oak Harbor, covering the river and its banks with a smelly, oily film. The river actually caught fire at Oak Harbor in June 1888. (Liske.)

Hartford was not the only town platted along the Portage River in the 1830s. The town of Port Oleron, which was to be even larger than Hartford, was surveyed and recorded in 1834. It was located near the corner of Benton-Carroll Road and State Route 105, west of Oak Harbor. Other towns platted along the river but never developed included Hallville, Moscow, Leatherport, and Whitestown. (Martin.)

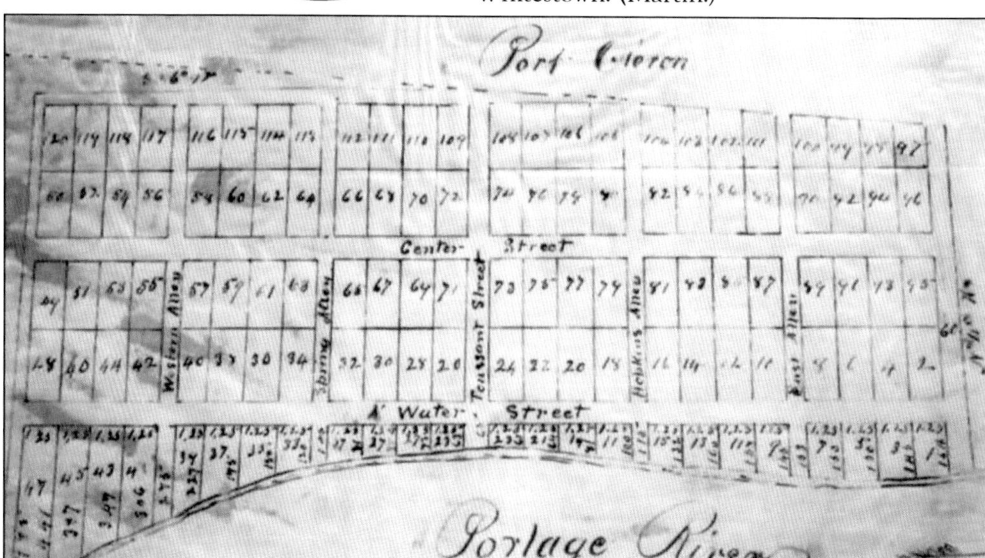

Three

Business and Industry

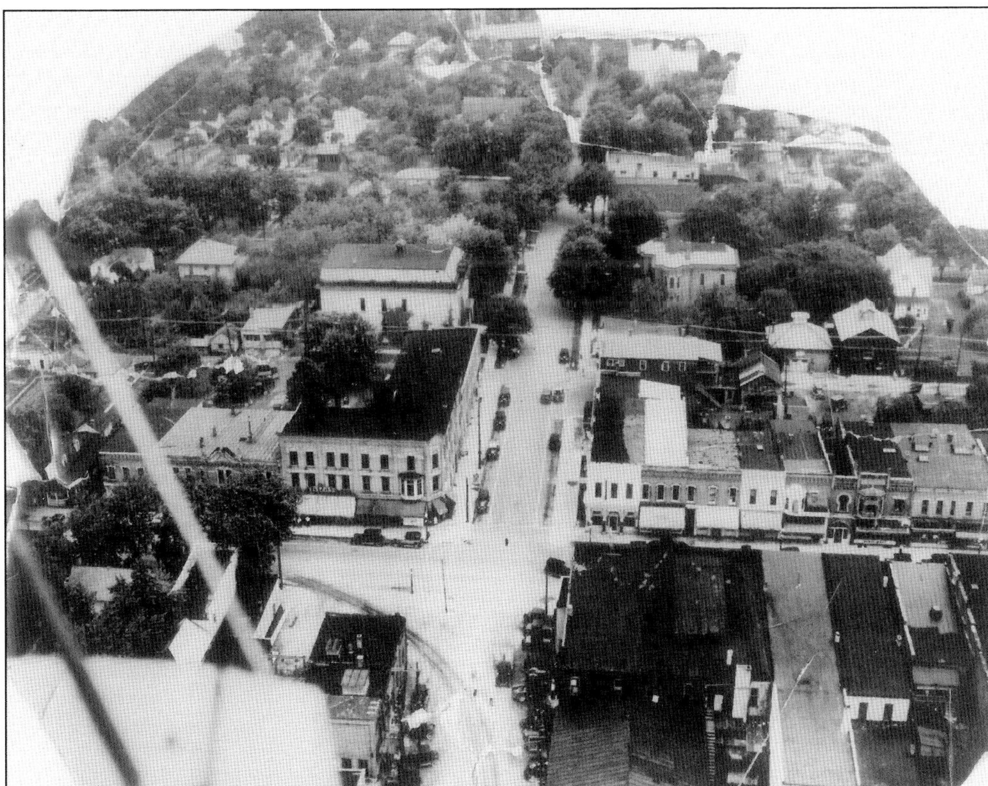

Flying over Oak Harbor in the late 1920s, this photographer captured a nice view of Oak Harbor's business district. Looking north up Church Street from the river, it clearly shows the Kuebeler Hotel and the interurban tracks turning the corner at Water and Church Streets. Also seen on the upper right is the Fought/Heller house, replaced in 1938 by the new post office. (Jack Kemp.)

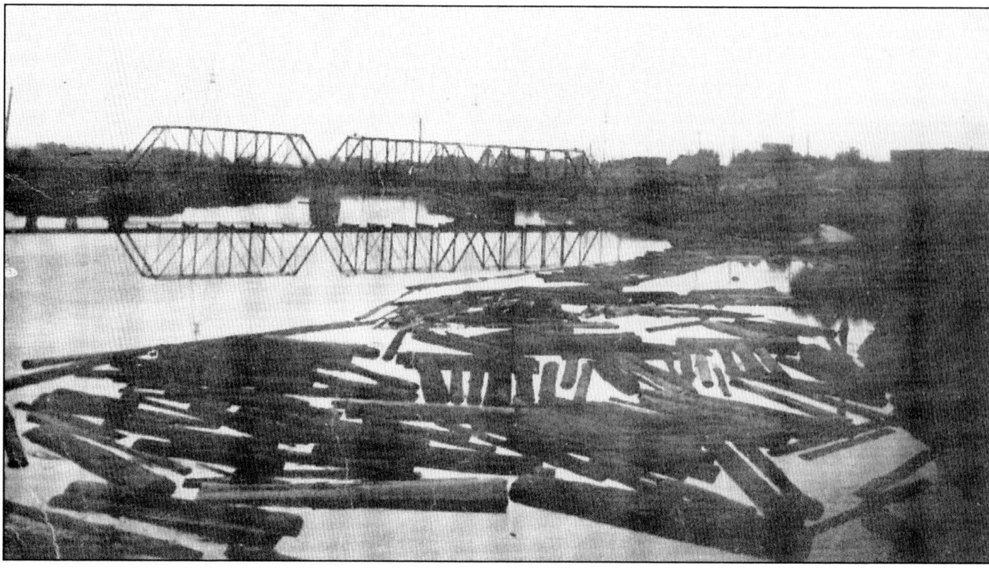

With the many hardwood forests surrounding Oak Harbor, sawmills, barrel and stave mills, and basket factories were major employers. The river was often used as a means of transporting logs to the various lumber and stave mills lining the riverfront. Here, logs in the river await milling at the stave or basket factory. (Bernita Hiles and Sharon Sweeney.)

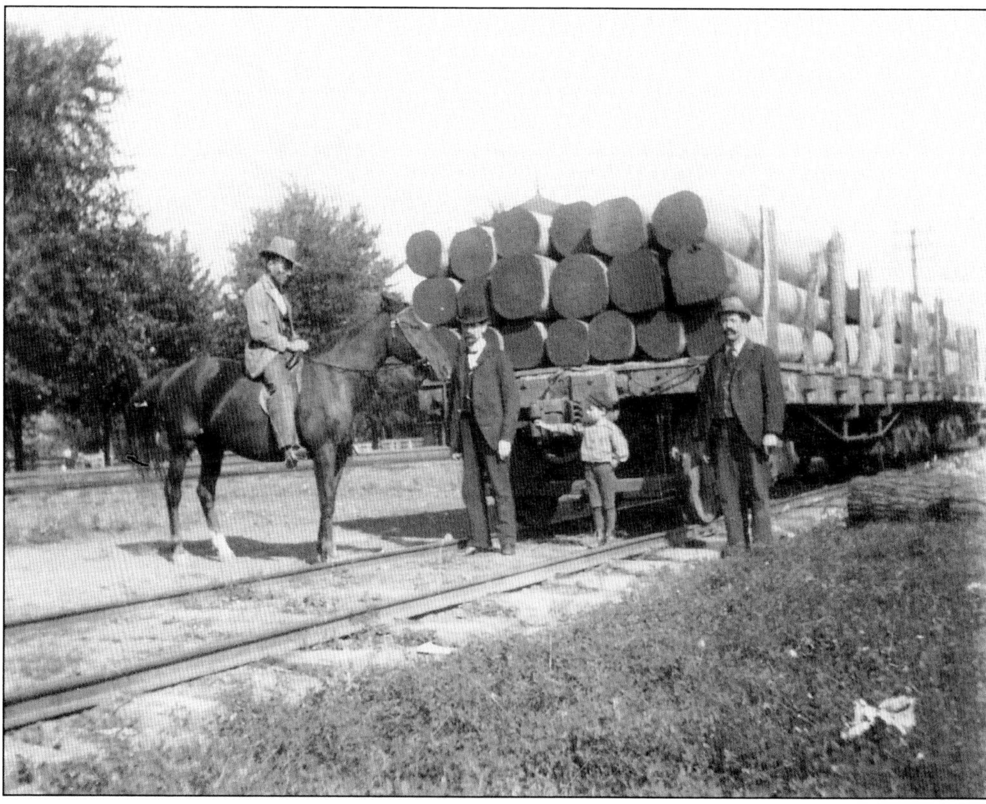

Timber was also shipped by rail from the Oak Harbor area to world ports. Here, a load of logs from Oak Harbor awaits rail shipment to a distant destination. (OCHM.)

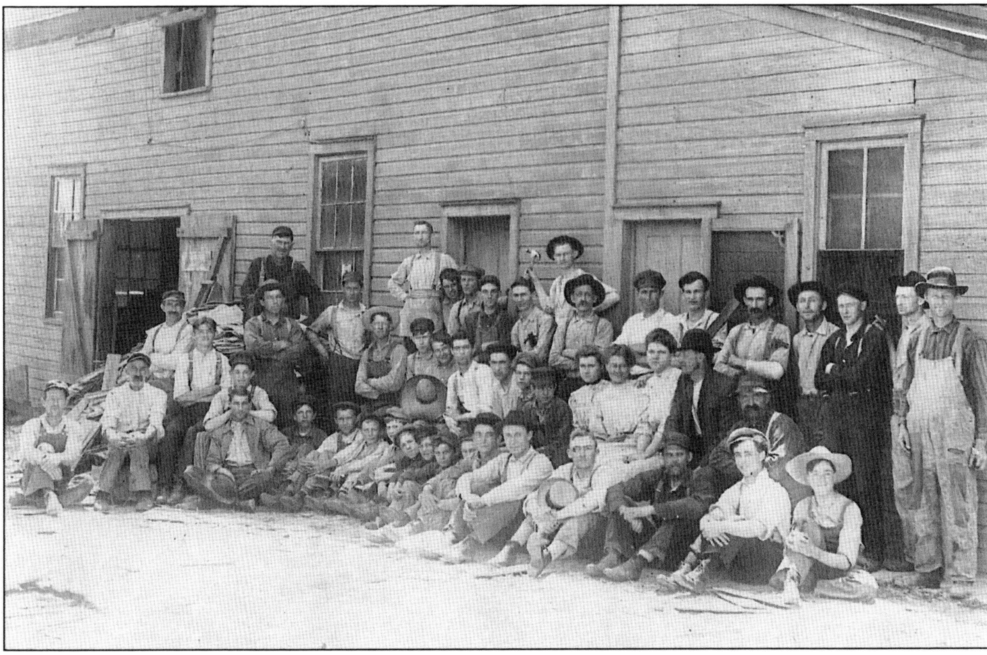

The Oak Harbor Basket Factory was founded in 1895 by Stephen Fetterly to meet the needs of the expanding local fruit industry. The company employed 90 hands at peak season. The company made a special seven-eighth-bushel "Detroit basket" for large city markets. The smaller basket looked like a regular bushel basket, but contained slightly less fruit. (Liske.)

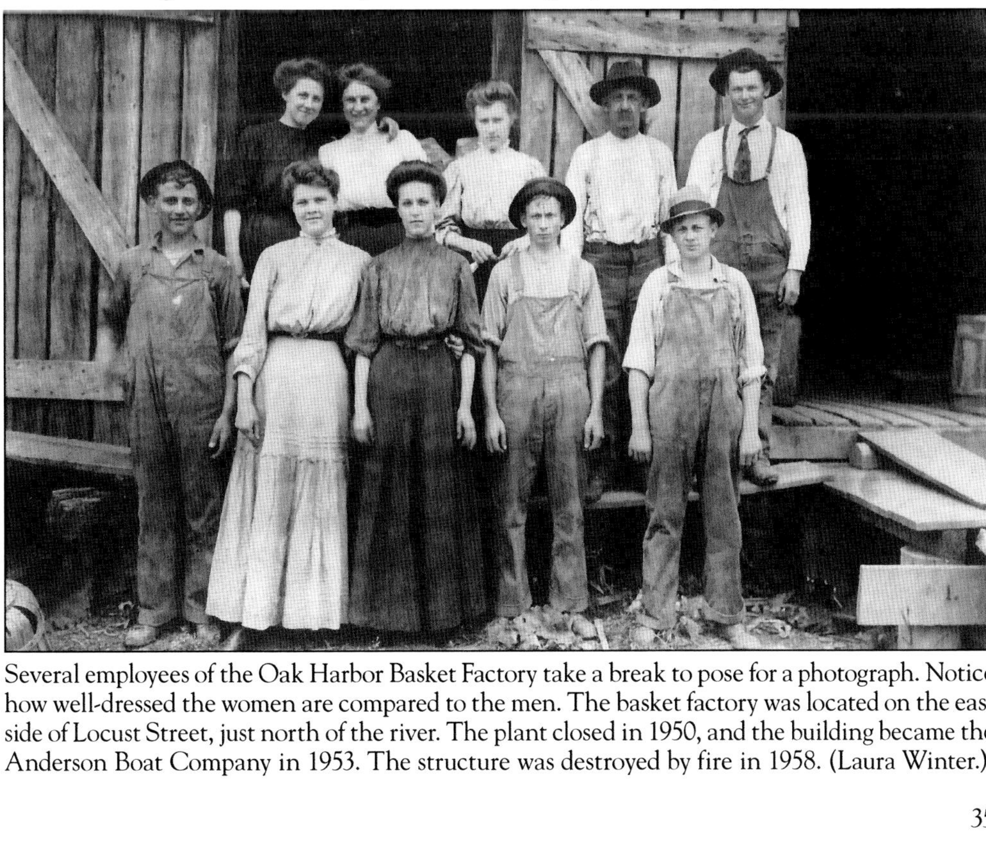

Several employees of the Oak Harbor Basket Factory take a break to pose for a photograph. Notice how well-dressed the women are compared to the men. The basket factory was located on the east side of Locust Street, just north of the river. The plant closed in 1950, and the building became the Anderson Boat Company in 1953. The structure was destroyed by fire in 1958. (Laura Winter.)

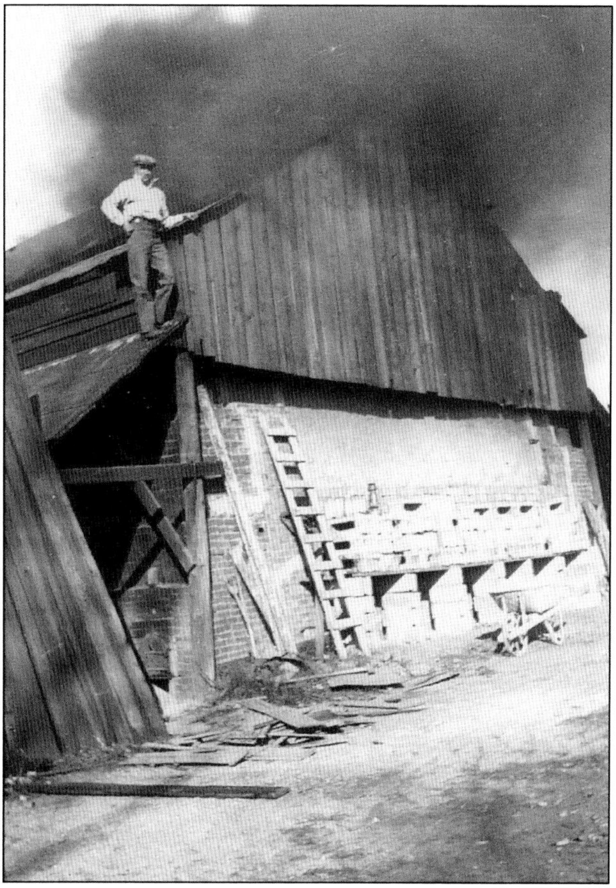

No, this building is not on fire. It is the Gleckler Tile and Brick Kiln, with Ray Gleckler standing on the roof. The business was begun by Ray Gleckler's father, Fred Gleckler, in 1900. First located on Locust Street, it later moved to East Water Street, along the river near the current sewage plant. Many buildings in Oak Harbor are made with Gleckler's Ottawa bricks. (Robert Gleckler.)

Russell Bordeaux was the owner of this cement block manufacturing business at 141 West Water Street. Taken prior to 1911, the photograph also shows Joseph Goetz, at left, standing in front of his jewelry store. Standing in front of Bordeaux's business are, from left to right, Frank Bordeaux, Roy Bordeaux, unidentified, John A. Fader, Rev. C.M. Morrison, and Russell Bordeaux. (Liske.)

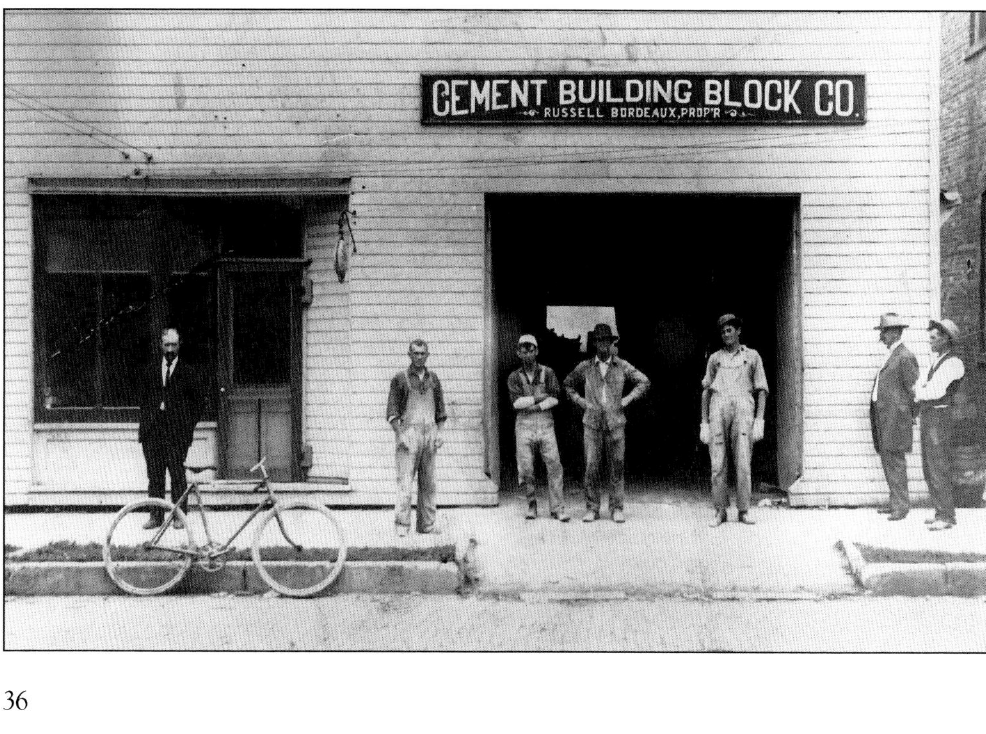

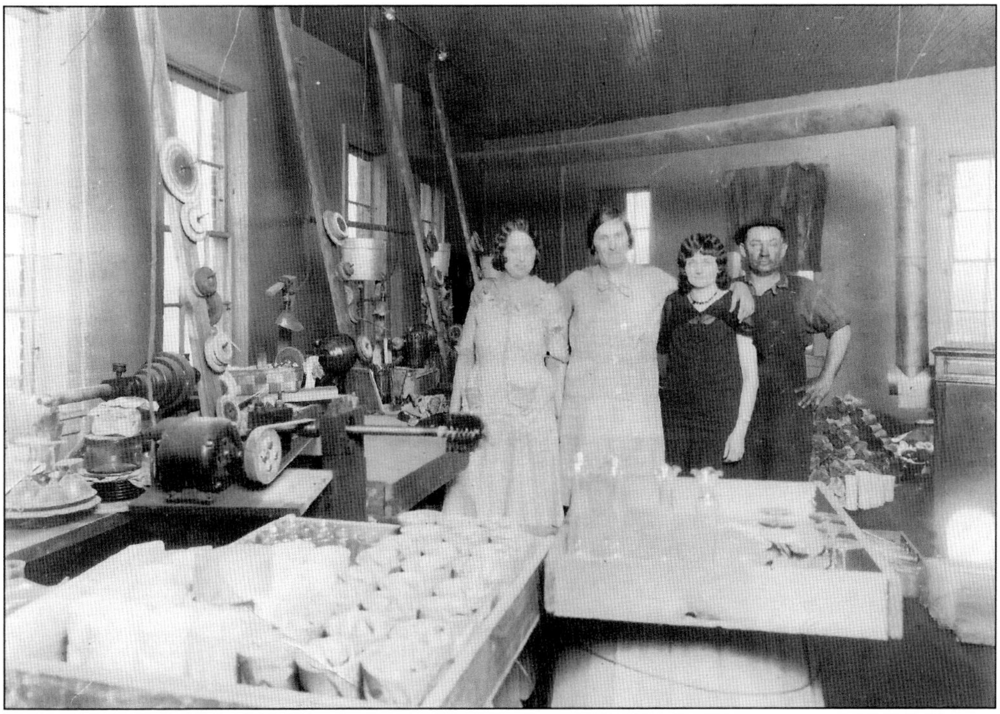

Although no glassware was ever produced in Oak Harbor, stemware called Oak Harbor glass is often seen in area antique stores. The glass was first produced in 1917, when the Brilliant Cut Glass Company moved to Oak Harbor from Toledo. Manufactured glassware was shipped to the Oak Harbor plant, where various designs were etched into the glass, as seen at right. Above, workers at the plant, located near Houghton Street along the Wheeling & Lake Erie Railway, take a break from their work. The factory was destroyed by fire on February 9, 1928. It briefly relocated to the room above the fire station before it moved to Fremont. The company ceased operations in 1930. (Above, Gaylyn and Robert Hofacker; right, OHPL.)

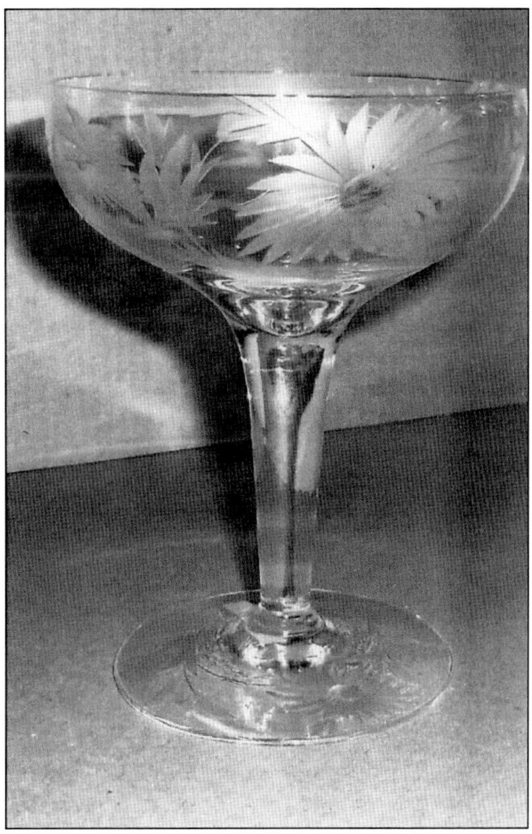

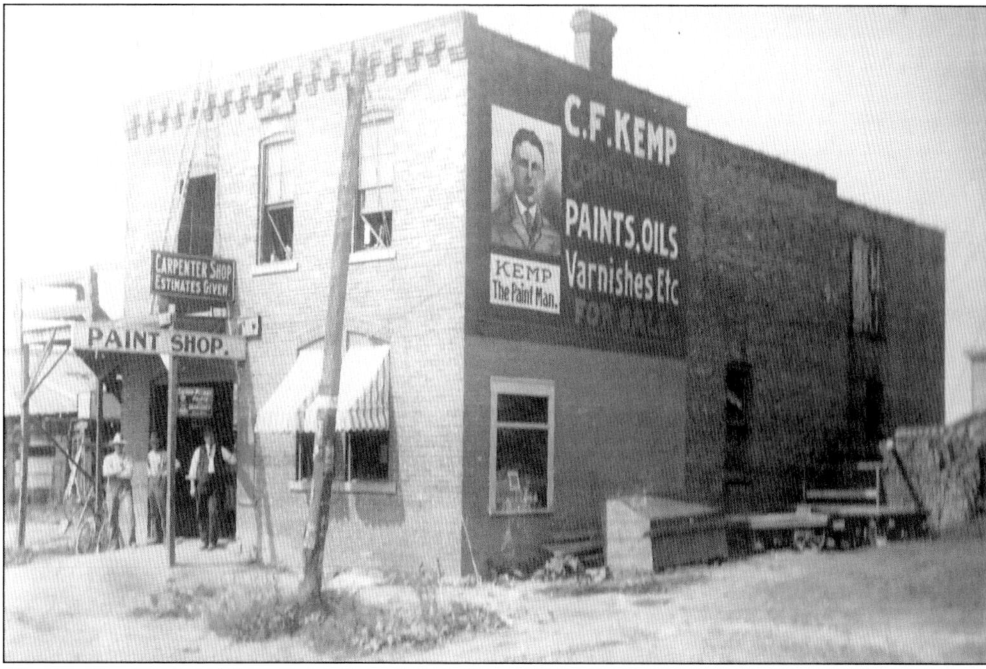

Charles Kemp owned this paint store, located on the west side of South Church Street near the river. The building was later used for storage until it was torn down for the construction of the former Oak Harbor State Bank in the 1970s. (Jack Kemp.)

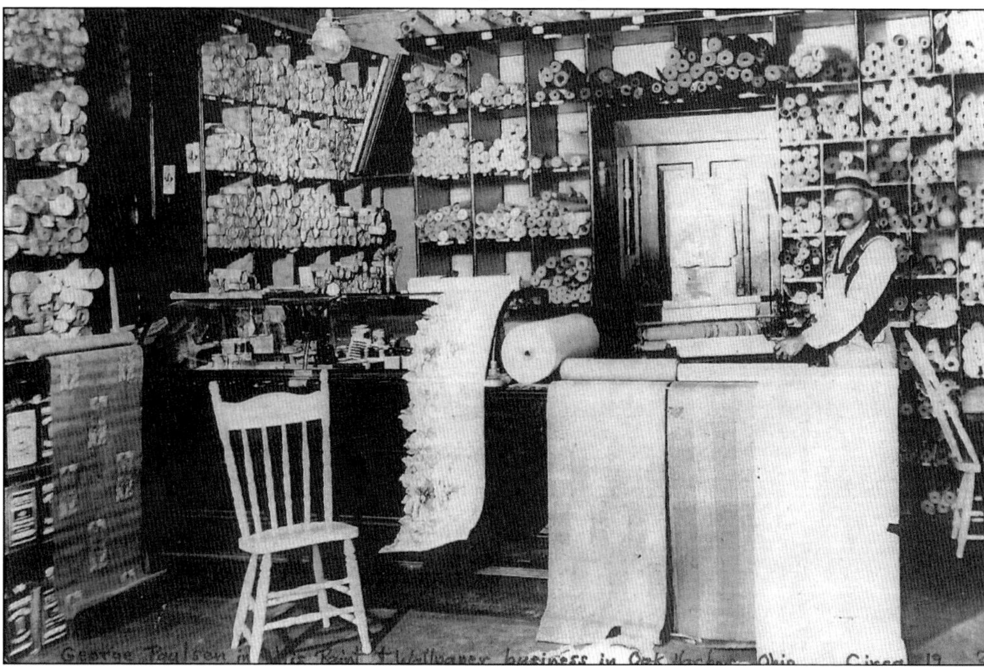

Wallpaper was apparently a hot commodity at the turn of the 20th century. Hundreds of rolls of wallpaper are seen here with George Paulsen in his paint and decorating store, located on the east side of Locust Street, midway between Water and Main Streets. The building, which later housed Oak Harbor Cleaners, no longer exists. (Mary Paulsen.)

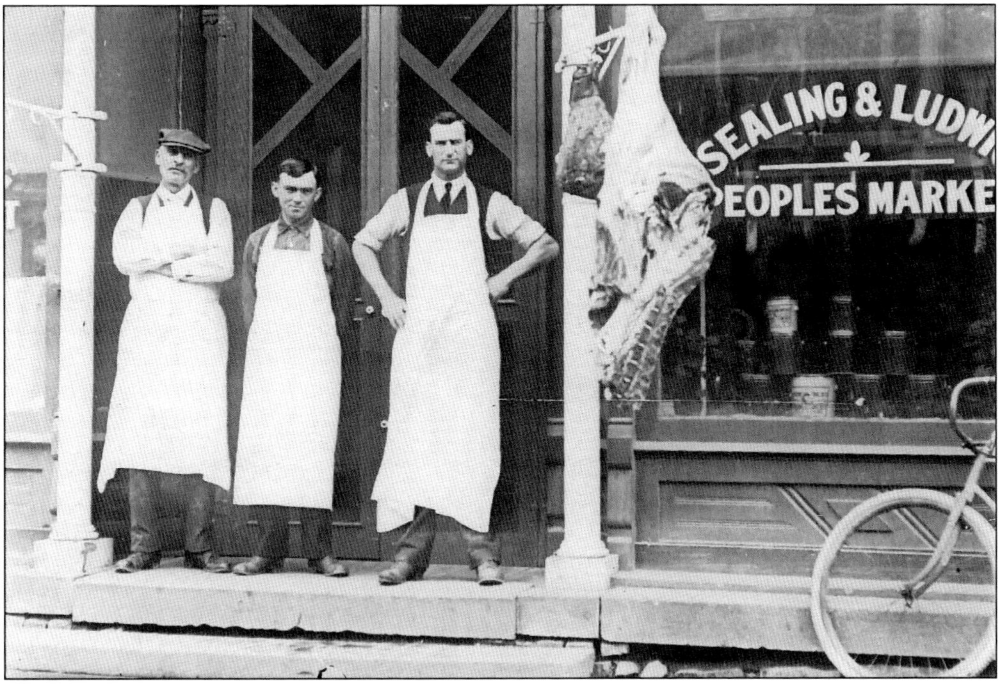

Without adequate refrigeration, food shopping became an almost daily chore for many housewives. As a result, many meat markets and grocery stores could be found in early Oak Harbor. Shown above is People's Market, owned by Sealing and Ludwig. Pictured are, from left to right, Otto Sealing, Harry Dunenee, and Otto Rose. The store was located on the south side of Water Street. Note the quarter of beef hanging outside. Below is the Bowersox and Son City Meat Market, owned by S.P. Bowersox, at 126 West Water Street. The bicycles were used to deliver meat and groceries to local homes, sometimes twice a day. (Above, Mary Paulsen; below, Liske.)

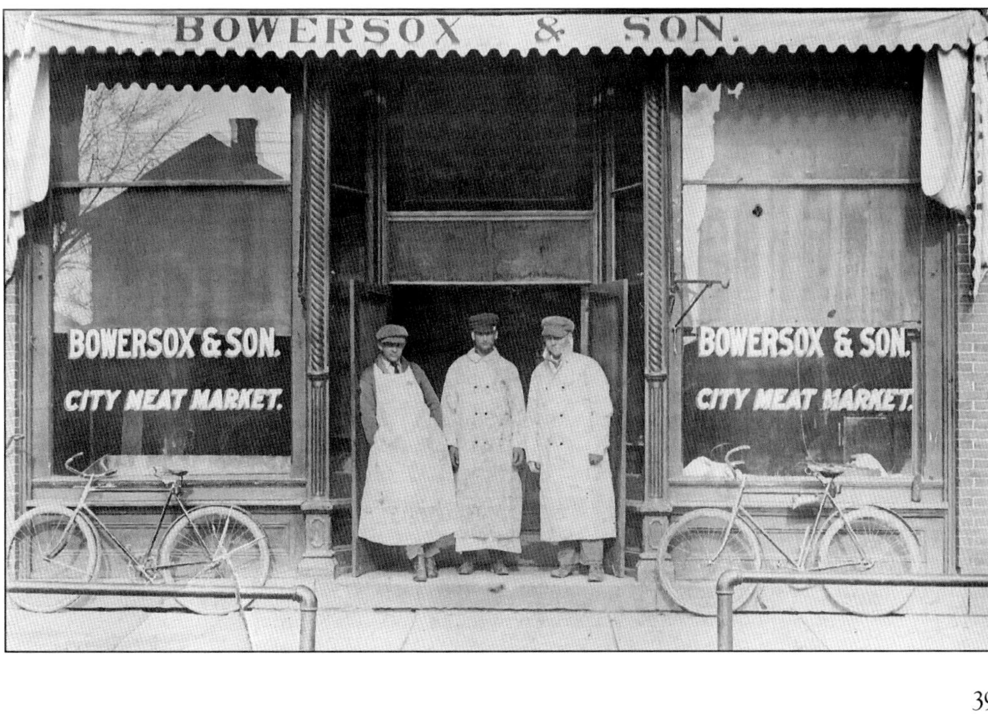

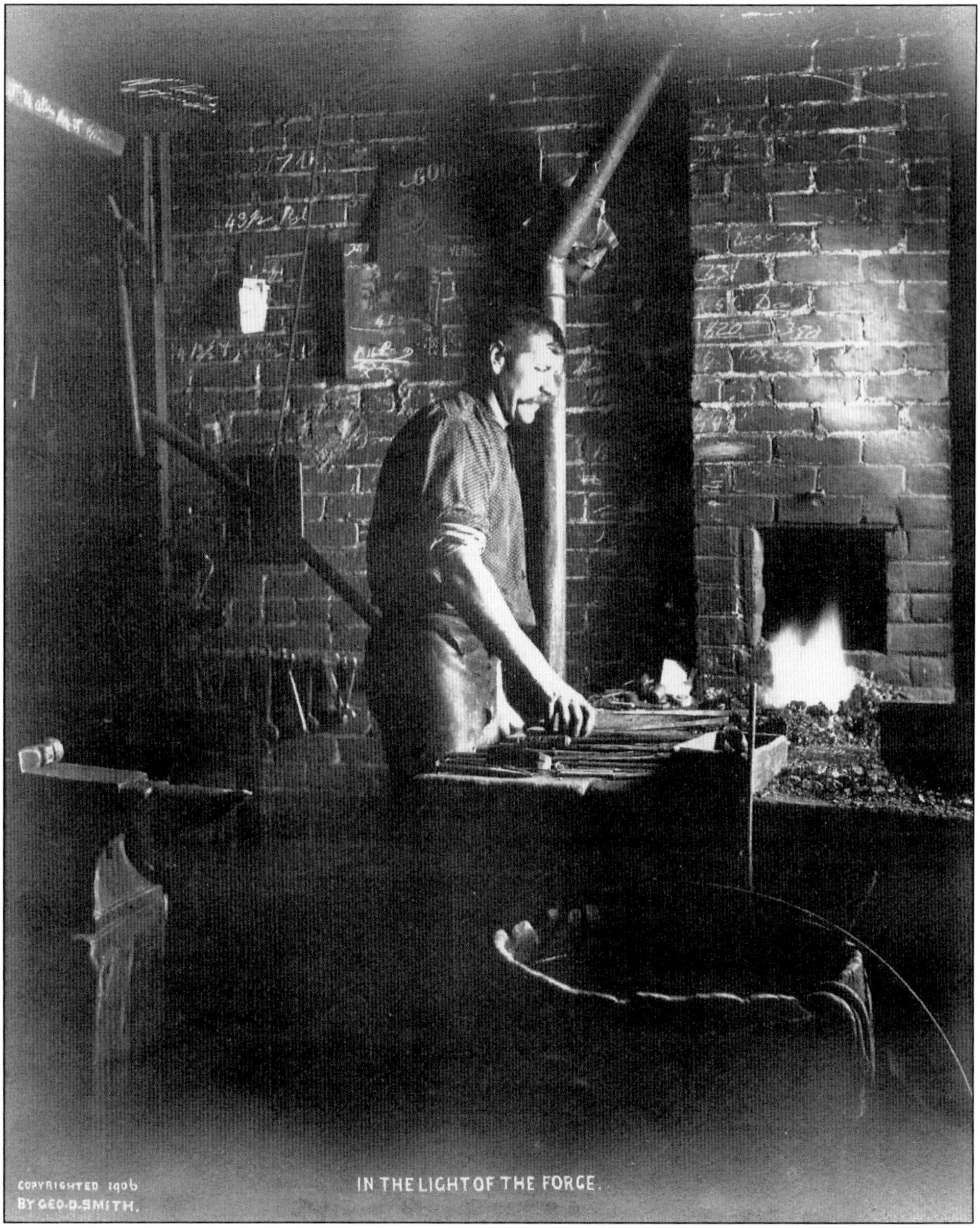

This award-winning photograph, entitled *In the Light of the Forge*, was taken by photographer George D. Smith in 1906 and depicts L.D. "Louie" Link, an Oak Harbor blacksmith and wagon builder. The Link Blacksmith Shop was located at 245 West Water Street, directly across from the present fire station. Link bought the blacksmith shop in the late 1880s from another blacksmith, Charles Leow. The original Leow/Link blacksmith building was destroyed in the 1894 fire. Link then erected a three-story building on the same site that served as his new blacksmith shop. After Link retired in the 1920s, the building was used for various enterprises until the early 1980s, when it was torn down for a parking lot expansion. This photograph is particularly interesting in that the only light comes from the fire of the forge. Given the detail apparent in the picture and the primitive film that was used at that time, this was quite an accomplishment. (OHPL.)

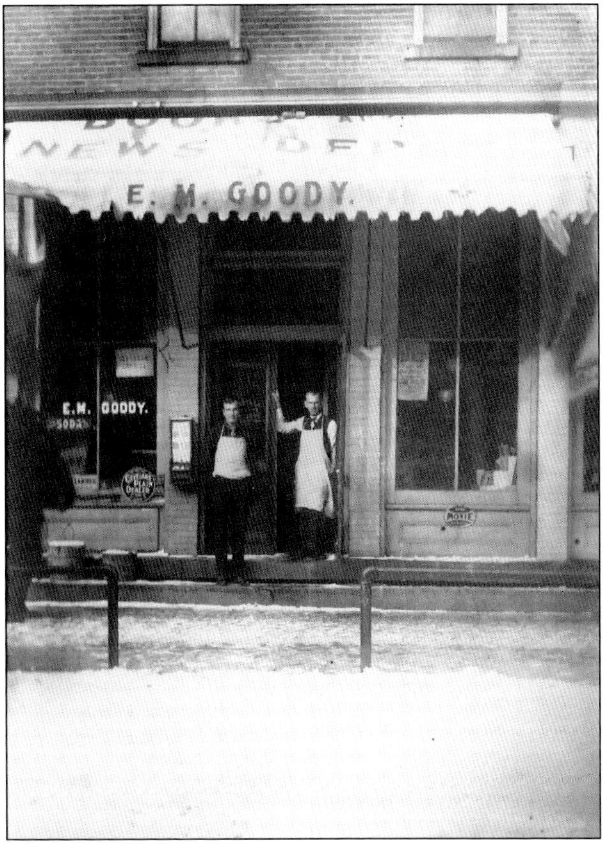

E.M. Goody ran an ice cream store and news depot in Oak Harbor for over 50 years. This 1908 photograph shows Goody (right) in front of his store at 168 West Water Street. The store even had a talking parrot in the back. The establishment was later moved to 148 West Water Street when it was sold to Stan Mylander. Goody died in 1934. (Gluth.)

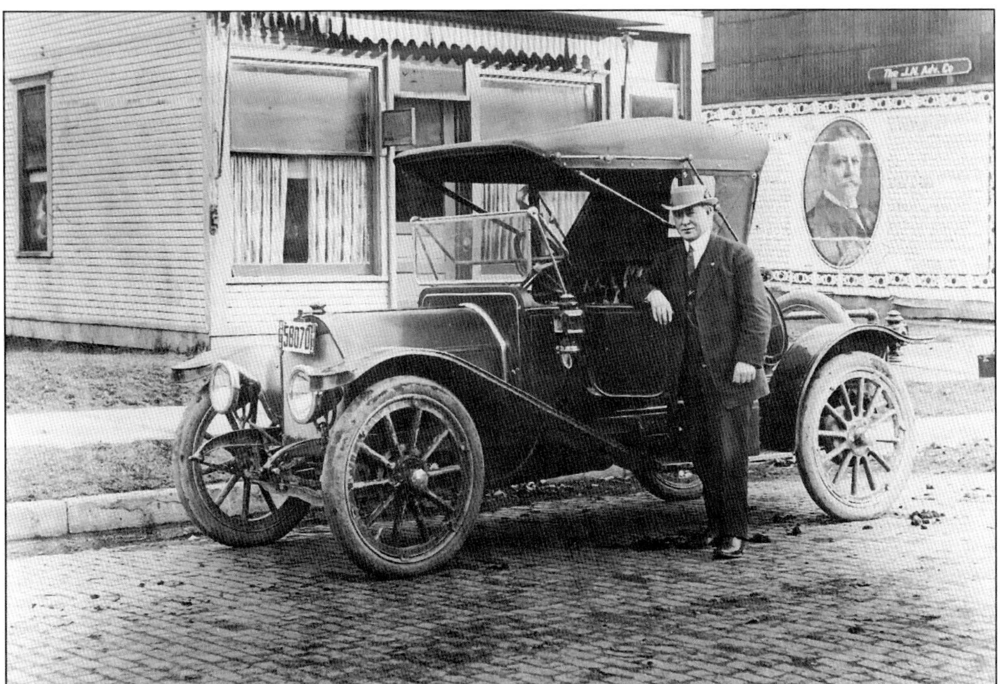

Dr. Frederick S. Heller practiced medicine in Oak Harbor for 56 years, from 1889 until three weeks before his death in 1945. He is standing with his Cadillac roadster in front of his office at 118 Church Street in 1912. That building still stands today as a beauty shop. Heller was said to be the first doctor in Oak Harbor to own a car. (OHPL.)

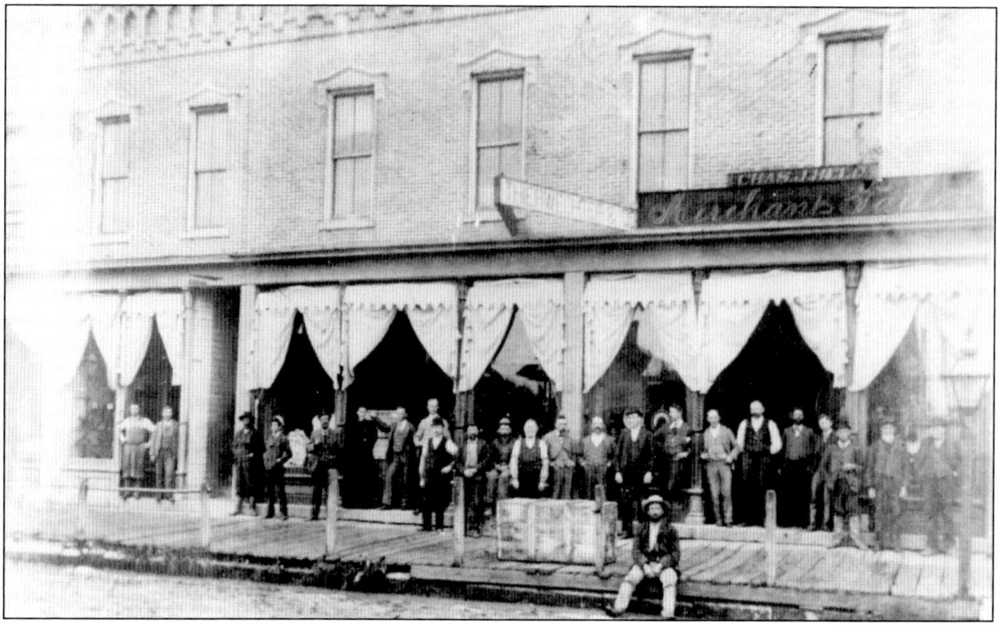

Michael Thierwechter opened a general store in Elmore in 1867 and expanded the business in 1877, when he rented a room from Adolphus Kraemer on Locust Street in Oak Harbor. In 1882, Thierwechter built this block-long establishment, which still stands at 142–148 West Water Street. When opened, it was reported to be the largest general store between Toledo and Sandusky. (Charles Hablitzel.)

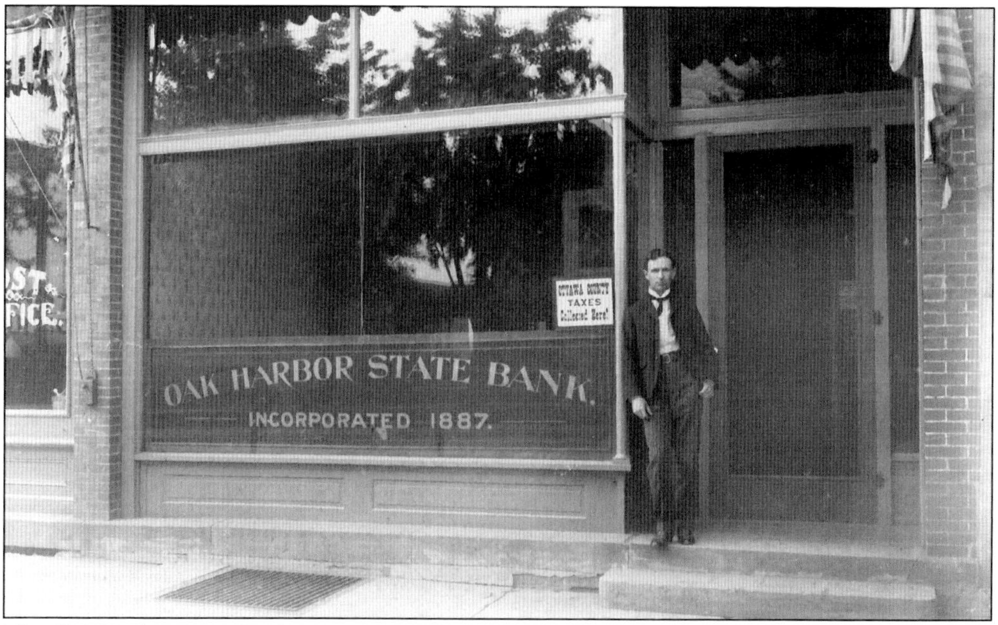

The Oak Harbor State Bank was organized in 1887 by Adelbert L. Spitzer and Ceilan M. Spitzer, Toledo bankers who saw a need for a bank in Oak Harbor. It was initially located at 208 West Water Street in the Bank Block, where this photograph was taken. In 1911, the bank relocated to the northeast corner of Water and Church Streets, the site of the former Jno O. Fought market. (Liske.)

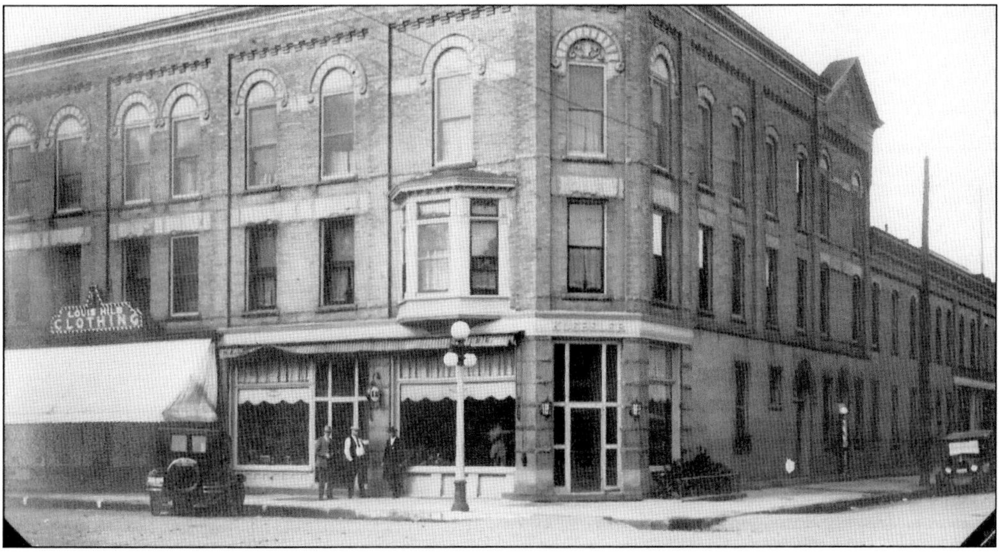

With rumors of a new interurban line coming through Oak Harbor and the need for more hotel rooms, the Kuebeler family of the Kuebeler-Stang Brewing Company of Sandusky started construction on this massive three-story hotel in 1899. The hotel was dedicated in a gala event on January 22, 1900. It boasted 35 guest rooms and toilet facilities on each floor with hot and cold running water. There was even a bowling alley in the basement. The building and furnishings cost upward of $50,000. In the below photograph, Cletus Kemp calmly smokes his cigar in his three-piece suit. Note the spittoon on the floor. The Kuebeler Hotel, under various names and owners, continued as a hotel for almost 100 years. The building now houses a restaurant and retail establishment. (Both, Jack Kemp.)

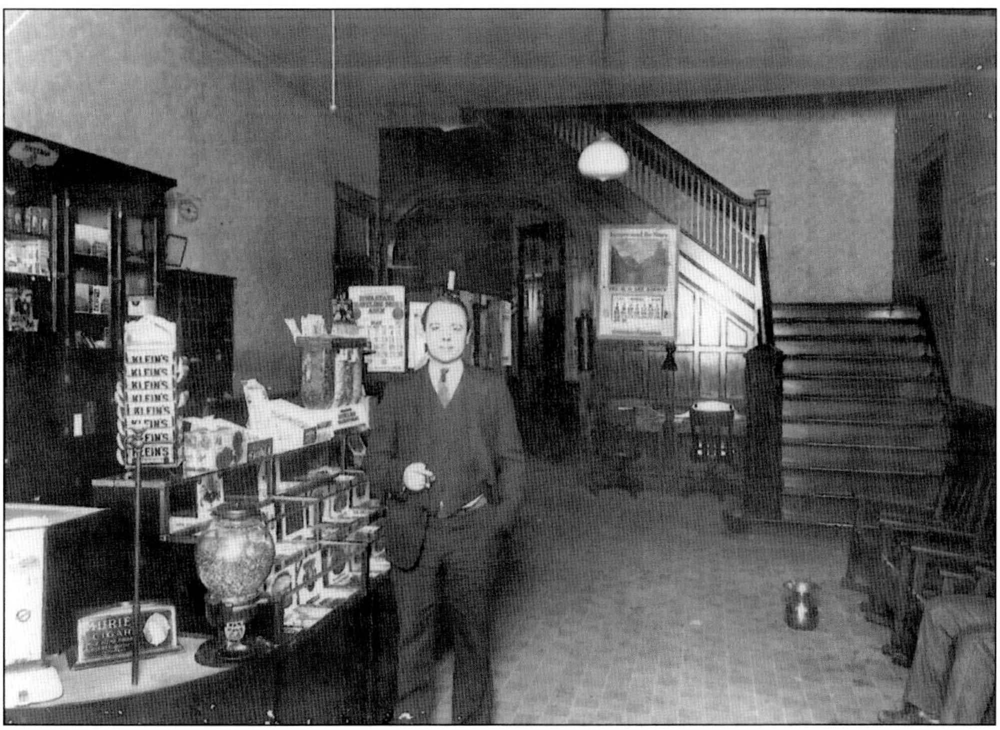

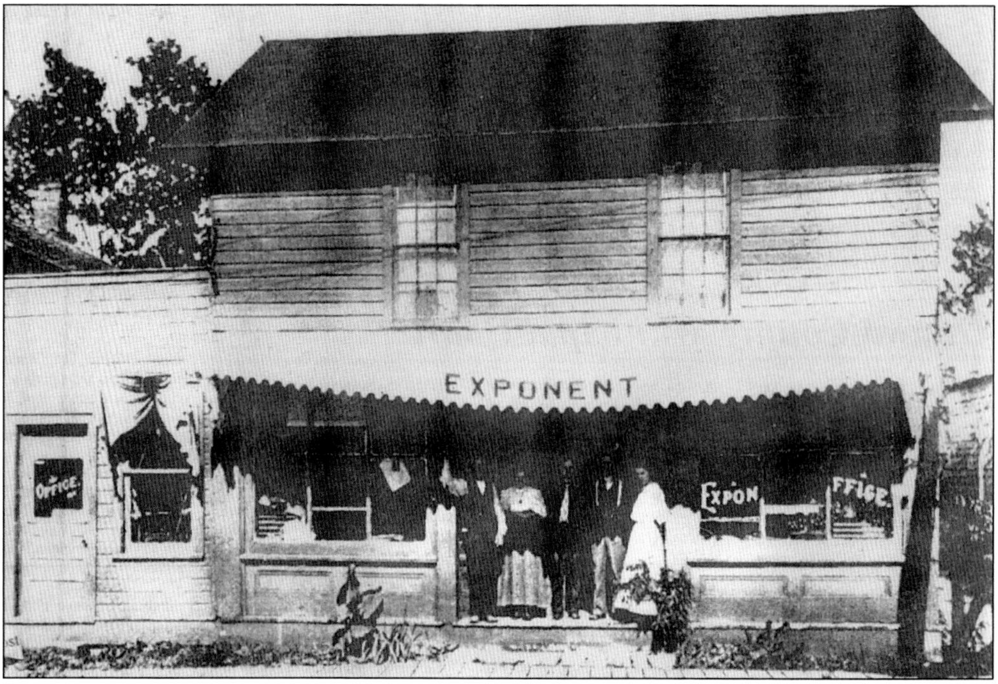

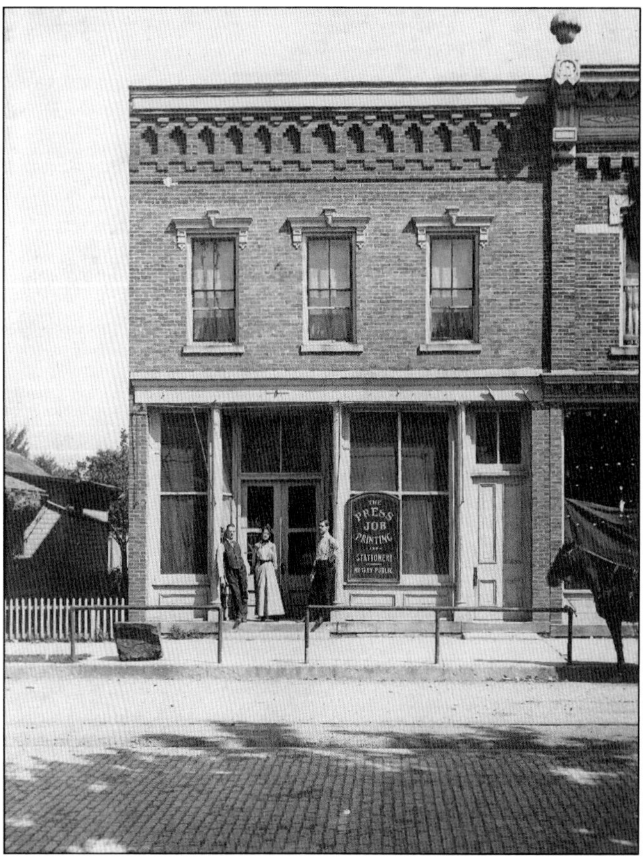

The *Ottawa County Exponent* has been in continuous publication since 1871. Its founding has been attributed to Adolphus Kraemer, although R. Stanbery was listed as the first editor and publisher. This building, one of the *Exponent*'s early offices, was located at 116 North Locust Street. Today, this is the site of a Laundromat. A new *Exponent* building was constructed just to the south in 1946. (Liske.)

A competing newspaper, the *Oak Harbor Press*, was started in 1873 by R. Harpham, although George Gosline, who acquired the paper in 1875, was best known as its editor. The *Oak Harbor Press* moved to this building at 218 West Water Street in 1898. Over the years, the building has had many uses; today, fittingly, it houses a print shop. (Liske.)

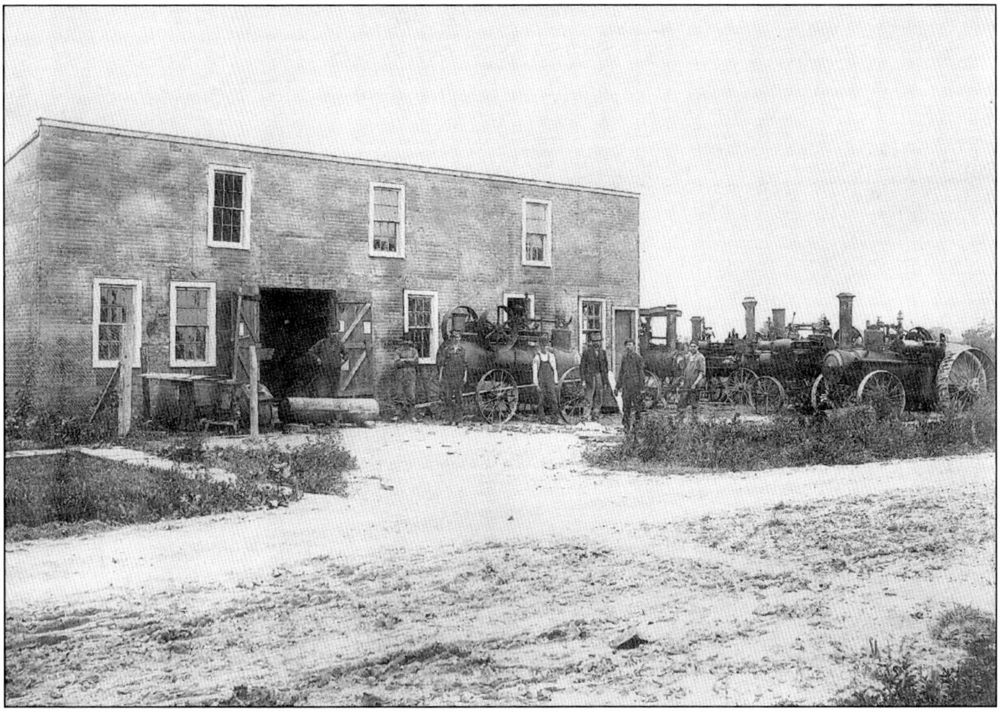

With the advent of mechanization and the automobile, machine and repair shops began to appear. The John H. Bense and Son Machine Shop was located along the Portage River at the foot of Toussaint Street. After 1906, the Bense Motor Company made a small gas engine called the "Bense" for marine and stationary use. (OHPL.)

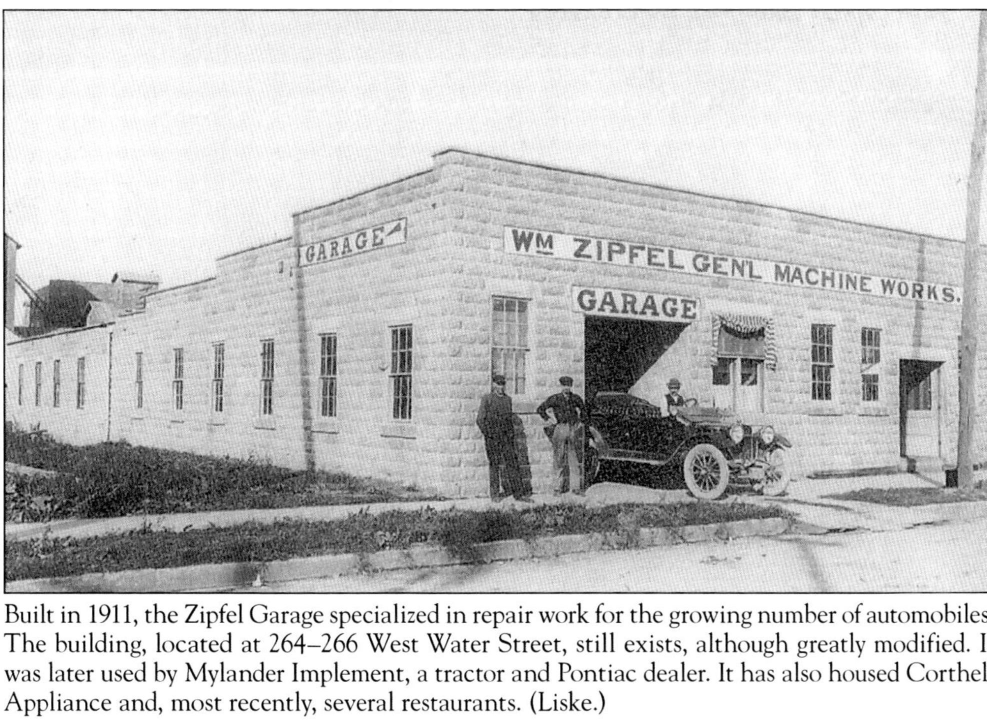

Built in 1911, the Zipfel Garage specialized in repair work for the growing number of automobiles. The building, located at 264–266 West Water Street, still exists, although greatly modified. It was later used by Mylander Implement, a tractor and Pontiac dealer. It has also housed Corthell Appliance and, most recently, several restaurants. (Liske.)

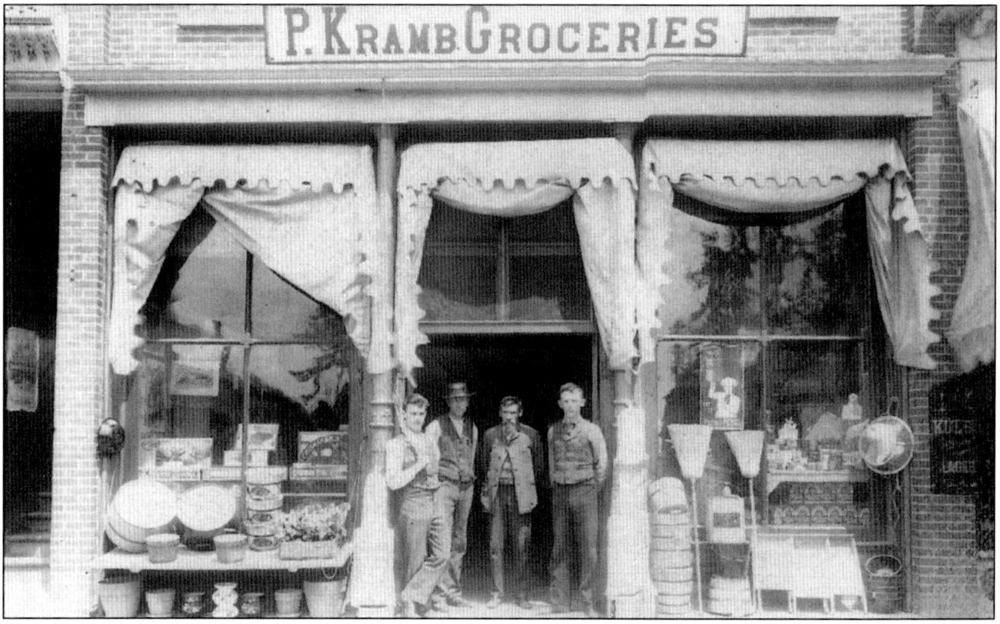

Philip Kramb started selling boots and shoes in Oak Harbor as early as 1865. By 1885, he had started a grocery business. This photograph was taken about 1895 in front of his store at 114 West Water Street. Shown here are, from left to right, Harmon Kramb, unidentified, Philip Kramb, and Albert Kramb. (Mary Paulsen.)

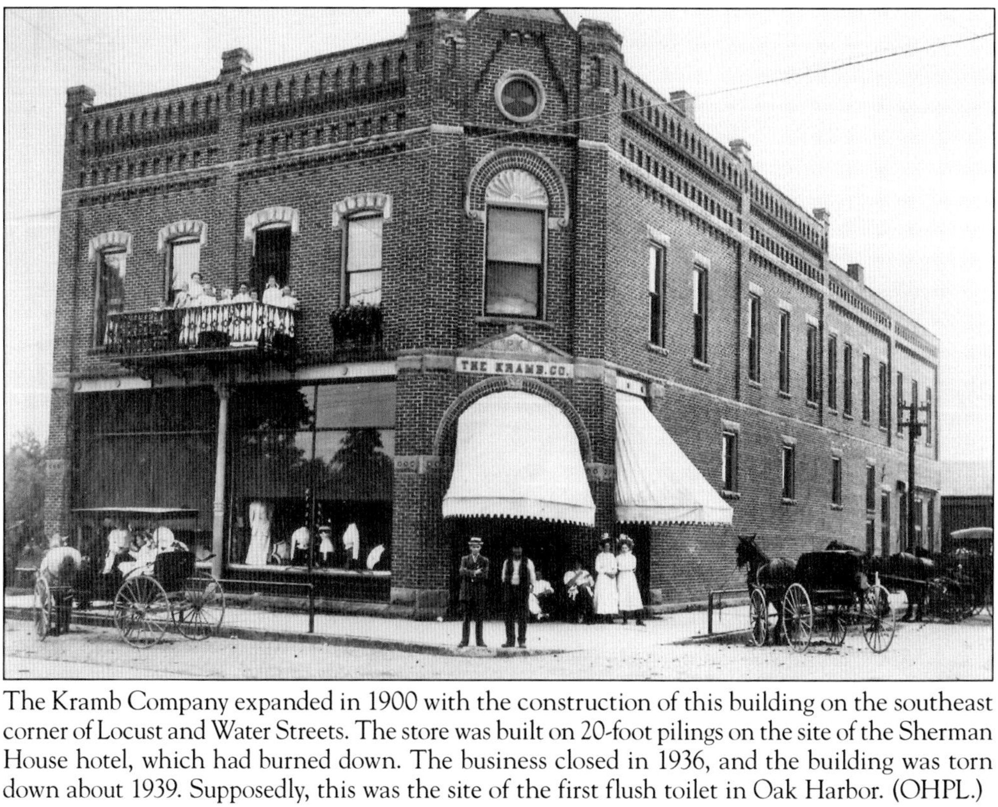

The Kramb Company expanded in 1900 with the construction of this building on the southeast corner of Locust and Water Streets. The store was built on 20-foot pilings on the site of the Sherman House hotel, which had burned down. The business closed in 1936, and the building was torn down about 1939. Supposedly, this was the site of the first flush toilet in Oak Harbor. (OHPL.)

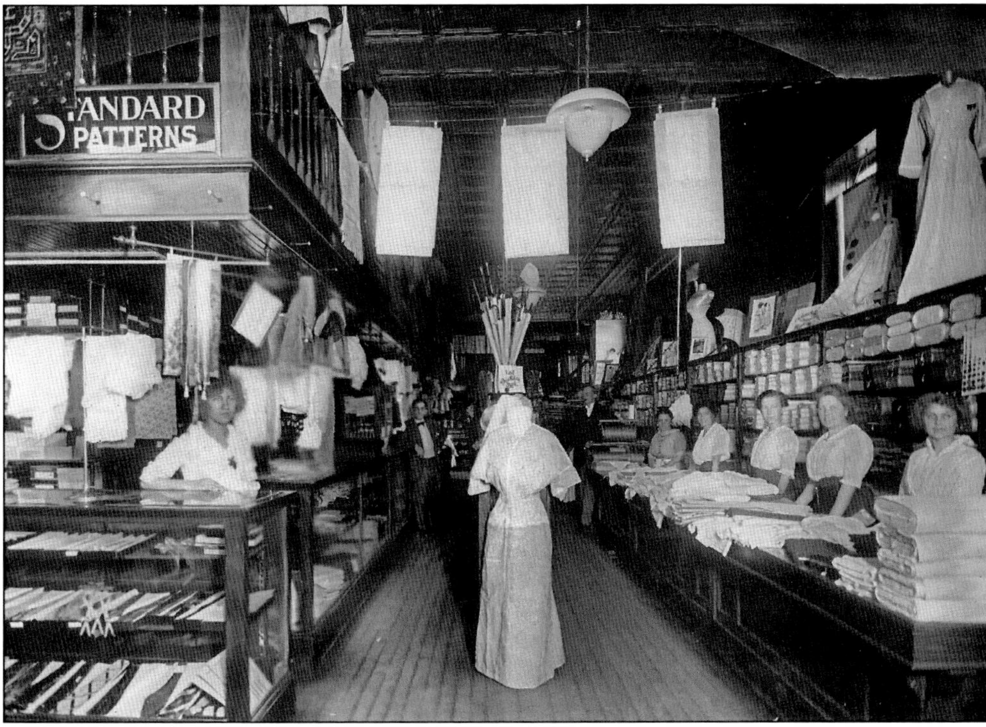

Inside, the Kramb store had a two-story ceiling with a second-floor balcony. As shown here, the Kramb Company specialized in clothing, dry goods, and sundries, and included a dress-making shop. Harmon C. Kramb is in the back, in bow tie with hand on his hip. Ida Kramb is the last woman along the counter on the right. (Mary Paulsen.)

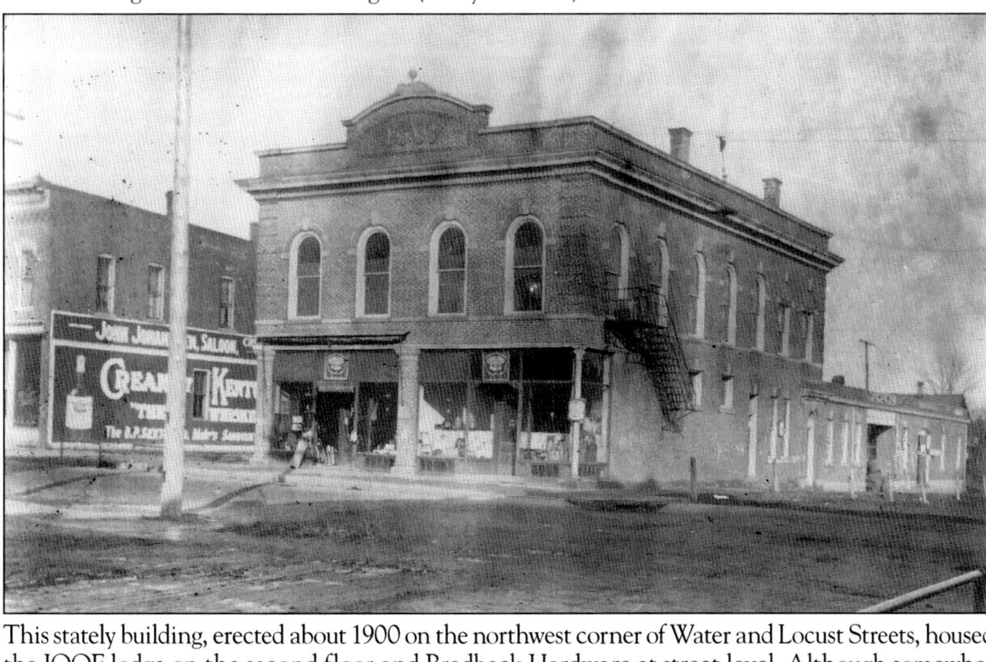
This stately building, erected about 1900 on the northwest corner of Water and Locust Streets, housed the IOOF lodge on the second floor and Bredbeck Hardware at street level. Although somewhat modified, the building remains today as a restaurant and commercial establishment. (Gluth.)

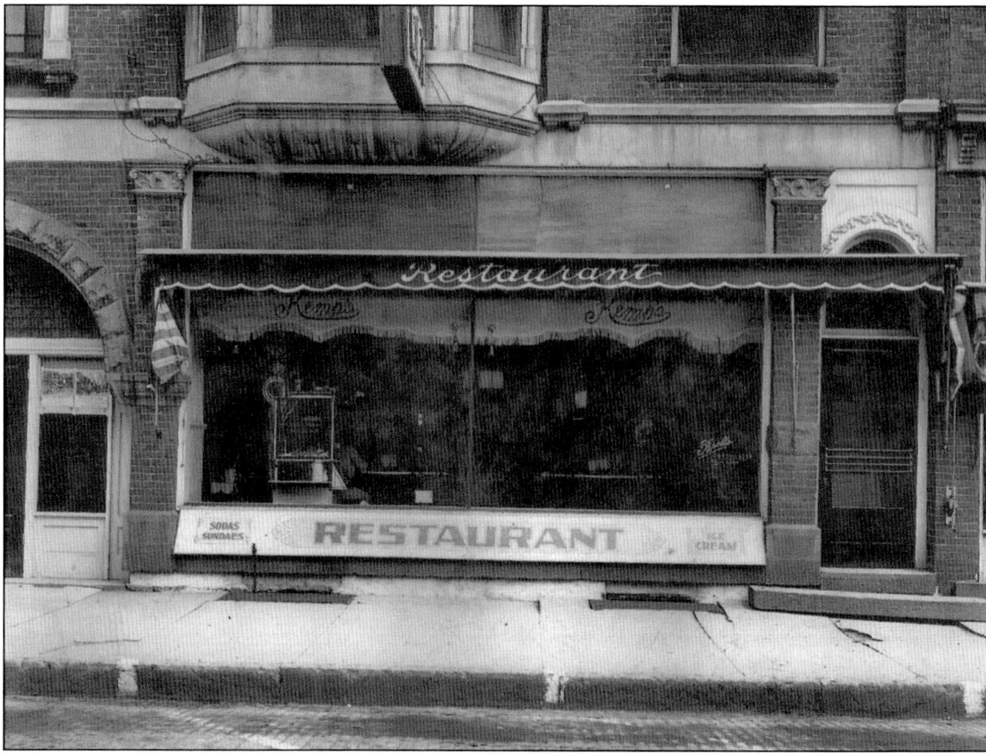

Charles Kemp owned a restaurant for many years at 160 West Water Street in the Von Thron Building. The restaurant, shown above in a 1920s photograph, served sandwiches, sodas, and ice cream. The photograph below is of the restaurant's unusual interior, complete with artificial palm trees. Local Oak Harbor businessman Nick Stevens is at the piano. The restaurant was later converted into an A&P grocery store, which operated until the early 1960s. (Both, Jack Kemp.)

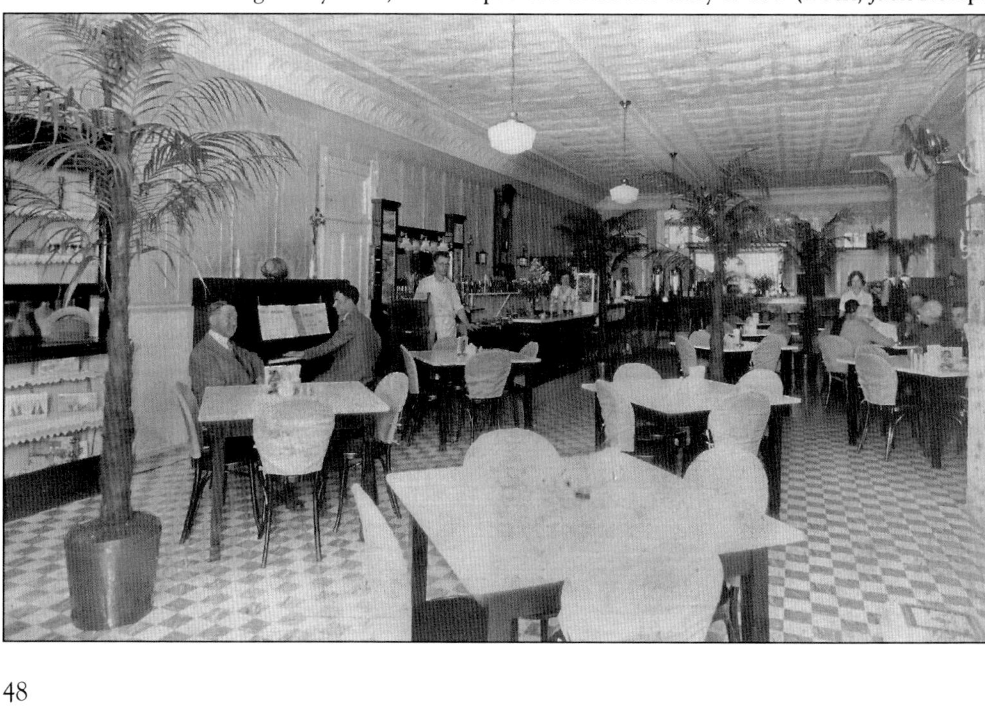

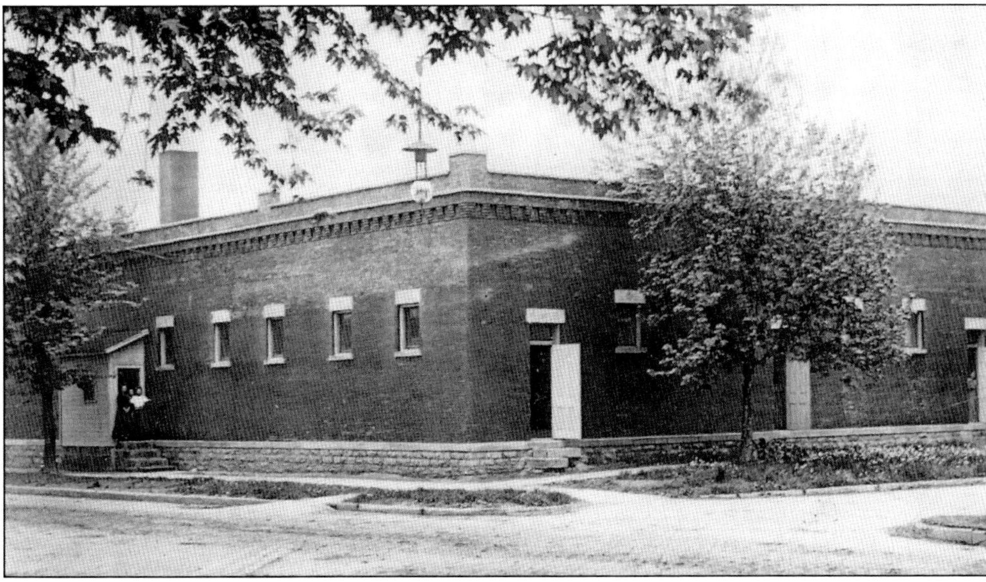

The "Mitten Factory," a branch of the Fremont Glove & Mitten Company, was established around 1908 in this building at the northeast corner of Main and Church Streets, previously the site of the Central Hotel. Newspaper reports indicate that the top two floors were removed from the hotel, resulting in this structure. The building was demolished in 1975 to make way for the new municipal building. (Liske.)

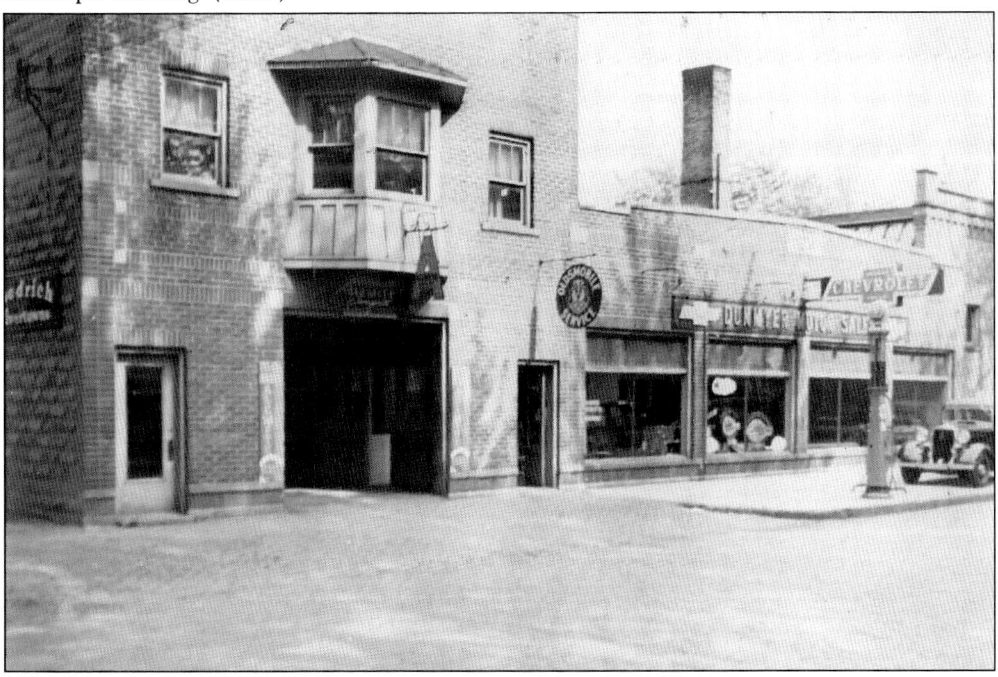

Blacksmith L.D. Link and his son Roy Link built this garage and repair shop around 1912 on the north end of the mitten factory. Roy and his wife lived in the apartment above the garage. Originally known as the Palace Garage, it later became Dunmyer Chevrolet. The structure had other uses, but, like the mitten factory, was torn down in 1975 to make room for the new municipal building. (Martin.)

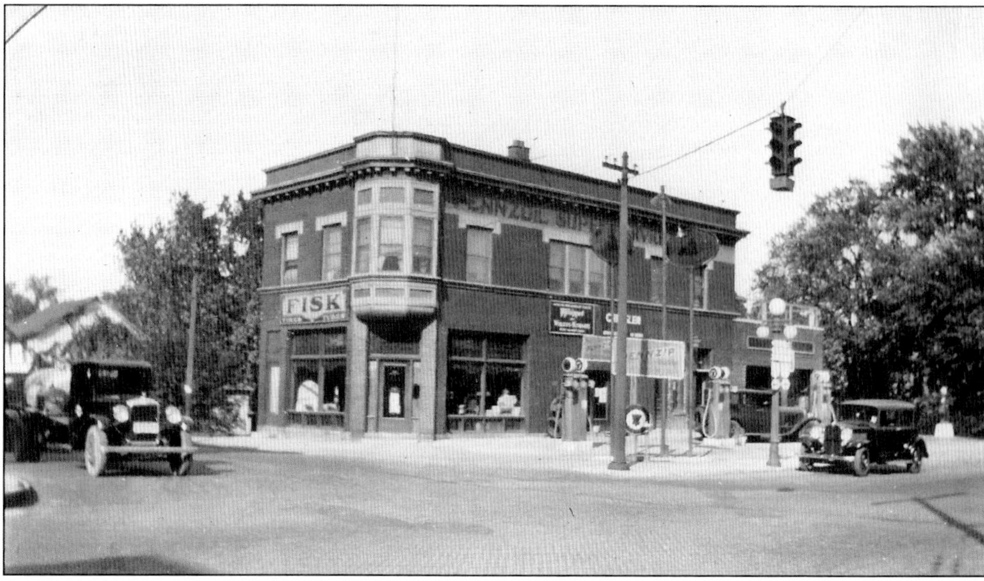

Erected about 1912, this building on the northeast corner of Locust and Water Streets was originally a grocery store. It initially stood right on the corner, but was moved about 30 feet to the north around 1929. Max C. Griest then opened a gas station and also sold Chrysler and Whippet automobiles. The building remains today as an automotive repair shop. (Elizabeth Milbrodt.)

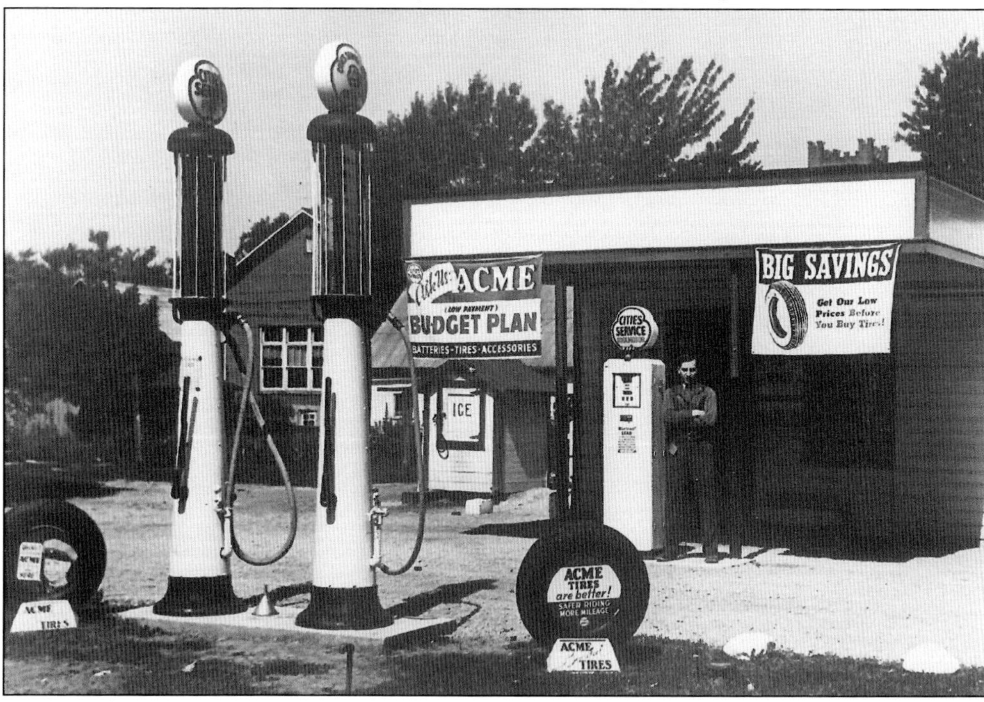

Lester Parkson built this gas station in 1923 on the northwest corner of Ottawa and Church Streets. It was the first drive-through service station in Oak Harbor. When this picture was taken in the late 1930s, it was Calvin Hetrick's Cities Service. This area is now a parking lot for the St. John's Lutheran Church. The building in the background is an early St. Boniface Church school. (Al Hemminger.)

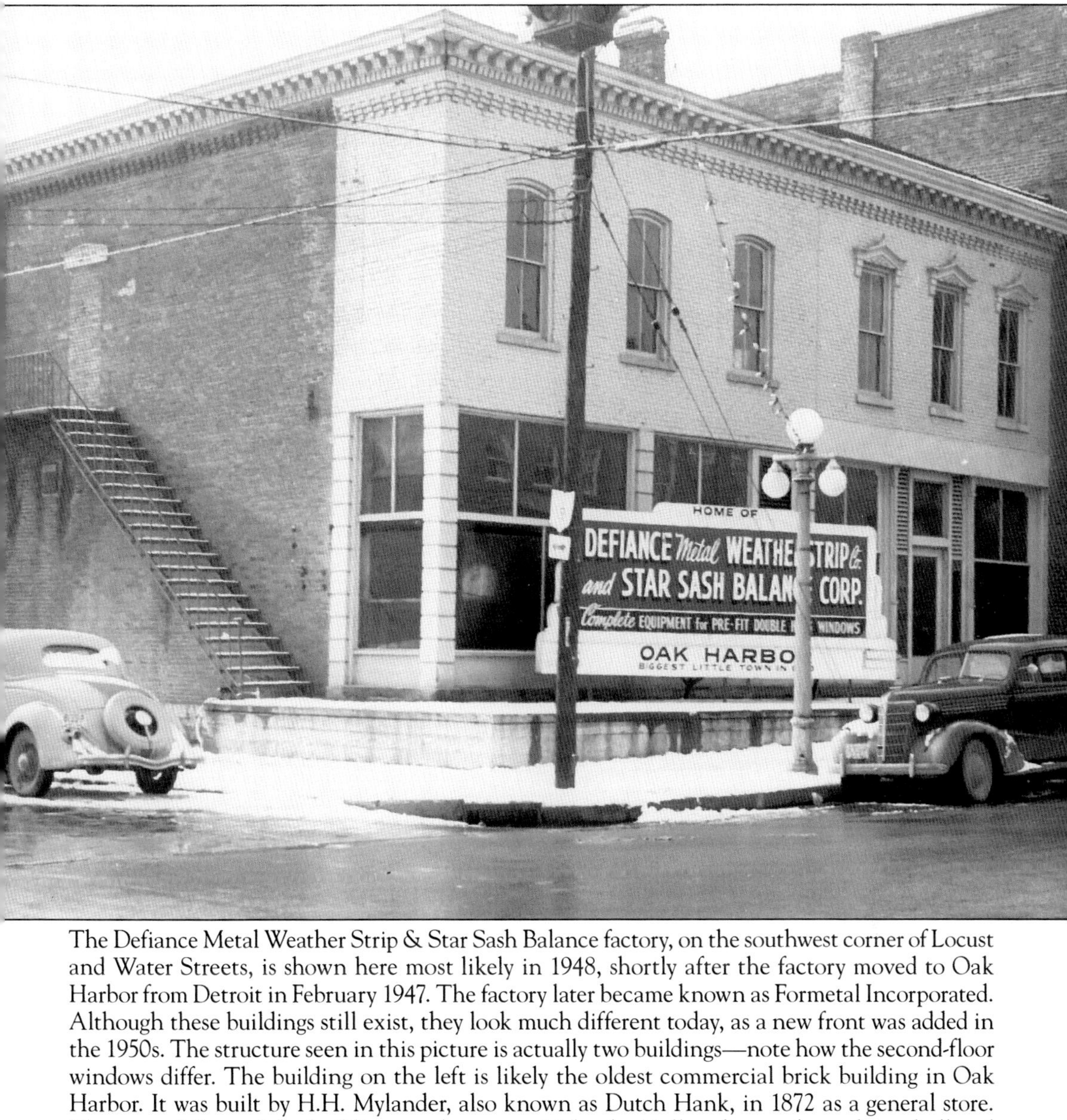

The Defiance Metal Weather Strip & Star Sash Balance factory, on the southwest corner of Locust and Water Streets, is shown here most likely in 1948, shortly after the factory moved to Oak Harbor from Detroit in February 1947. The factory later became known as Formetal Incorporated. Although these buildings still exist, they look much different today, as a new front was added in the 1950s. The structure seen in this picture is actually two buildings—note how the second-floor windows differ. The building on the left is likely the oldest commercial brick building in Oak Harbor. It was built by H.H. Mylander, also known as Dutch Hank, in 1872 as a general store. The second floor of the building was known as Mylander Hall and was a large dance hall and assembly area. The dedication of Mylander Hall took place on New Year's night, 1873, in a gala affair. This was also the location of the first Masonic hall in Oak Harbor. (Liske.)

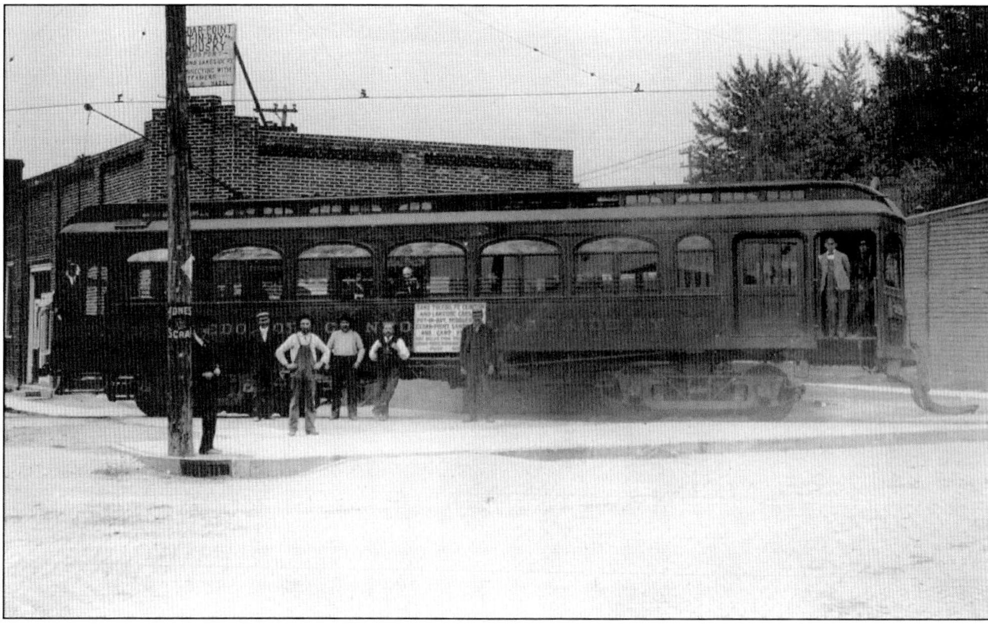

After several years of discussion, the Toledo, Port Clinton and Lakeside interurban electric railway began carrying passengers through Oak Harbor in 1904. The line went from Toledo through Genoa, Elmore, Oak Harbor, Port Clinton, and Lakeside. Here, eastbound car No. 22 has stopped in front of the Oak Harbor station, on the southwest corner of Water and Church Streets. (OCHM.)

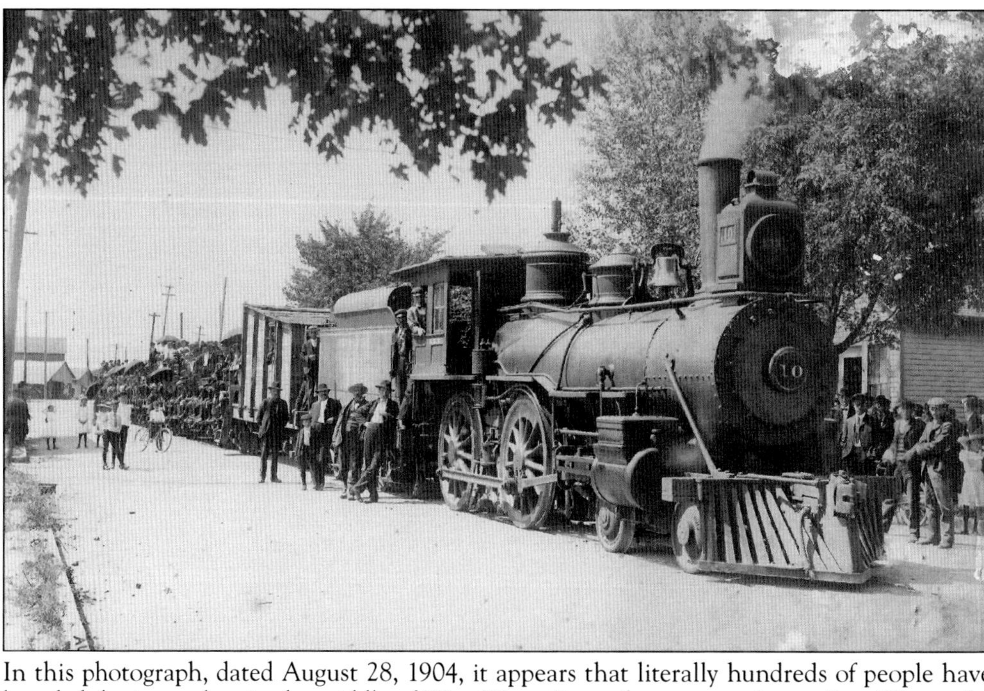

In this photograph, dated August 28, 1904, it appears that literally hundreds of people have boarded the interurban in the middle of West Water Street for an excursion to Port Clinton for a baseball game. These were the first paying passengers to use the new interurban line. Note that the open passenger cars are being pulled by a steam construction engine. (OHPL.)

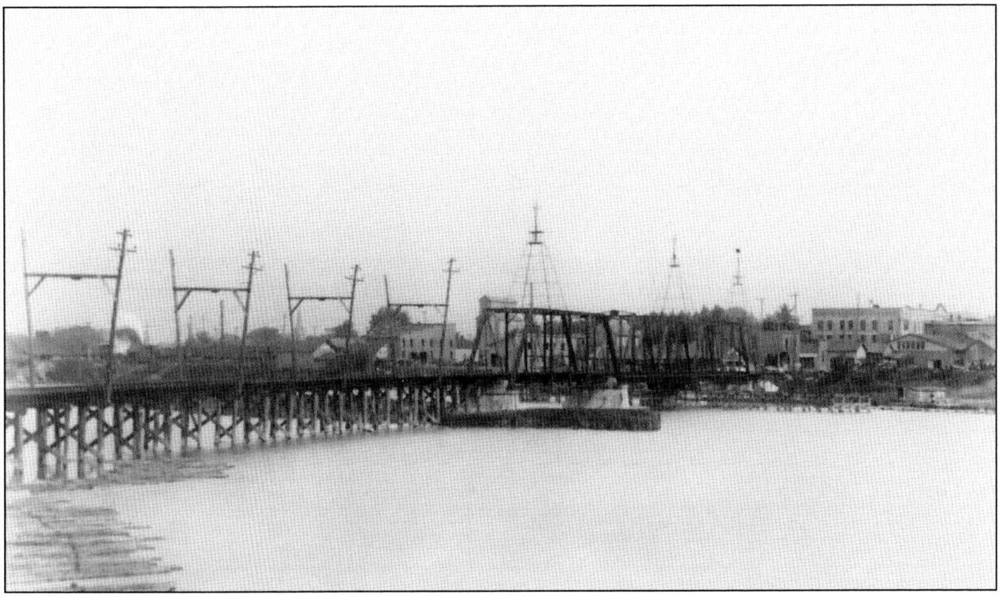

In order for the interurban to cross the Portage River, a swing span bridge was constructed. A 60-foot tower was mounted on the revolving center so that the electric lines were not disturbed when the bridge was open. With the advent of the automobile, the interurban through Oak Harbor ceased passenger operations in 1939 and freight traffic in 1946. The bridge was torn down in 1946. (OHPL.)

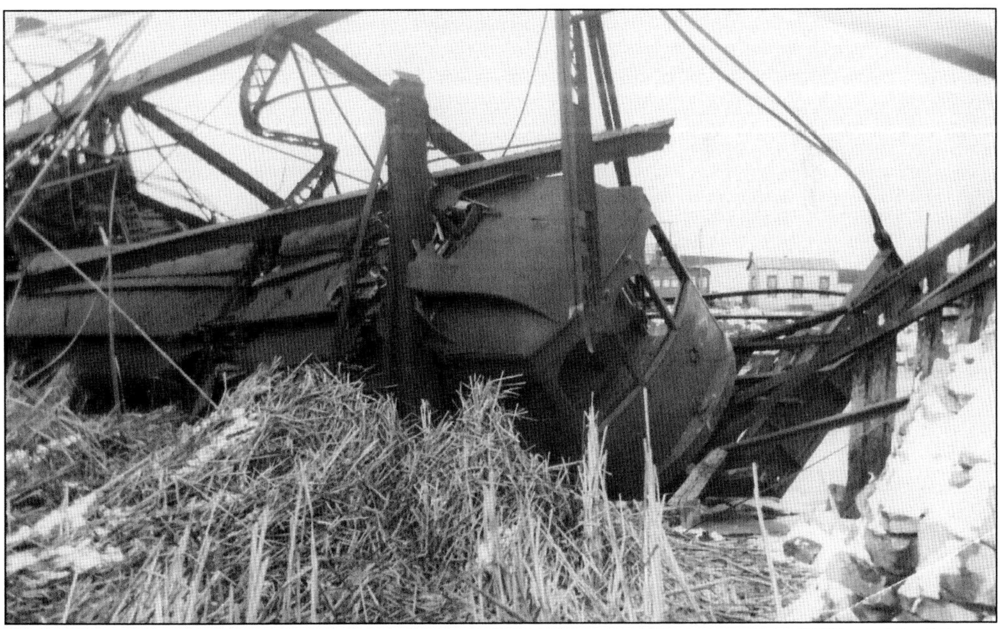

Tragedy was averted on March 7, 1923, when westbound car No. 20, operated by William Pluckhorn, motorman, and William Tremmer, conductor, derailed on the bridge, collapsing it into the Portage River. Amazingly, no one was seriously injured. Passengers were transported over the river by bus until the bridge was repaired. Car No. 20 was not repaired. (OHPL.)

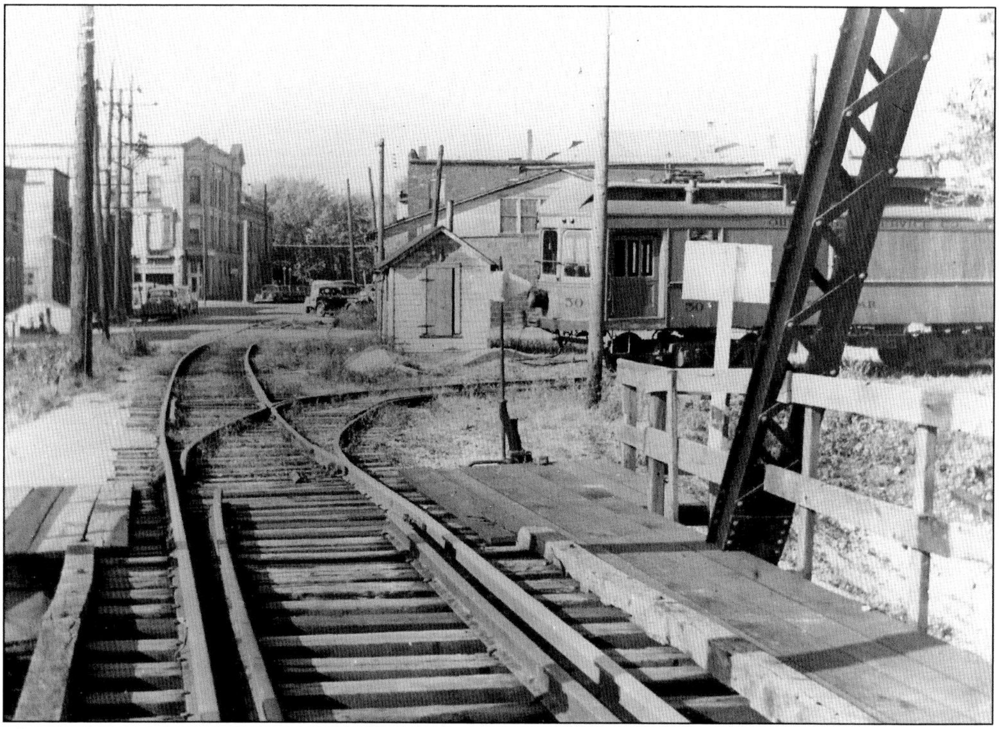

Shown here is the approach to Oak Harbor from the south across the Portage River on the interurban bridge. The main track went straight ahead, while the spur to the right went to the interurban carbarns on Mill Street. The carbarns were used by the interurban to repair streetcars from 1915 to 1946, when the tracks were removed in Oak Harbor. (Mary Paulsen.)

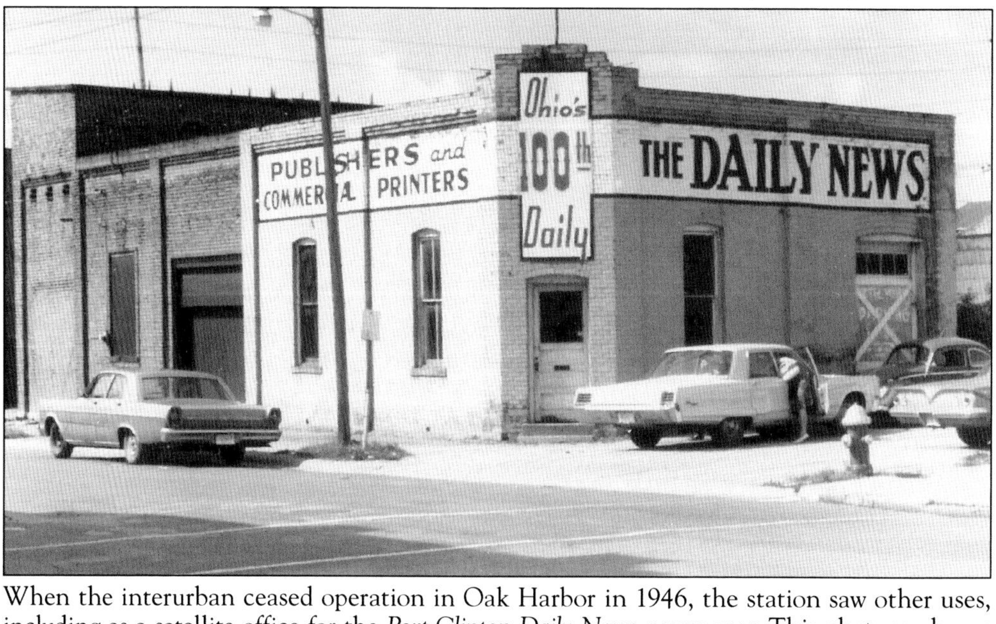

When the interurban ceased operation in Oak Harbor in 1946, the station saw other uses, including as a satellite office for the *Port Clinton Daily News* newspaper. This photograph was taken just prior to the building being razed in 1968. Today, a bank is located on this corner. (Charles Hablitzel.)

Four

To Protect and to Serve

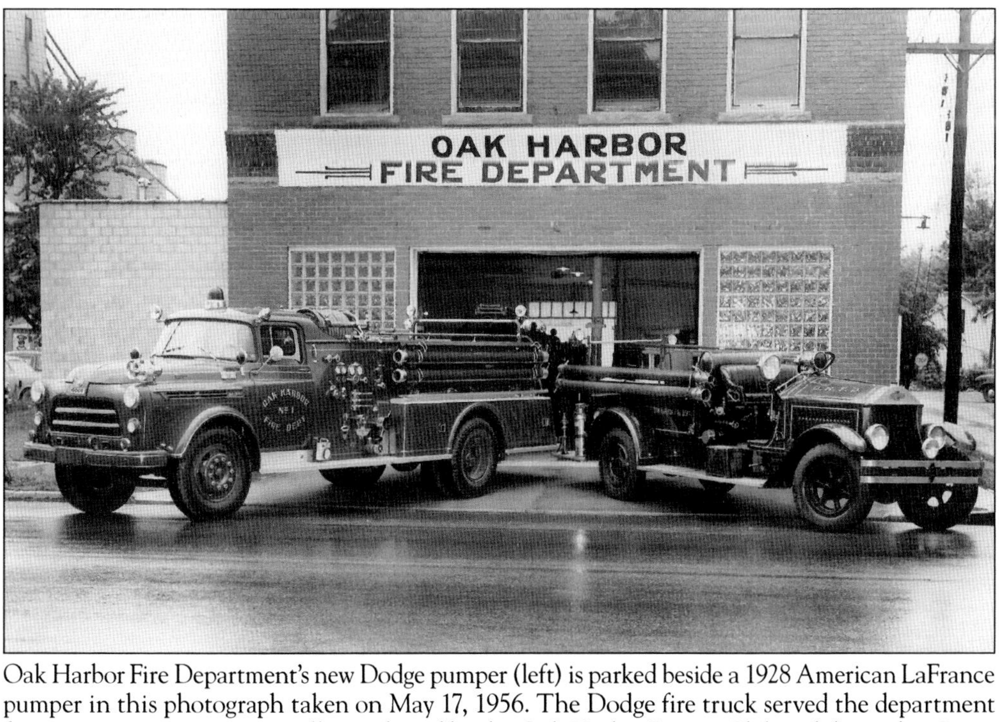

Oak Harbor Fire Department's new Dodge pumper (left) is parked beside a 1928 American LaFrance pumper in this photograph taken on May 17, 1956. The Dodge fire truck served the department for many years. It was eventually purchased by the Oak Harbor Rotary Club and shipped to Santa Anna, El Salvador, in 1988 for continued service in that country. (Harry Striker.)

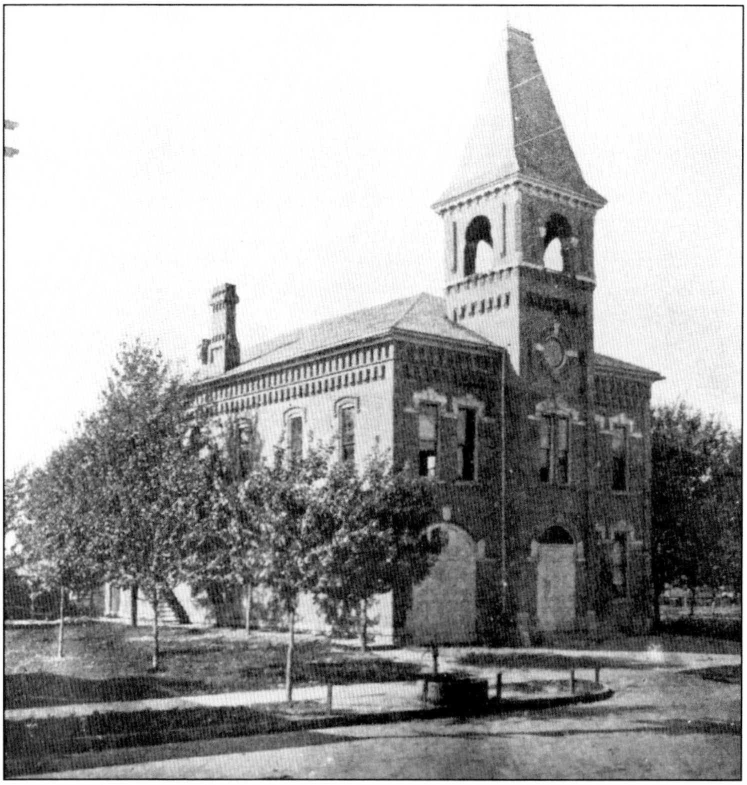

Oak Harbor's first town hall, built in 1883, was located on the west side of Church Street between the alley and Main Street, now Adolphus Kraemer Park. There was a fire bell in the tower, and the steamer fire pumper was kept behind the large door on the left. The building also contained a jail and meeting rooms. It was torn down in 1907 when the new town hall was constructed. (Liske.)

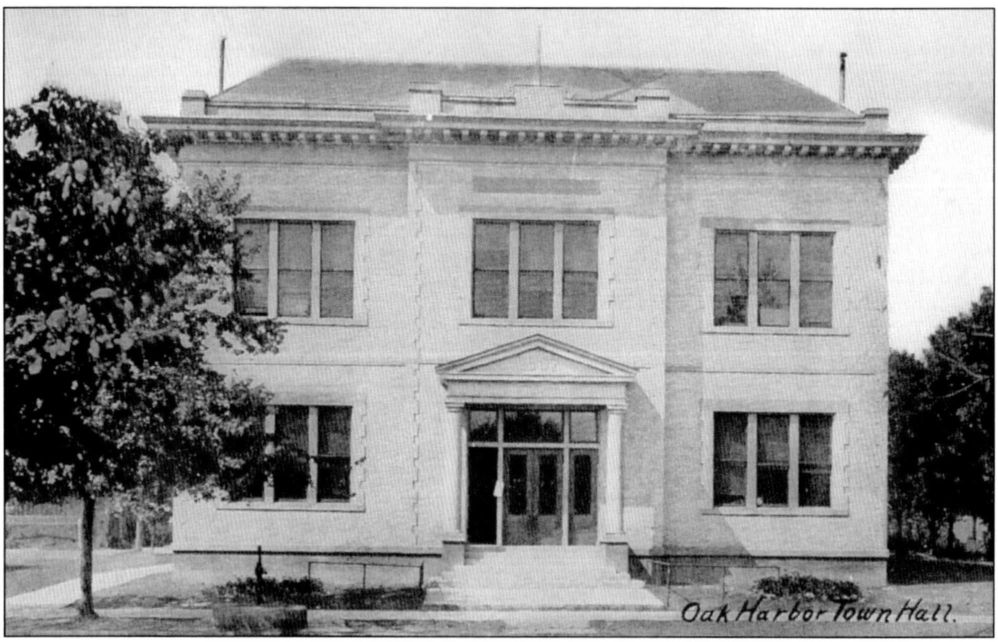

When the 1883 town hall began to deteriorate in 1907, a new town hall was constructed on the same site. The fire department was located in a small building in the alley behind the new town hall. The construction cost was $13,773, and the brickwork was done by Russell Bordeaux. The building was torn down in 1996. (Liske.)

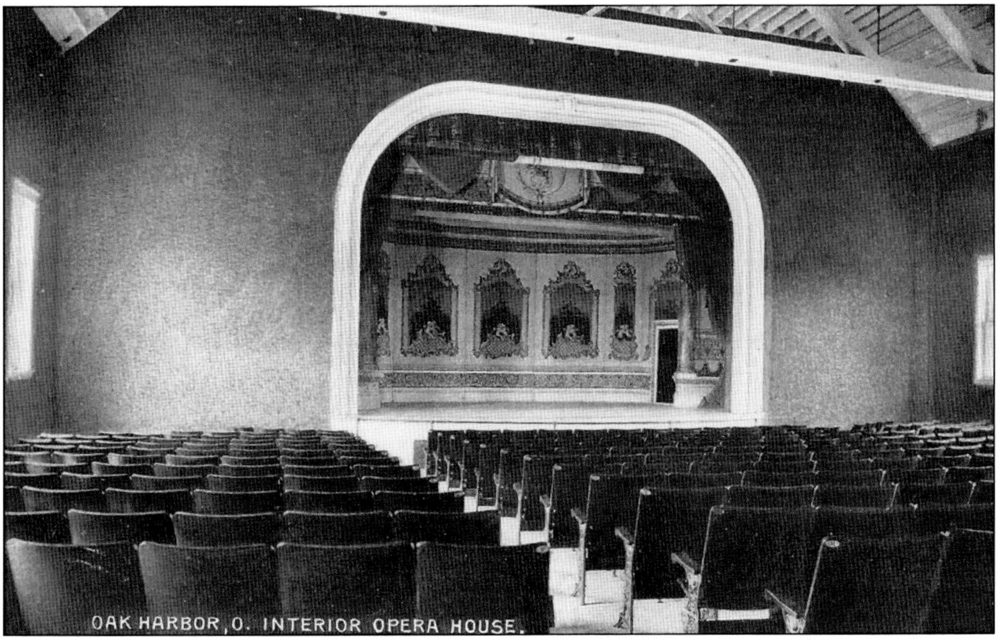

The second floor of the 1907 town hall contained a beautiful opera house auditorium, with a sloping floor and 400 permanent wooden seats. The stage was 25 feet high with a diamond motif arch. The opera house was used for high school class plays, graduations, farmers' institutes, and other gatherings for many years. (Liske.)

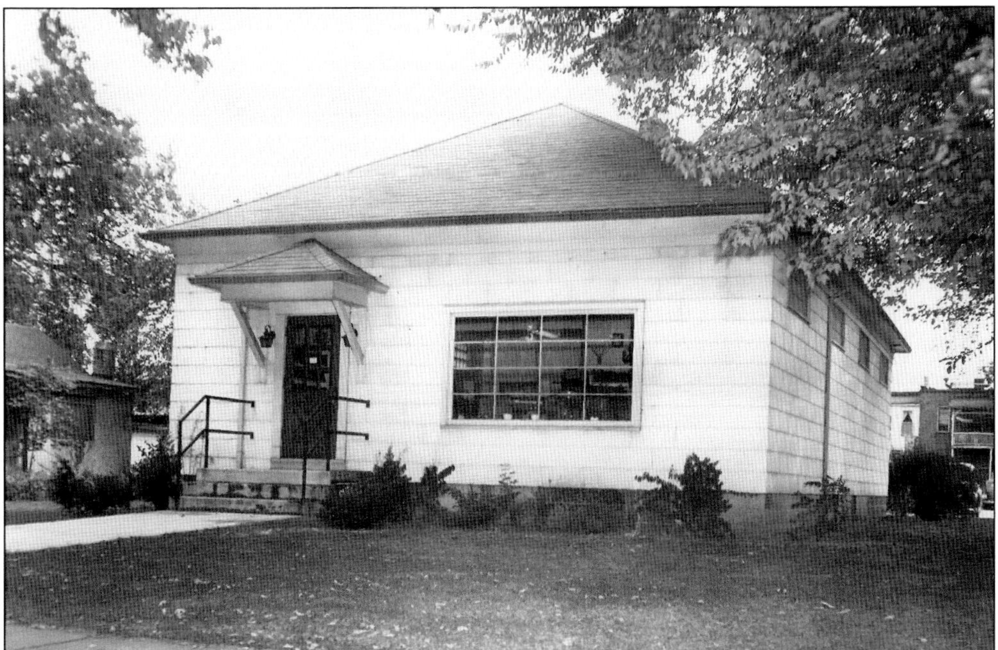

A public library in Oak Harbor dates back to at least 1875, when a subscription library was started in the high school. The library moved to this building in 1942 when it was a two-story house. A fire on March 23, 1944, destroyed the second floor, and the library was rebuilt to this one-story structure. It was torn down in 1987 when the new library was built. (OHPL.)

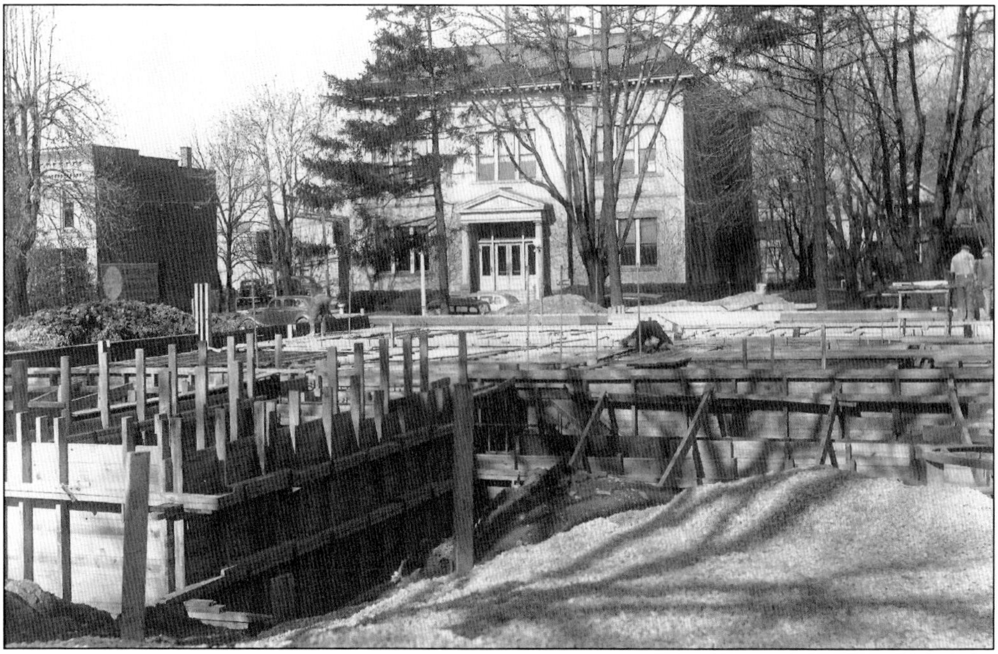

The Oak Harbor Post Office was housed in many locations over the years, including sites on Water Street and in the Kuebeler Hotel. However, in 1938, federal funds were provided to construct a new post office building on the southeast corner of Church and Main Streets. The 1878 Fought/Heller house was purchased, and the new post office was built at that site. The above photograph shows the initial construction in March 1939. The 1907 town hall is in the background. The c. 1950 photograph below shows the completed building, which still serves as Oak Harbor's post office. (Above, Oak Harbor postmaster; below, OHPL.)

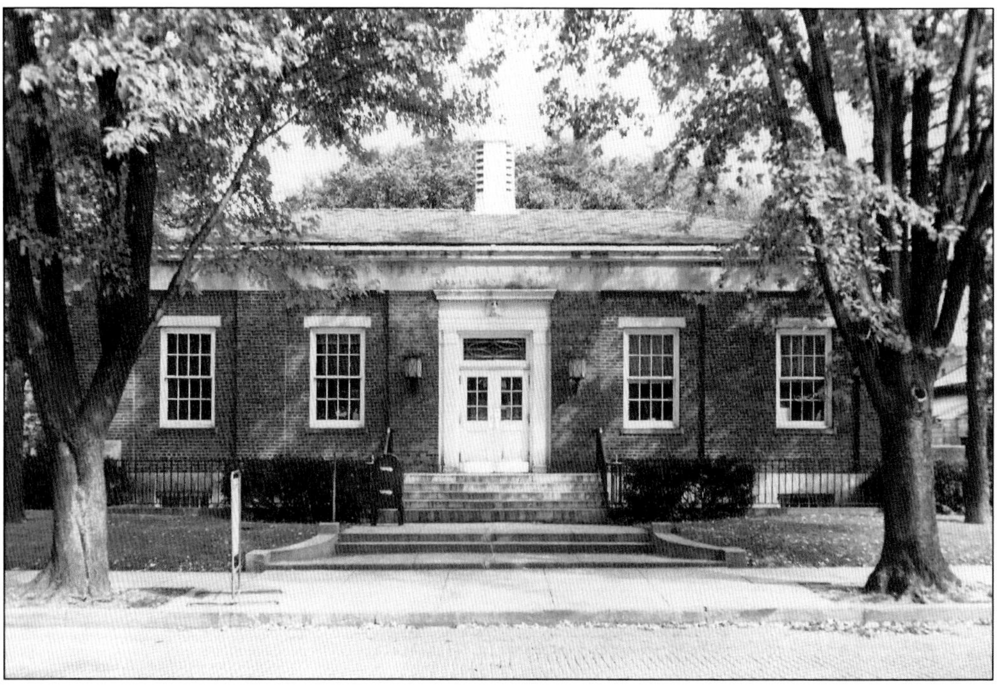

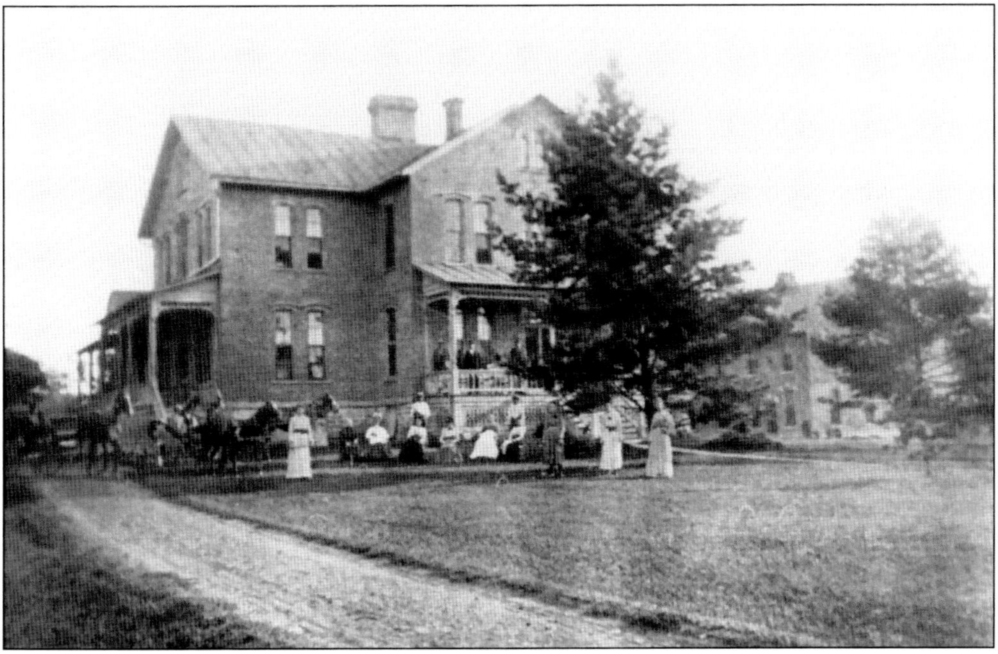

Commonly known as the "poorhouse," the Ottawa County Home, or Infirmary, was located just east of Oak Harbor in Salem Township. The three-story infirmary, home to 42 "inmates," was built in 1871 and used until the mid-1960s, when a modern county home was built. It was torn down in 1969. The site had its own cemetery, which still exists today. (OCHM.)

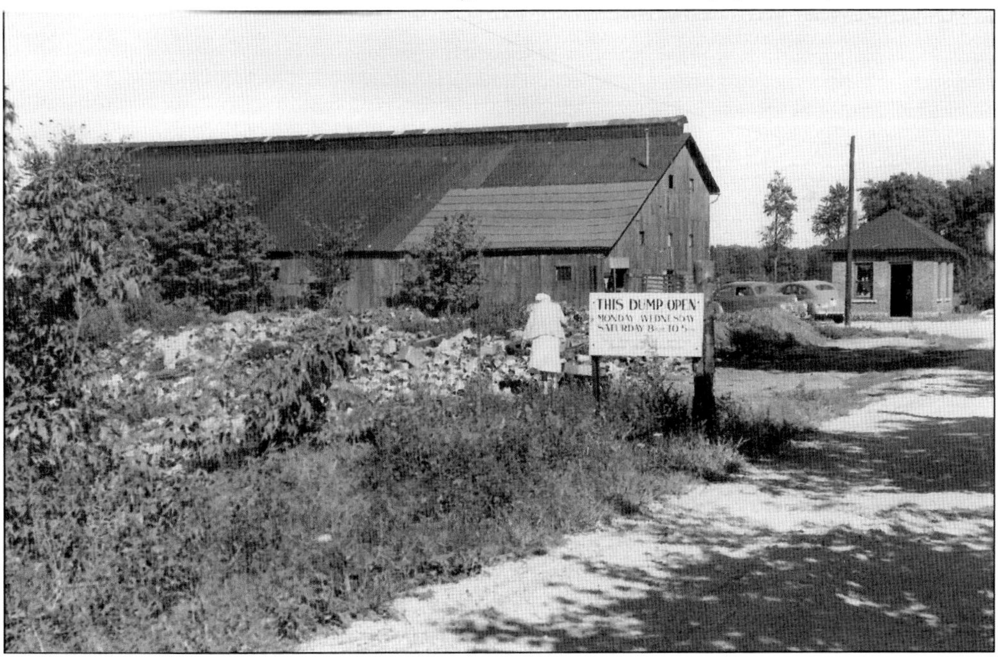

Before the days of sanitary landfills, every town had a dump. Oak Harbor was no exception. Over the years, dumps were located at various sites, including some areas along the river. This early 1950s photograph is of the town dump on the east end of Walnut Street. The building in the background is the old Oak Harbor stockyard. (OHPL.)

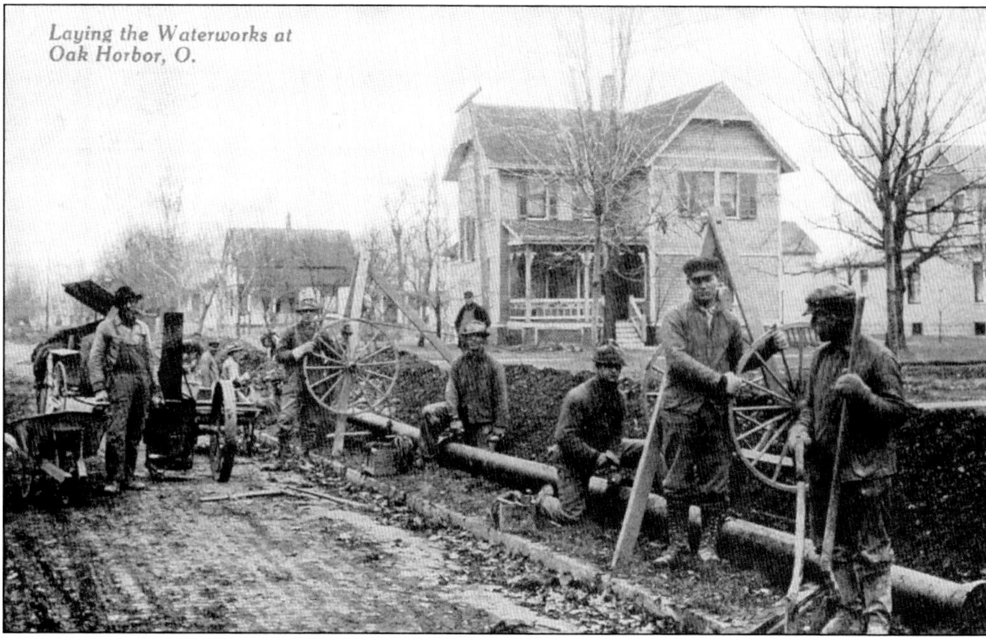

A growing community needed a reliable municipal water system, and in 1911, Oak Harbor installed its own. Shown above is early water main construction, most likely on Church Street near Walnut Street. In order to provide water pressure, a water tower, shown below, was also built in 1911, along the railroad tracks behind the high school. This 50,000-gallon elevated tower cost $2,980. The tower still remains, although the bowl and roof have been replaced. Some may remember when the roof of this water tower blew off in the July 4, 1969, storm. Note the two men standing precariously on the tower's crossbar. (Both, Liske.)

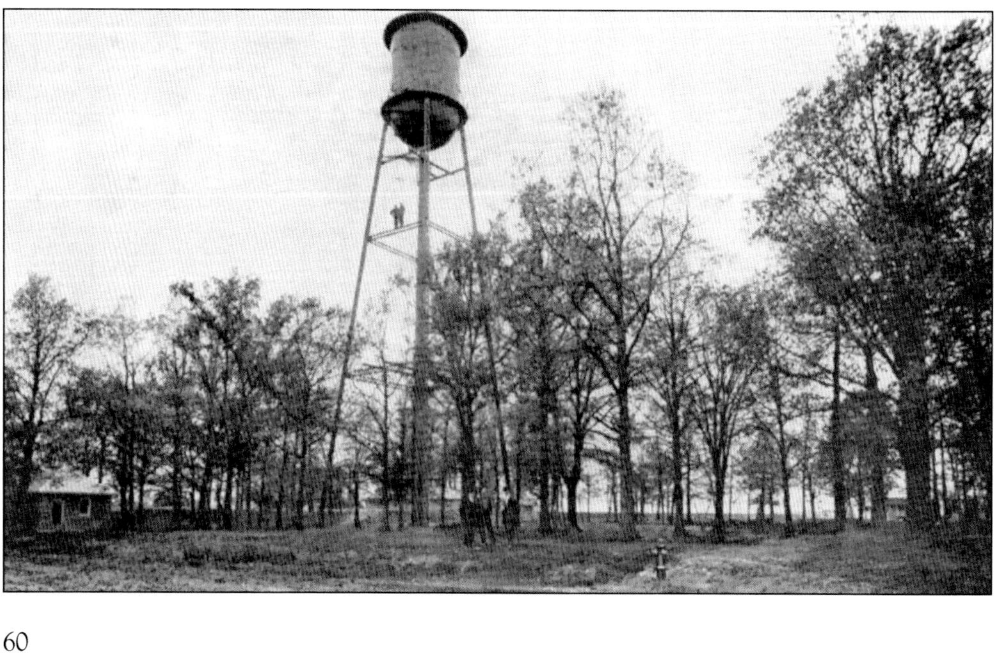

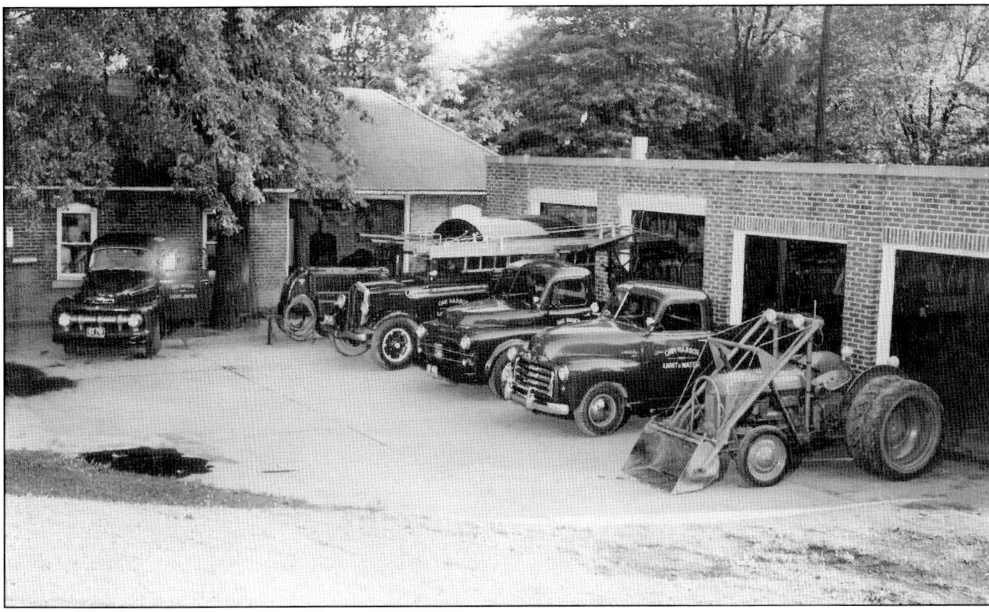

The Oak Harbor Light & Water Department, located on Park Street, brought out its equipment for this 1951 photograph. The water department began in 1911, and the electric department, in 1917, when the village purchased the Mylander power plant and built its own distribution system. (Irene Wood via Ted Foust.)

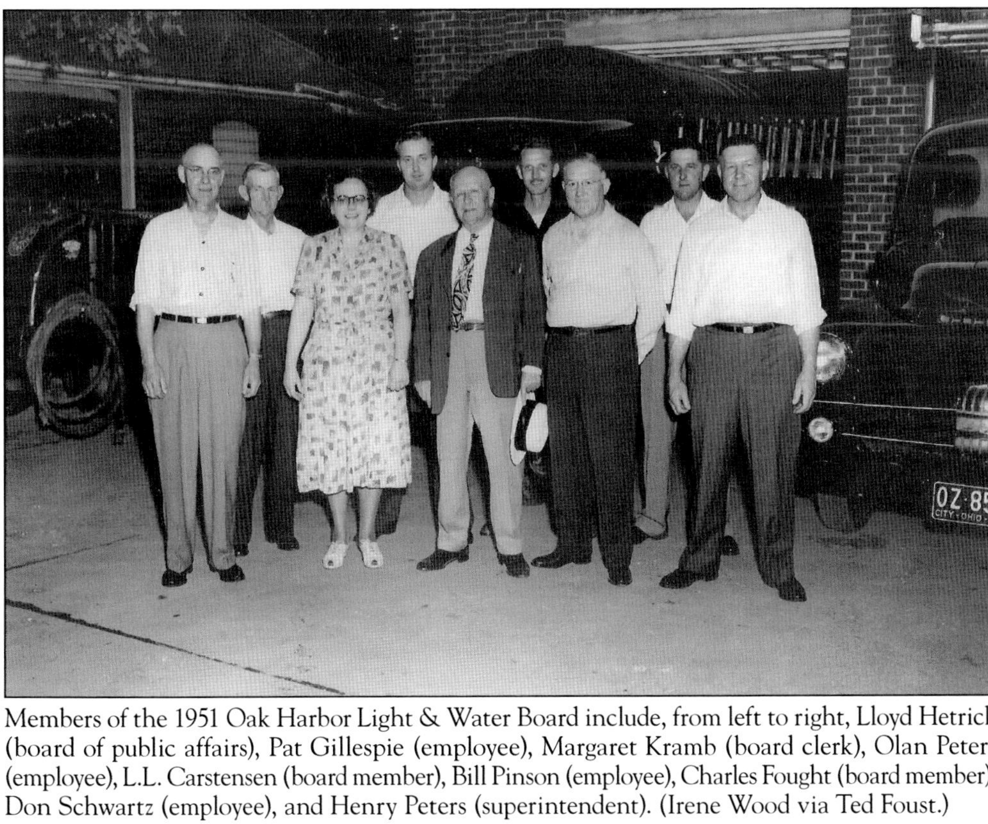

Members of the 1951 Oak Harbor Light & Water Board include, from left to right, Lloyd Hetrick (board of public affairs), Pat Gillespie (employee), Margaret Kramb (board clerk), Olan Peters (employee), L.L. Carstensen (board member), Bill Pinson (employee), Charles Fought (board member), Don Schwartz (employee), and Henry Peters (superintendent). (Irene Wood via Ted Foust.)

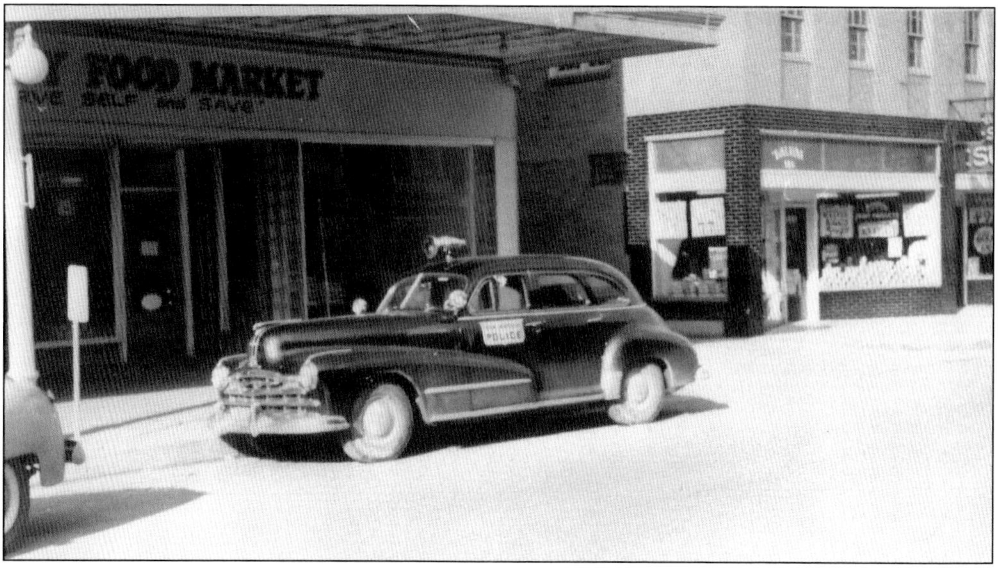

Although Oak Harbor had a village marshal or police department dating to the mid-1800s, the town did not have a police car until early 1949. Prior to that date, police officers were expected to patrol and answer calls in their personal vehicles. In late 1948, the village council voted to purchase the 1948 Pontiac seen above. It was delivered in January 1949, and it served the force until 1955, when a Dodge (below) was purchased as a replacement. Early police cars did not have two-way radios. When a call came in for the police on patrol, light bulbs would be lit at the corners of Church and Water Streets and Locust and Water Streets. Upon seeing the lights, the officer would stop in at the station to see what the problem was. (Both, Oak Harbor Police Department via Steve Weirich.)

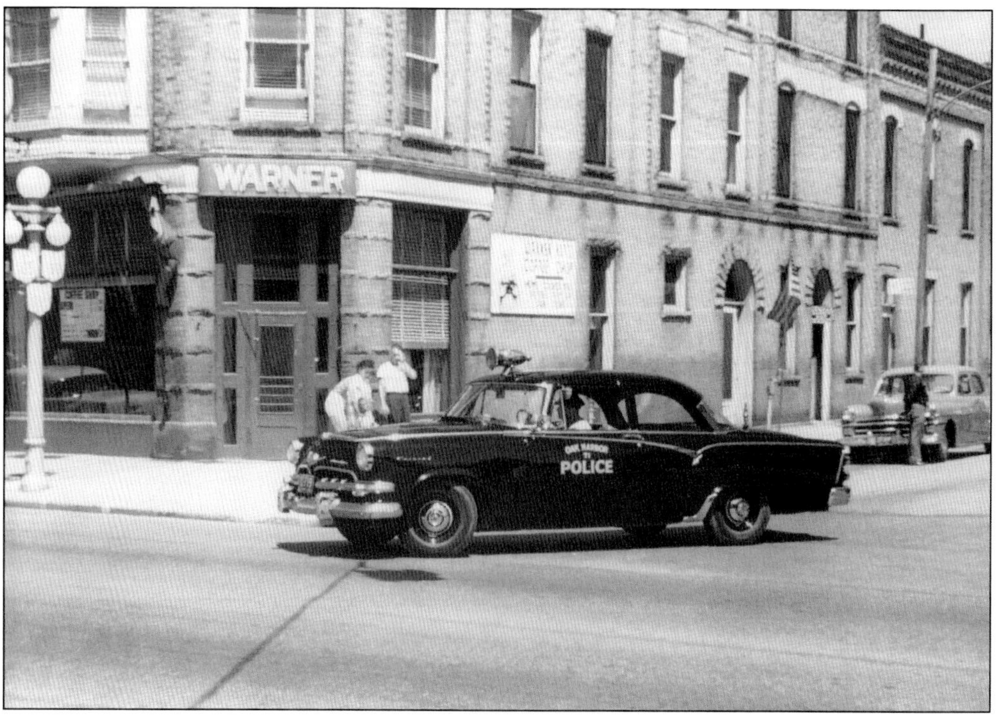

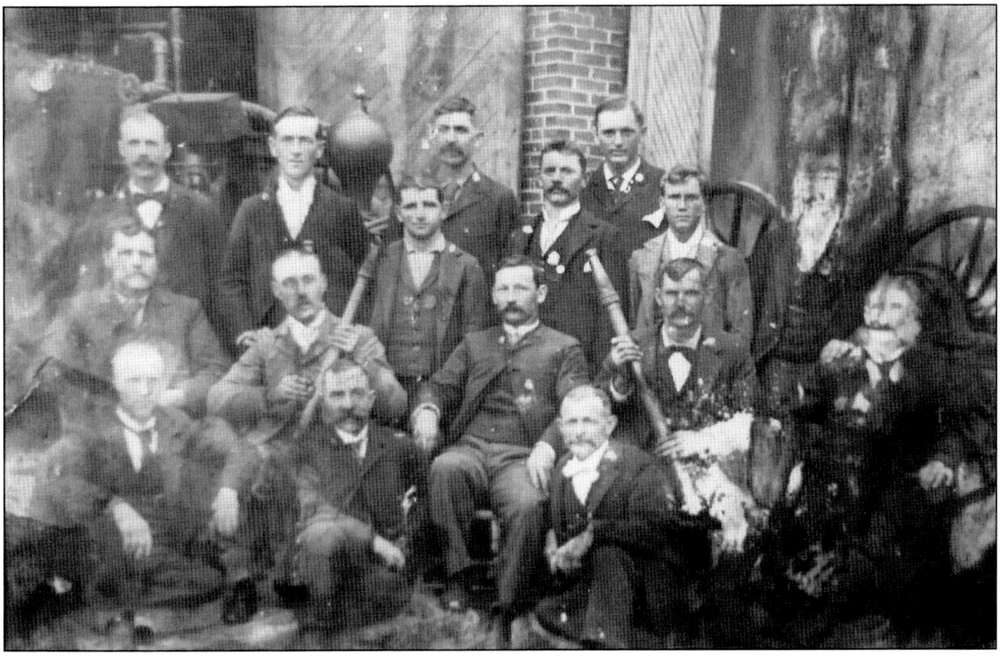

Oak Harbor's first fire department was the Roose Hose Company. Established in 1866, it consisted of workers at the Roose, Mylander, & McGrath stave factory. In 1873, it became part of the newly formed Portage Fire Company, pictured here after the 1883 town hall was built. Today, the fire department that serves Oak Harbor is still called the Portage Fire District. (Harry Striker.)

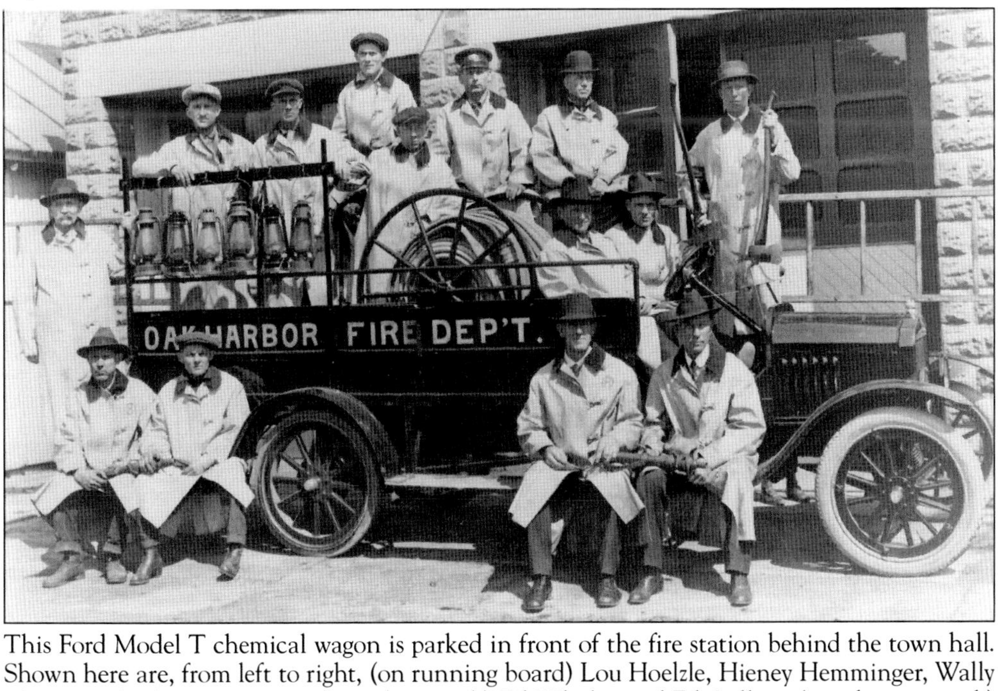

This Ford Model T chemical wagon is parked in front of the fire station behind the town hall. Shown here are, from left to right, (on running board) Lou Hoelzle, Hieney Hemminger, Wally Bloom, and Glorence Leaser; (seated in truck) Ed Whaley and Ed Collins; (standing in truck) George Probel, Al Frank, Otto Leucht, Rube Ross, Irv Overmeyer, Frank Palmer, George Schroeder, and Pat Cullenen. (Harry Striker.)

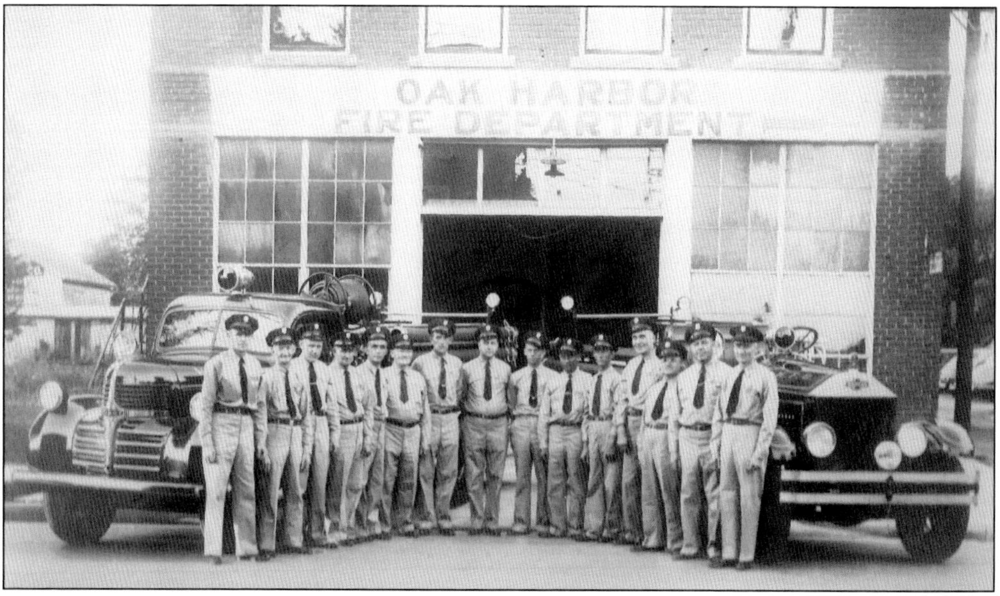

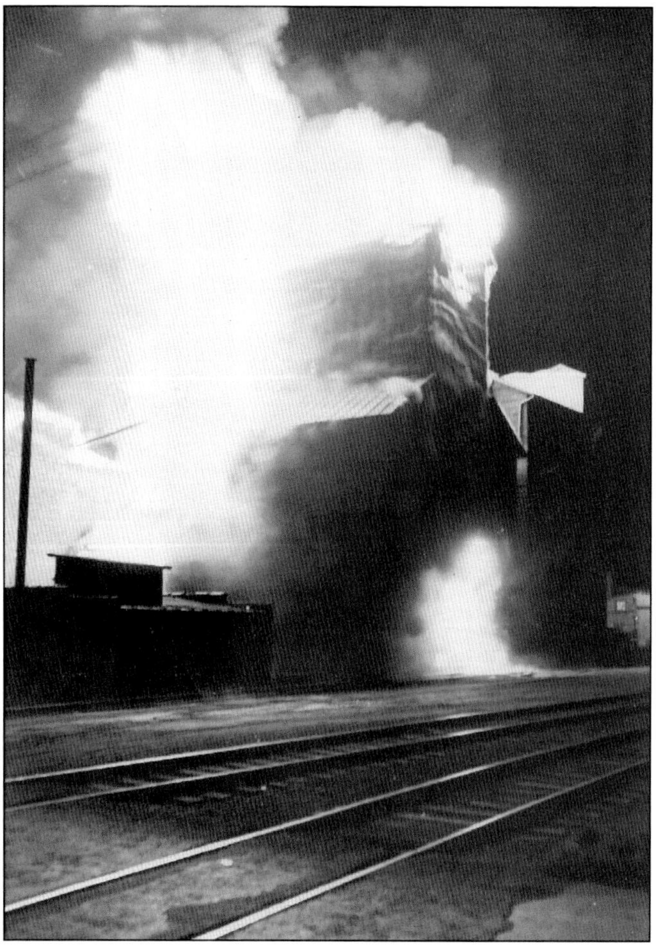

By the early 1940s, additional equipment had been added and new facilities were provided for the fire department. Equipment included a new 1941 Dodge pumper and a 1928 American LaFrance pumper. In the late 1930s, the department moved into this new facility, the Sutter Building, at 240 West Water Street. Greatly expanded, this structure still serves the fire department today. (Helen Pfeiffer.)

A major fire struck the Ottawa County Cooperative grain elevator on April 19, 1949. This was one of two major fires that night, both of which were determined to be arson. The Ottawa County Cooperative was formerly the Emery Theirwechter Company elevator. Grain elevators at that location, on the south side of West Main Street by the railroad, were also destroyed by fire in 1900 and 1929. (OHPL.)

The Anderson Boat Company moved to Oak Harbor in 1953 and established a boat-building business in the old basket factory building east of Locust Street along the river. The company, run by Olaf Oscar "Andy" Anderson, produced 14-, 16-, and 20-foot-long wooden boats. At 8:00 p.m. on December 23, 1958, fire broke out at the plant. Due to the age of the building (1895) and the accumulation of wood dust, shavings, and paint supplies, the fire burned hot and fast. Anderson Boat Company did not rebuild, and later moved to Indiana. Note that the "turn-out gear" the firemen in the right photograph are wearing is really nothing more than rubber raincoats. (Both, Robert Liske.)

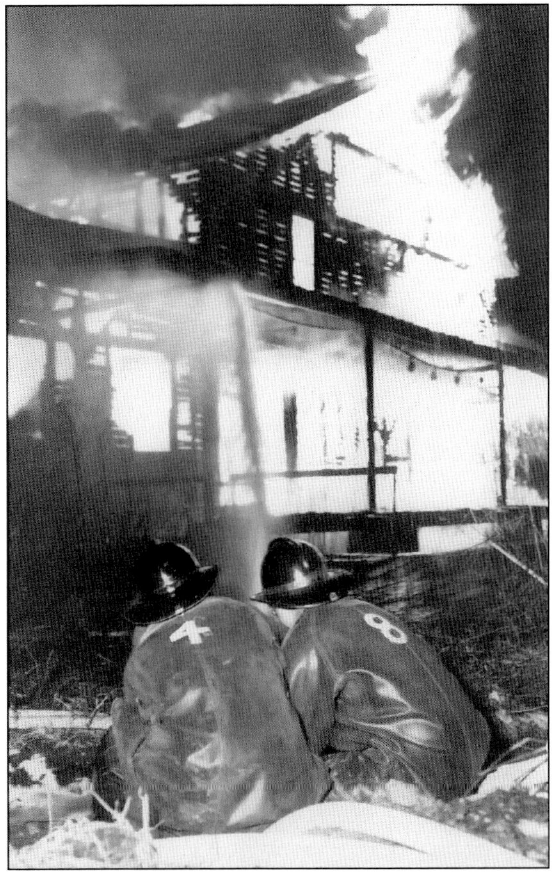

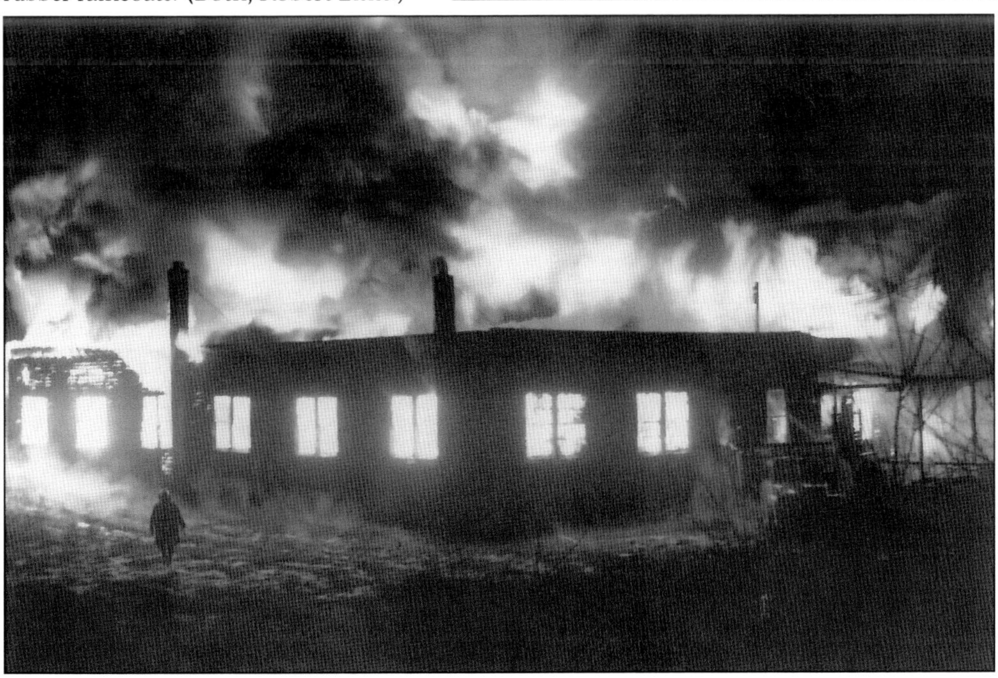

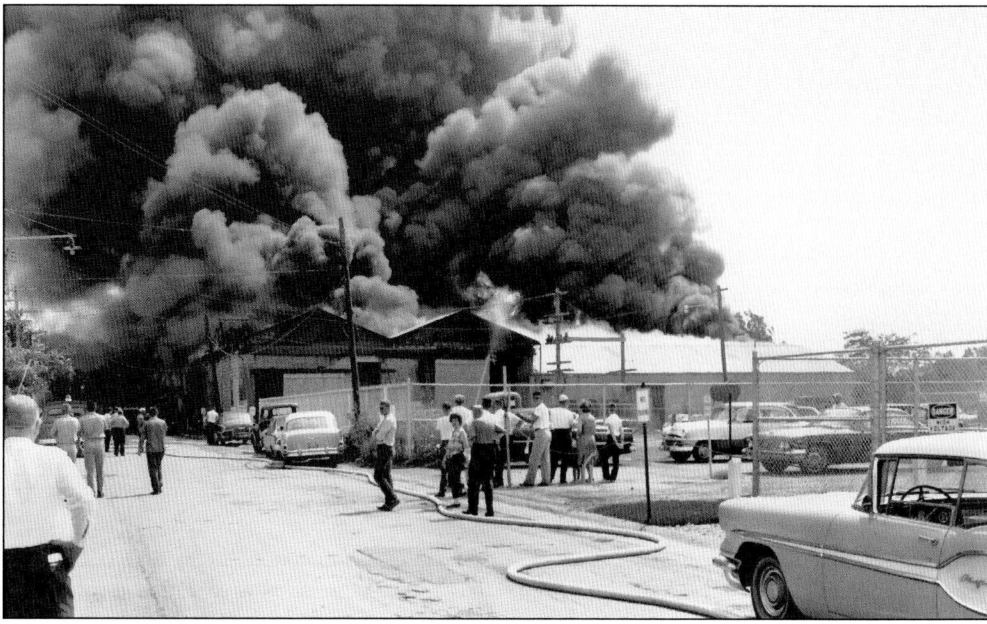

The Myca Products Company moved to Oak Harbor in 1955 to establish an extruded rubber products plant. The factory was located on Mill Street along the river in buildings that at one time housed a repair shop for the old interurban lines. Ironically, on August 23, 1963, workers installing a fire suppression system accidently ignited a flammable substance, and a major fire erupted. Given the petrochemicals used in the manufacturing process, a very hot and smoky blaze was created. The above photograph was taken on Mill Street looking east shortly after the fire started. Fearing the fire would spread, school buses being repaired at the local Dodge dealer were moved out of harm's way, as seen in the below photograph. (Both, Robert Liske.)

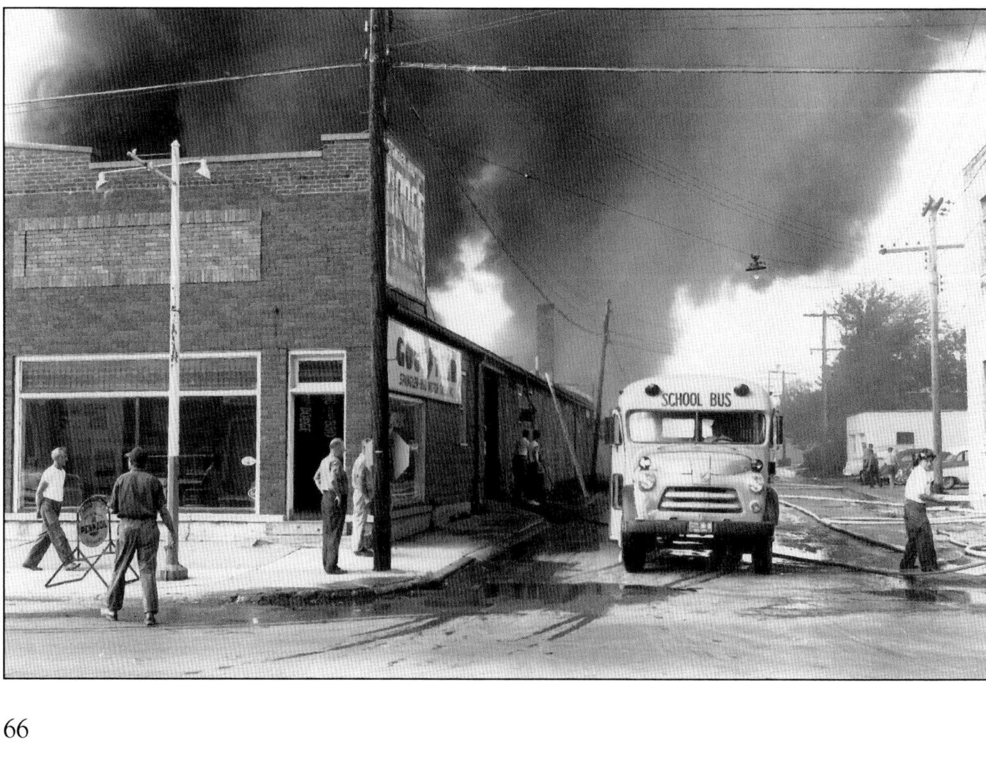

Five

Down on the Farm

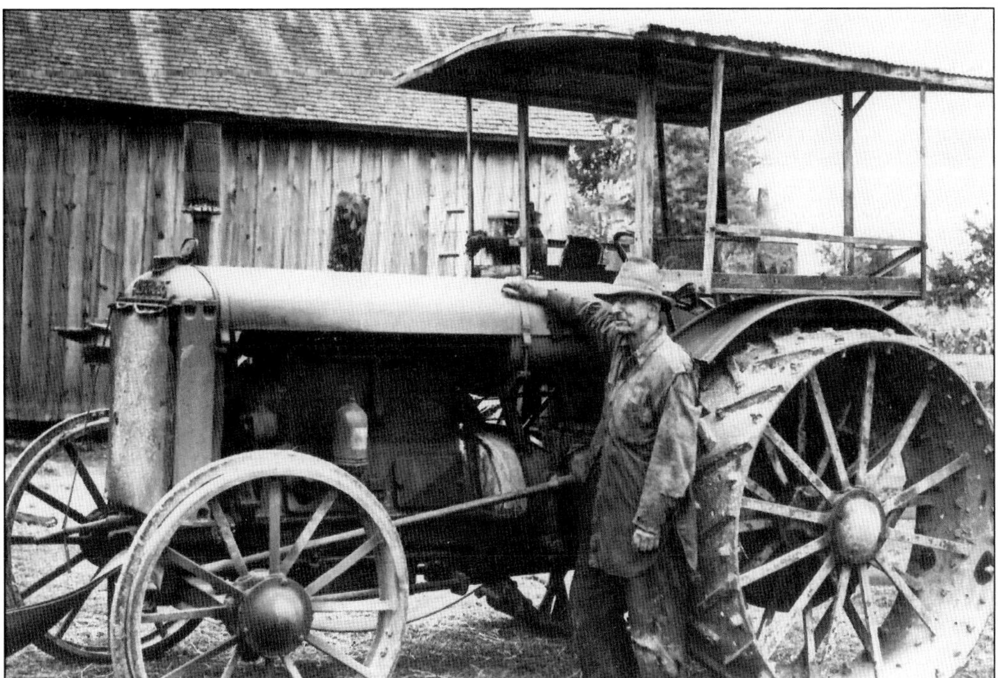

Tractors were beginning to replace horses as a means of power on area farms in the early 1900s, although many farmers continued to use horses until the early 1940s. Here, George Wagner, a farmer and threshing machine operator, stands beside his early model Allis-Chalmers tractor, complete with steel wheels and a homemade cab. (Linda Dehring.)

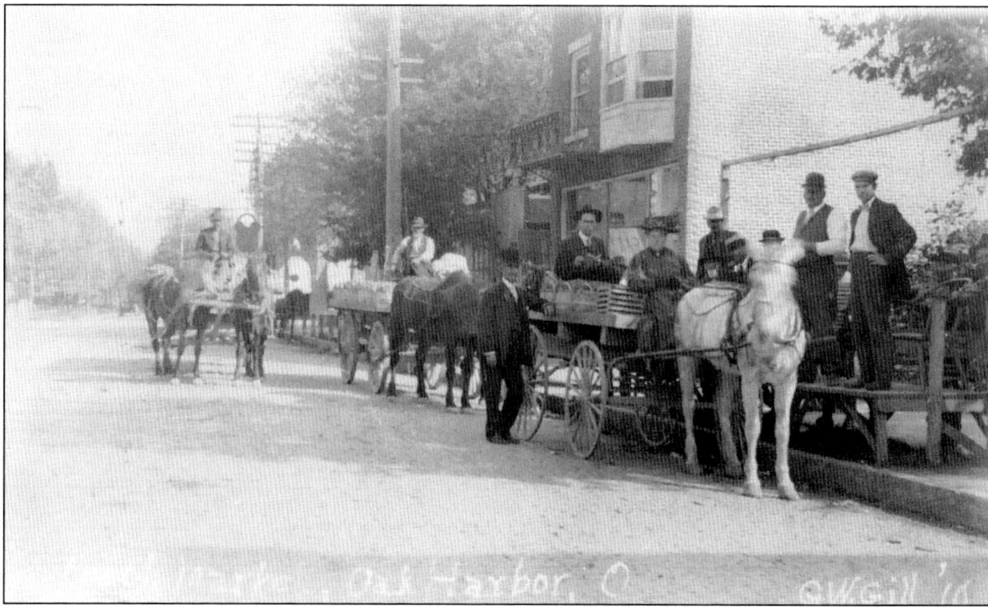

Farmers often marketed their crop at auctions. In the above photograph, taken in 1910, peaches and other fruit are being auctioned on West Water Street by Keach Mylander, son of H.H. Mylander. Fruit was then shipped by rail or boat, often to Detroit markets. Note that the three-story Huck Building had not yet been constructed. Below, farmers line up with their hay wagons on West Main Street. This was all baled hay destined for market, as opposed to loose hay, which was put in haymows with ropes, pulleys, and slings. Many of the homes on the left side of the photograph remain today. (Both, Liske.)

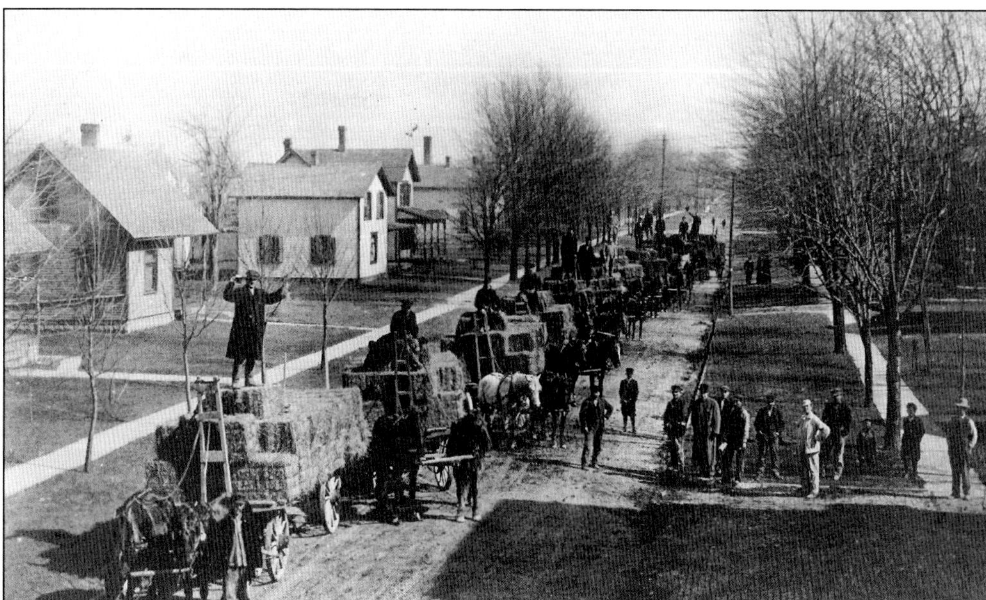

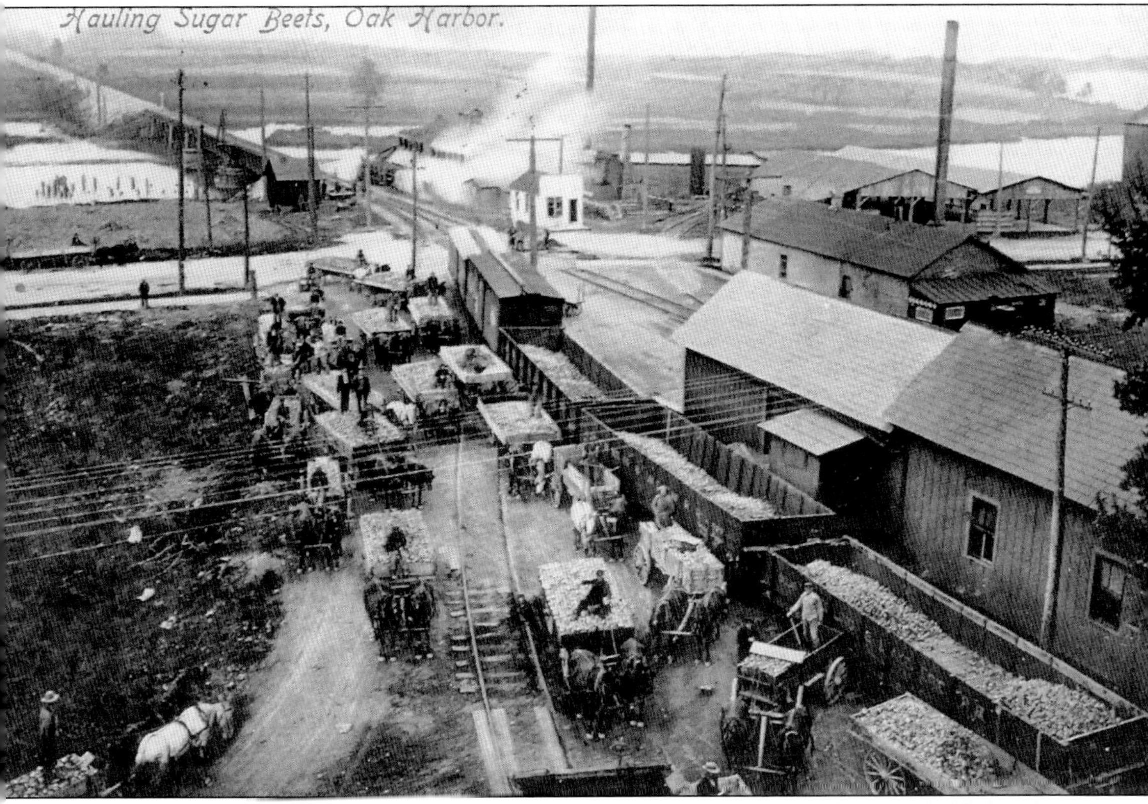

At one time, sugar beets were a major cash crop in northwest Ohio. This photograph, likely taken from the top of the Emery Theirwechter Company elevator, shows farmers shoveling their sugar beets onto railcars that were probably destined for the sugar beet processing plant in Fremont. Also visible is the Michigan Headlining and Hoop plant, which made wooden barrelheads. The plant was located along the river west of the railroad. The building on the right with the smokestack is the Mylander electric power plant, which provided electricity for the village until 1917, when the municipal electric system was installed. Finally, the building on the immediate right is the Oak Harbor railway station for the Wheeling & Lake Erie Railway, which first came through Oak Harbor in 1882. (Liske.)

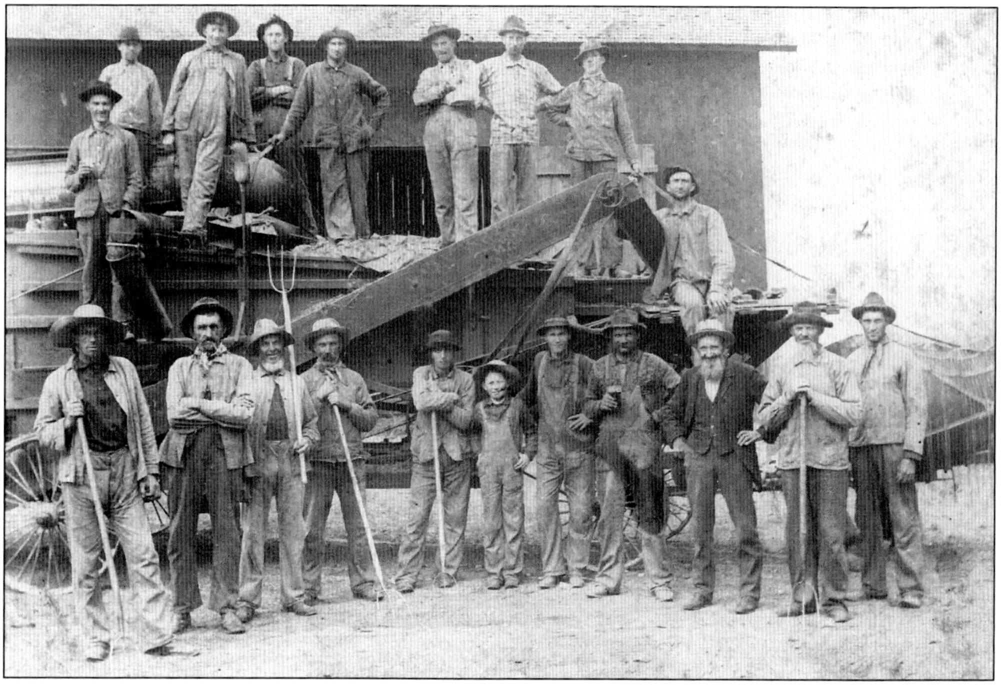

Neighbors helped each other at threshing time. Shown here are, from left to right, (first row) Otto Michael, John Denk Sr., Fred Michael, Carl Shellhouse, August Koepke, Leon Beier, Carol Rohda, Paul Genzman, Fred Beier Sr., Christ Muirhead, and Henry Peters; (second row) Fred Dank, Charles Beier, Will Schultz, Fred Beier Jr., August Genzman, John Denk, H.A. Mylander, Otto Rohda, and John Denk Jr. (OHPL)

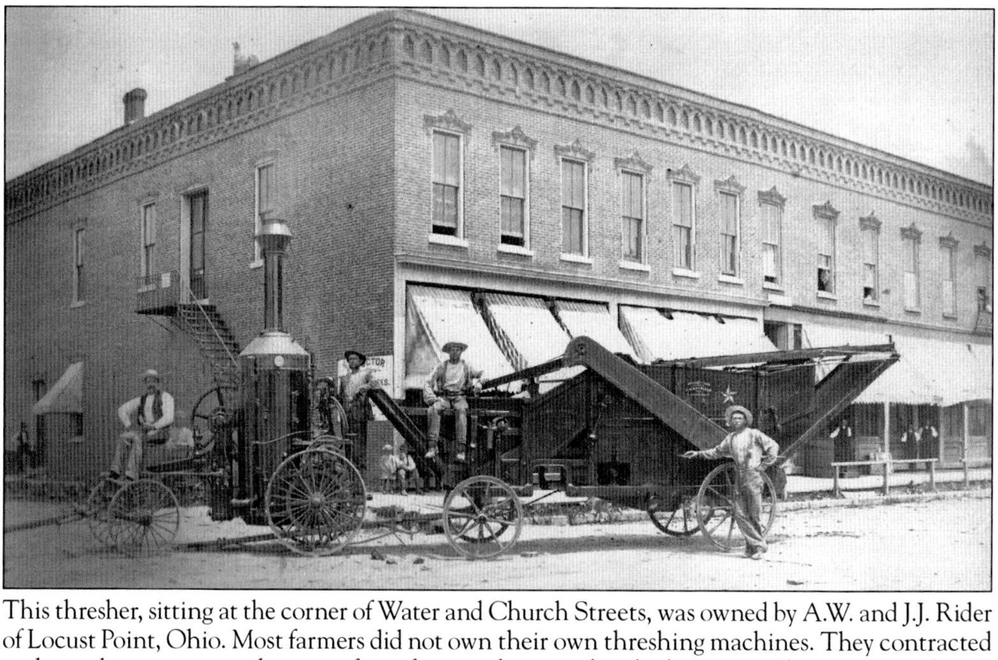

This thresher, sitting at the corner of Water and Church Streets, was owned by A.W. and J.J. Rider of Locust Point, Ohio. Most farmers did not own their own threshing machines. They contracted with machine owners, who went from farm to farm to thresh the grain. This photograph was taken between 1882 and 1894. (OHPL.)

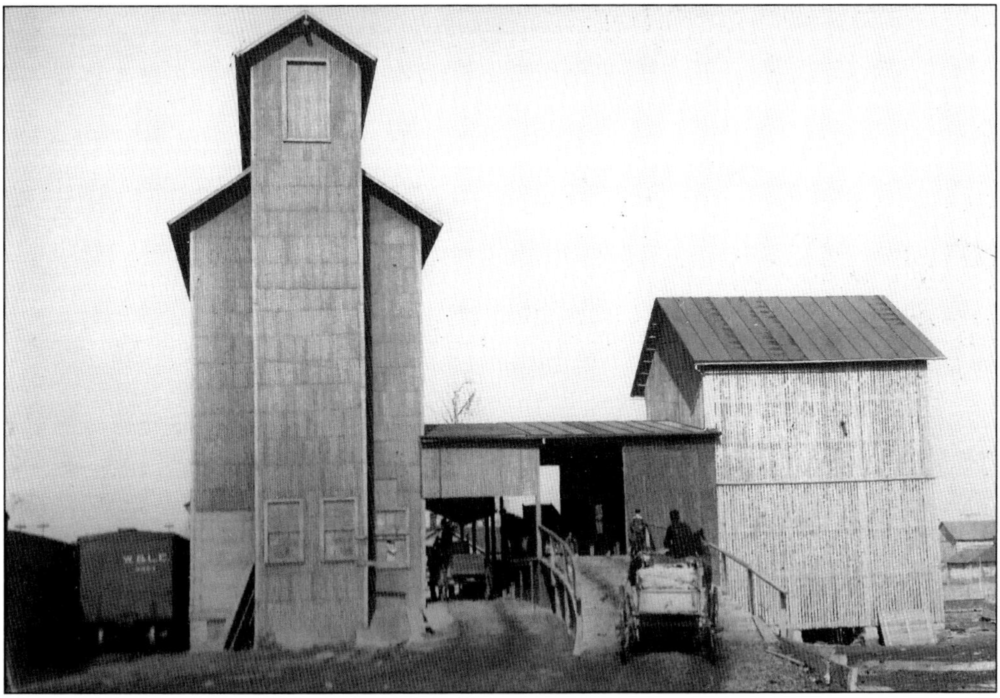

Michael D. Thierwechter constructed a grain elevator and mill sometime after 1882 along the Wheeling & Lake Erie Railway south of West Main Street. This elevator (above) was destroyed by fire in 1900. It was rebuilt, but burned again in 1929. Following the 1929 fire, the elevator was rebuilt and operated by the Ottawa County Cooperative. Another fire in 1949, determined to be arson, destroyed the elevator. It was then rebuilt as a concrete structure, which was torn down in the 1990s. The Thierwechter mill, a three-story brick structure located next to the elevator, produced flour known as Portage Flour (right). (Above, OHPL; right, Liske.)

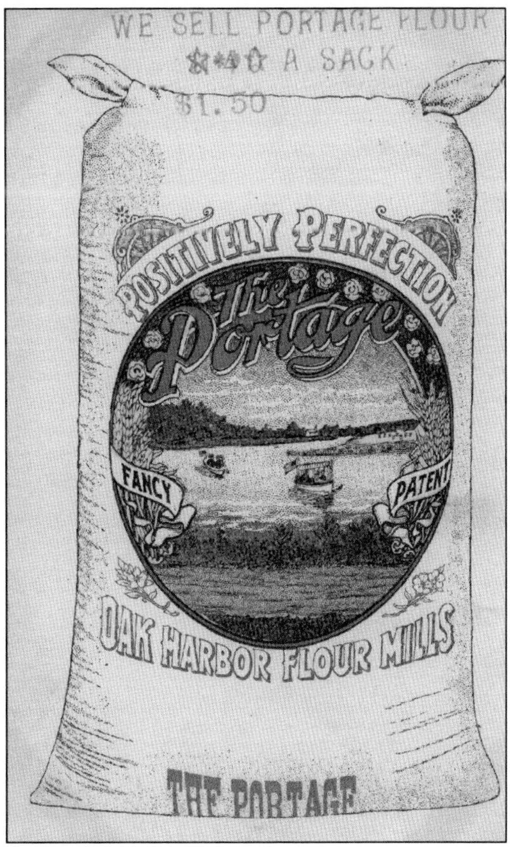

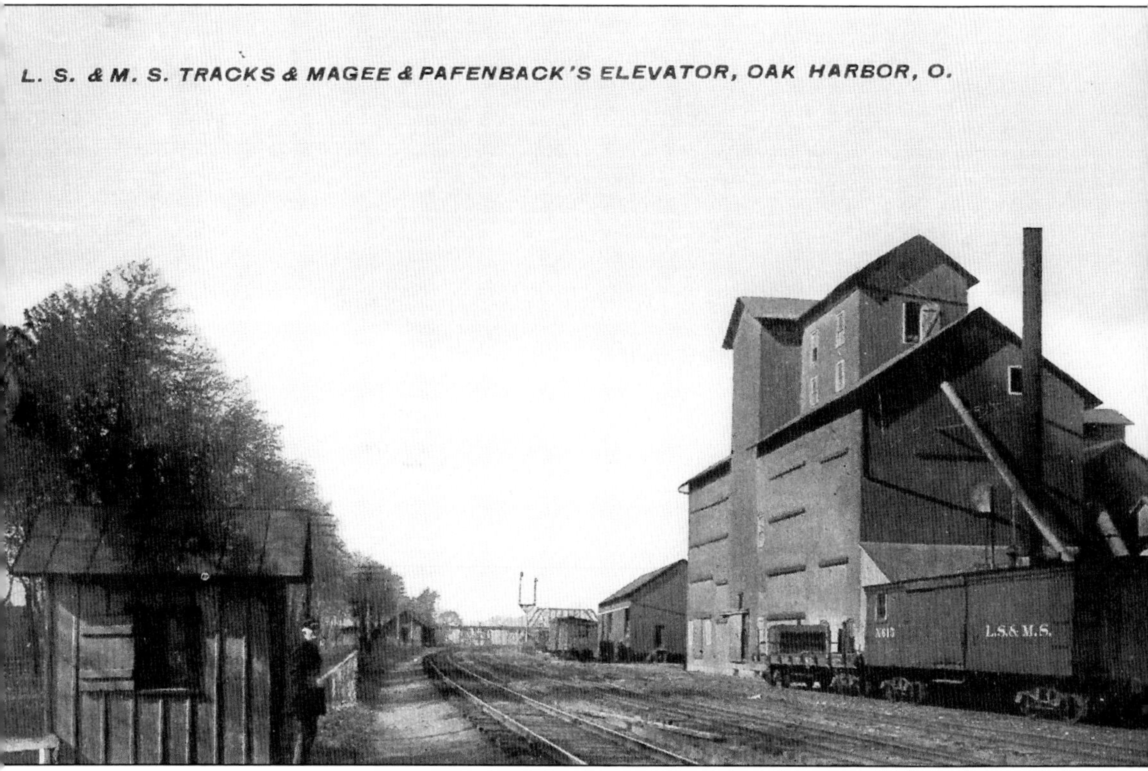

Henry Paffenbach of Elmore and John McGee of Toledo contracted with William Lipstraw of Oak Harbor to build this imposing grain elevator in 1902 along the Lake Shore & Michigan Southern Railway on North Locust Street in Oak Harbor. It stood on or near the site of the Kirk and Payne elevator, which was destroyed by fire in January 1883. In 1914, it incorporated as the Oak Harbor Cooperative and was eventually sold to Luckey Farmers. Amazingly, this was likely the only wooden grain elevator in Oak Harbor that did not burn down. It was torn down in 1994. Also seen in this photograph is the small shanty for the crossing guards at the Locust Street intersection with the Lake Shore & Michigan Southern. In 1924, a terrible accident occurred at this crossing, when a bus carrying 4-H members from Seneca County returning from Locust Point was hit, killing 10 children and adults. (Liske.)

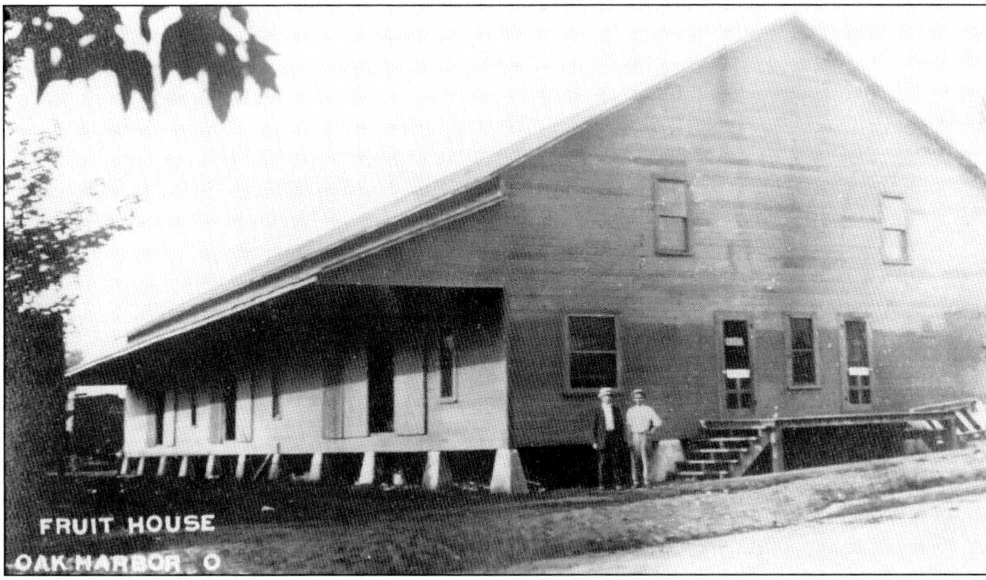

The Oak Harbor Fruit Company, formed in 1912, was a cooperative of growers and shippers who handled peaches, apples, pears, and plums. The Oak Harbor headquarters, shown above, was a 60-by-120-foot building just east of the Wheeling & Lake Erie tracks between Main and Ottawa Streets. Frank Bowersox was the manager, and the company used the 7/8-bushel Detroit basket. Peak time for employment was from mid-August to October 1. The company also had a branch in Lacarne. This building burned in 1930 and was not rebuilt. The below photograph of the employees was taken on Ottawa Street looking to the north. (Above, OHPL; below, Liske.)

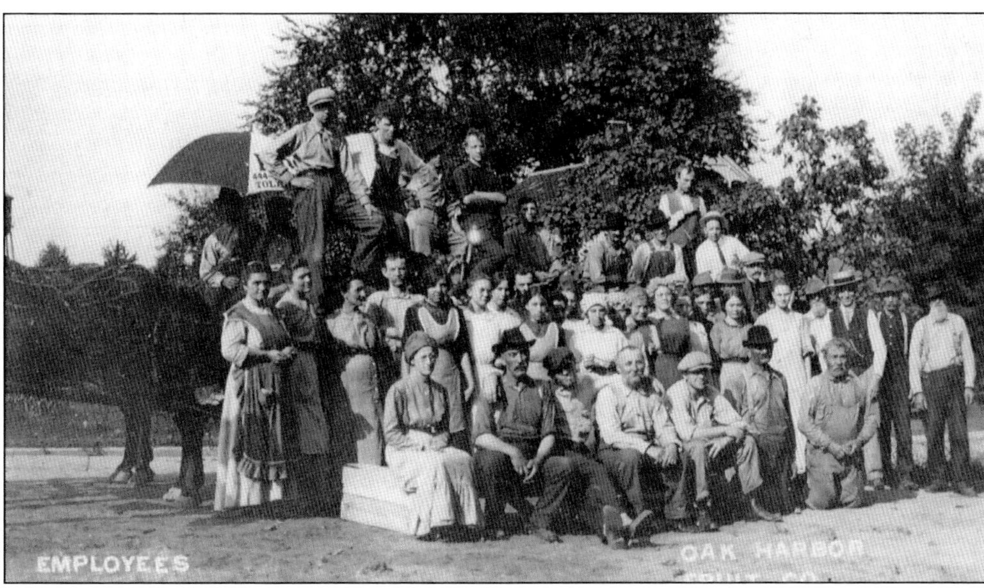

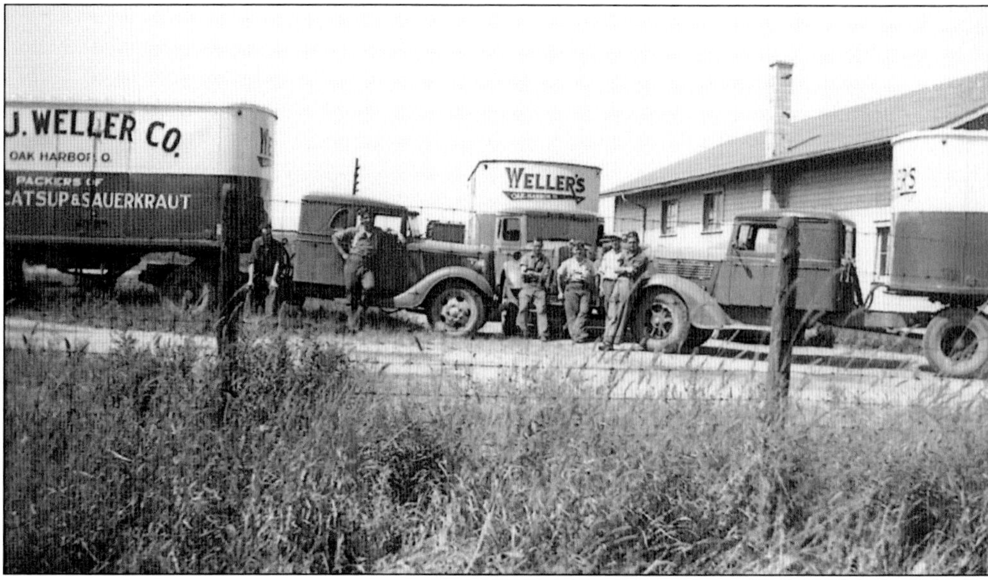

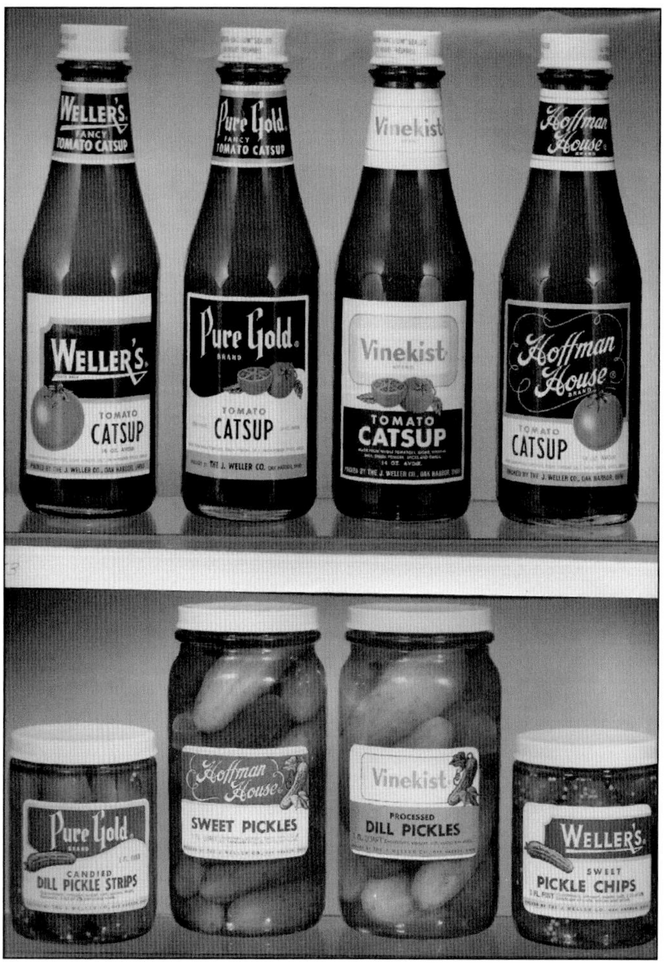

The J. Weller Company came to Oak Harbor from Cincinnati in 1898–1899 to process tomatoes and pickles grown by area farmers. The plant was located on the east side of the Wheeling & Lake Erie Railway, between Washington and Houghton Streets. The plant had 56 vats for curing pickles, and the sweet smell of tomato sauce being cooked is an autumn odor many residents remember. Weller products, shown in the left photograph, were trucked to major markets in the Midwest. The August 1938 scene in the above photograph shows some of the trucks and drivers. (Both, OHPL.)

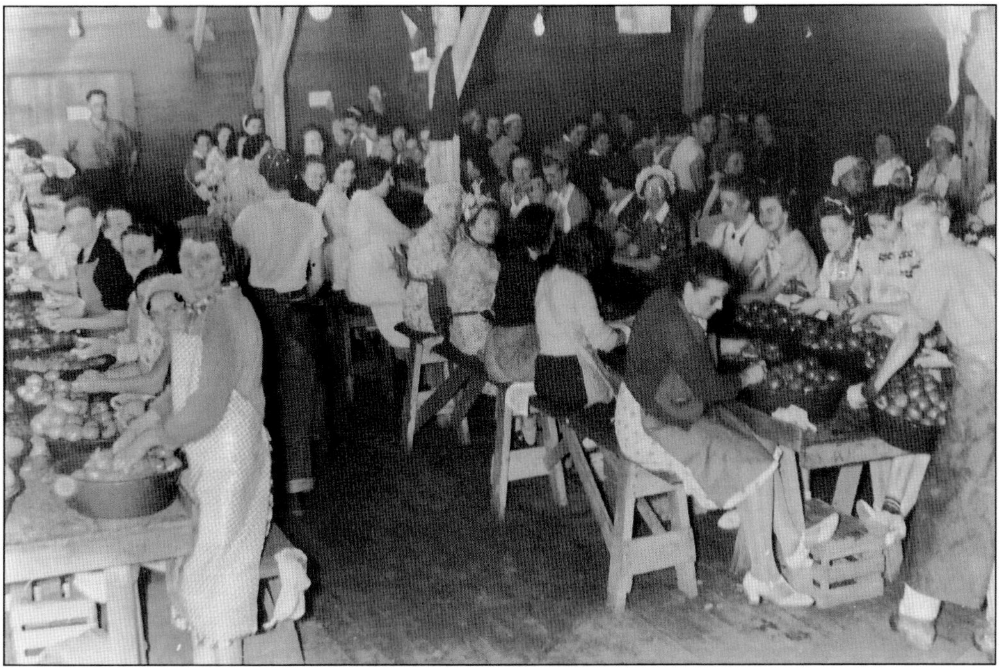

The J. Weller Company provided seasonal employment for many housewives in the area. In the above photograph, women peel huge panfuls of tomatoes in preparation for processing catsup. Below, pickles are graded by hand in the pickle processing room. In 1965, Wellers was running 18,000 gallons of catsup a day. Wellers produced not only its own brand but brands for other companies as well. The plant was sold to Hille Farms in 1980 and went out of business in 1984. (Both, OHPL.)

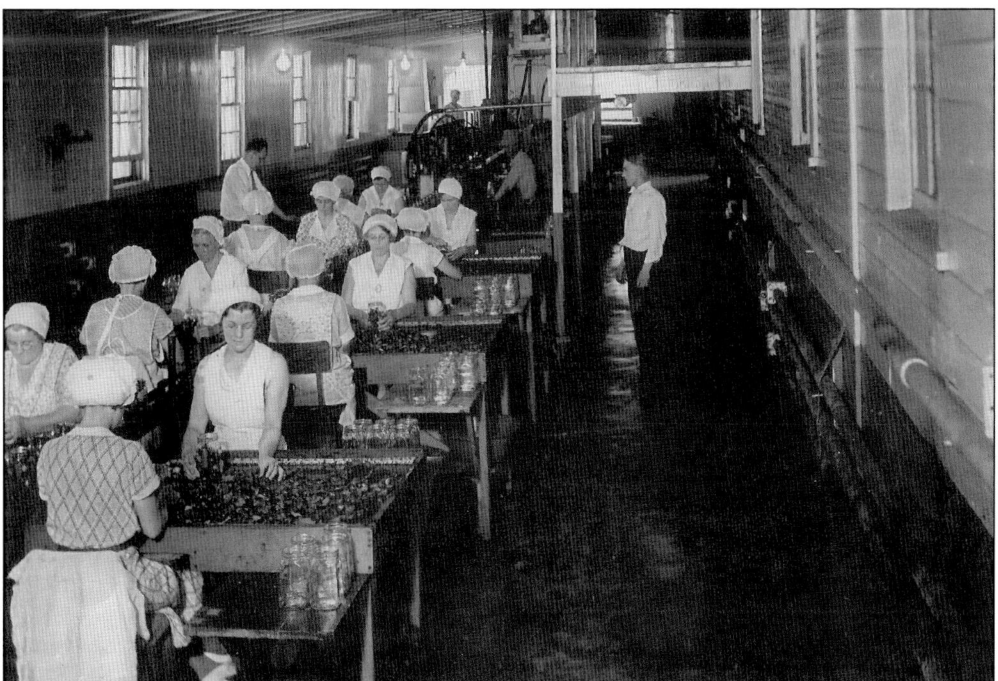

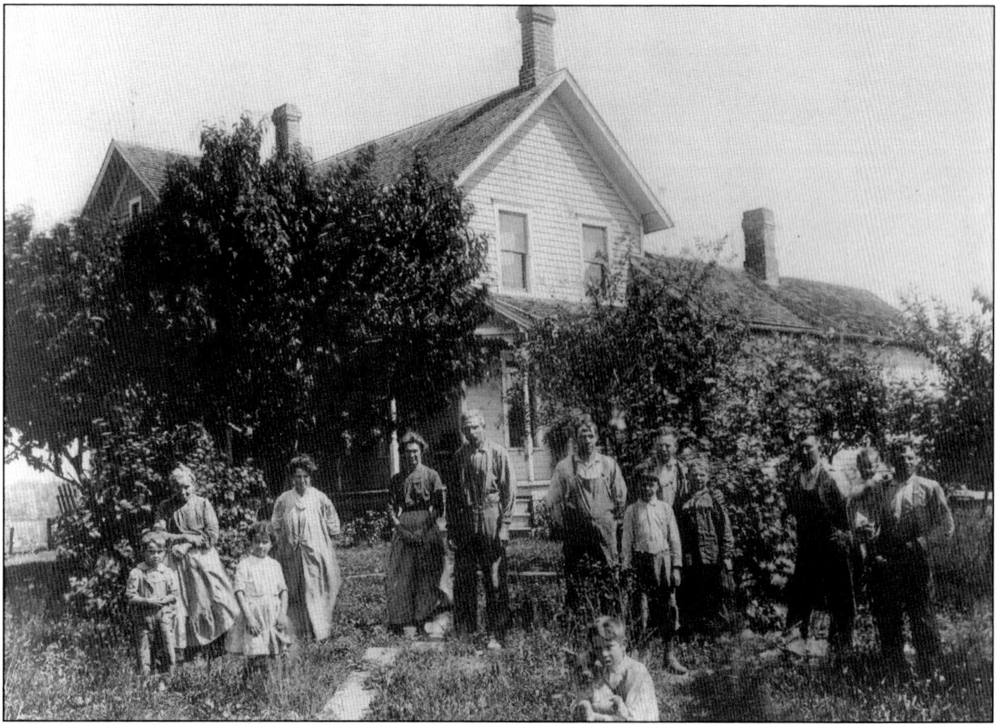

This Louis Risch farmstead on Four-Mile House Road in Salem Township is typical of the prosperous farms developed around the Oak Harbor area after the forests were depleted. Coming from the lowlands of Germany in 1853, the Risch family undoubtedly knew how to drain and farm the swampy land found in the Oak Harbor area. Like many early settlers, the family first settled in a log house when they bought the farm in 1883. By 1903, Louis had built this beautiful house and barn. These 1914 photographs appear to have been taken at a Risch family gathering. Tragically, the home burned in 2008. (Both, Linda Dehring.)

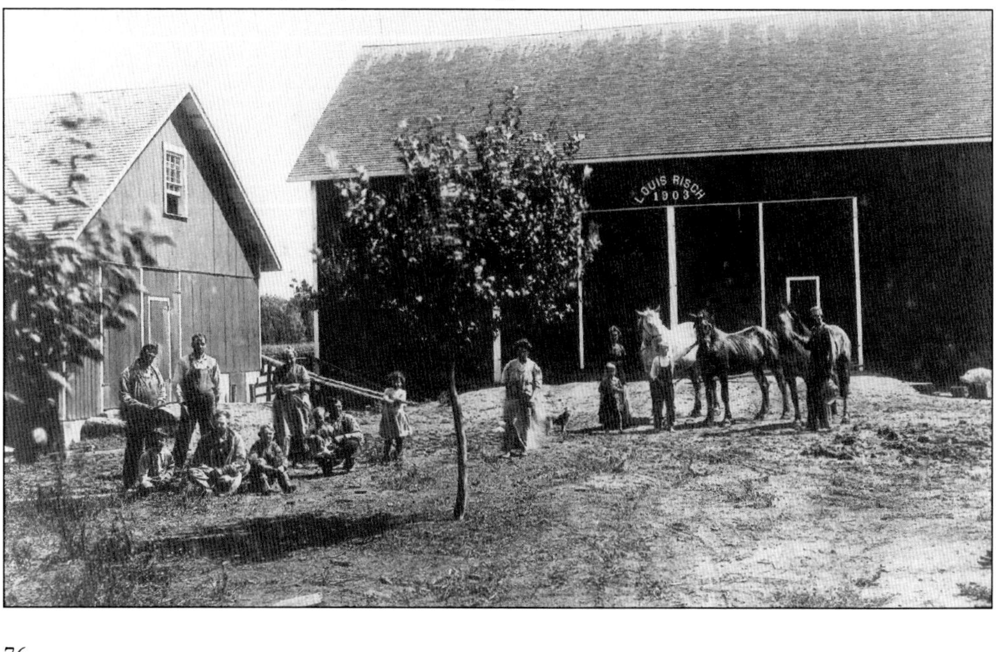

Six

SERVICE TO GOD AND COUNTRY

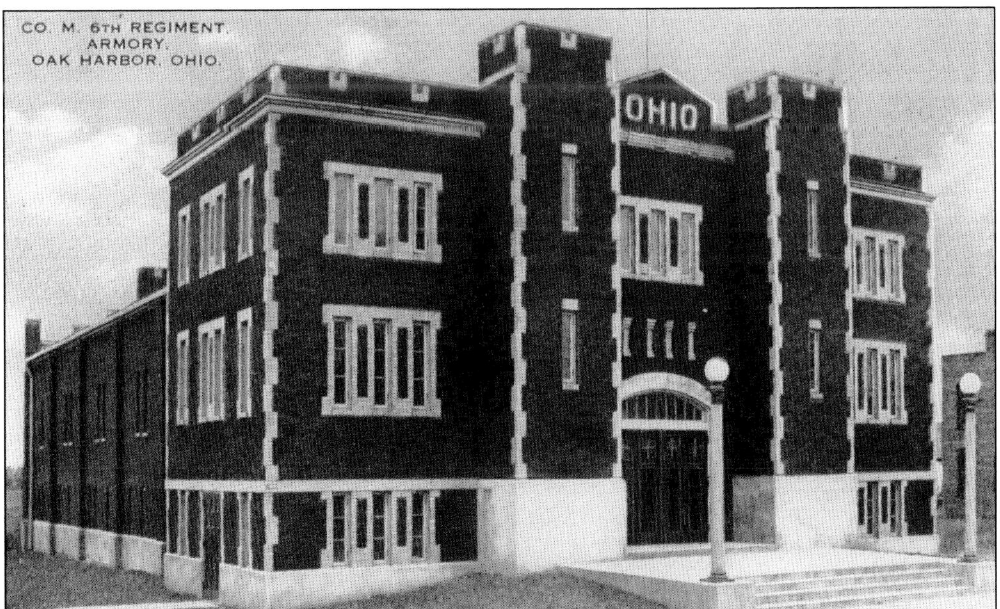

The Oak Harbor Armory was built in 1914 and dedicated on December 2, 1915. Its main function was to provide a meeting and training site for the local National Guard units. It was the home to Company M, 6th Ohio National Guard unit. Basketball games, wedding receptions, and many other memorable events were held here. The building was razed in 1988. (Liske.)

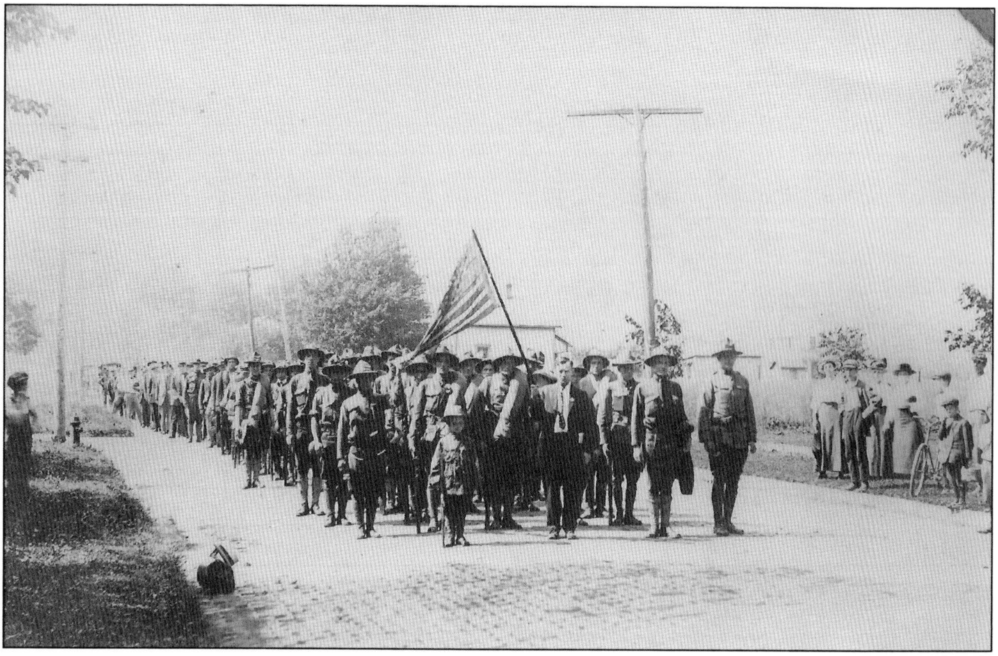

On the morning of July 1, 1916, Company M, 6th Regiment Ohio National Guard, is seen marching on Church Street to the New York Central Railroad depot, formerly the Lake Shore & Michigan Southern depot, on South Railroad Street. The unit had been called to serve along the United States–Mexico border prior to US involvement in World War I. (OHPL.)

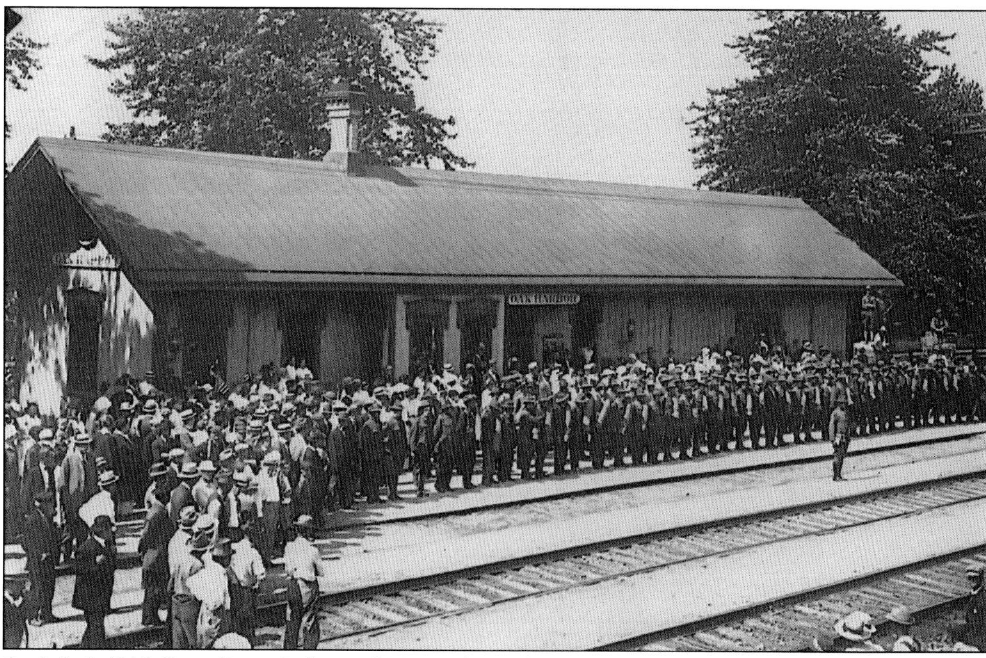

On July 1, 1916, Capt. Peter Gulau and 83 members of Company M, 6th Regiment await deployment at the New York Central depot on the north end of Oak Harbor. From here, the troops went to Camp Willis in Columbus, Ohio, to be mustered into federal duty on the Mexican border. Later, they would see service during World War I in France and Belgium. (Liske.)

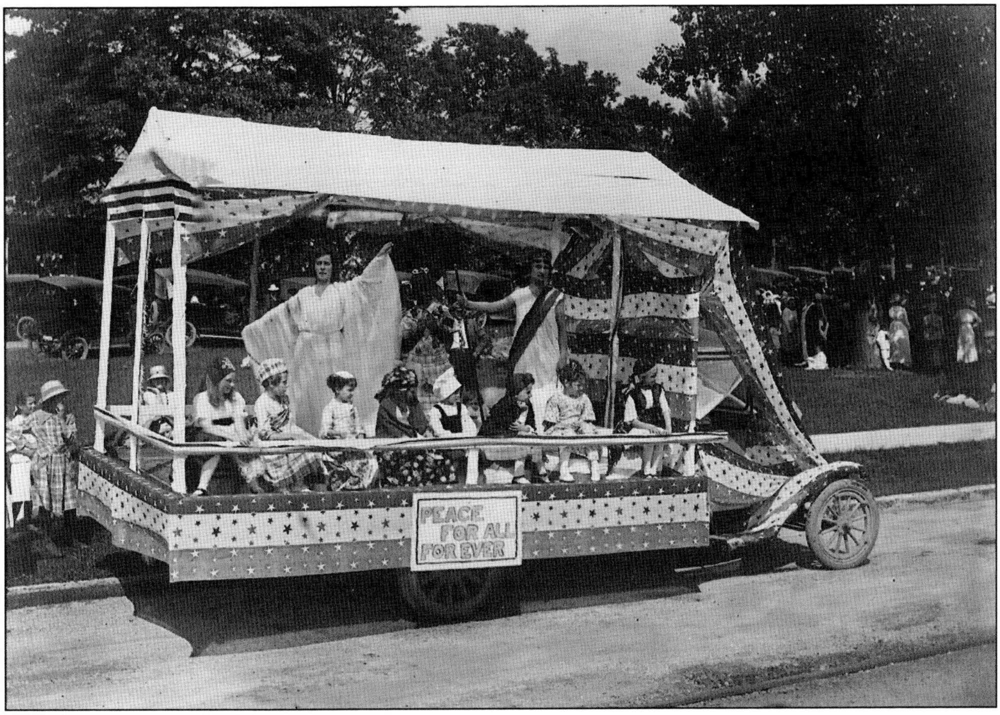

Oak Harbor celebrated the end of World War I and the return of "our boys" with a grand parade and the dedication of a monument at Flat Iron Park on Labor Day 1919. The float depicts the Goddess of Peace (Thelma Kramb) on the left and the Goddess of Liberty (Dorothy Sperling) on the right, along with a sign reading "Peace for All For Ever." Others on the float include, in no set order, Jane Newman, Catherine Bowersox, Frances Kramb, Margaret Kramb, Dorothy Dicken, Lillian Weirich, Margaret Jessen, Rose Franck, and Katherine Bell. The monument (below) was dedicated to the dead and veterans of the Great War. Today, the monument and park are the site of many events honoring all of Oak Harbor's military veterans. (Above, Liske; below, OHPL.)

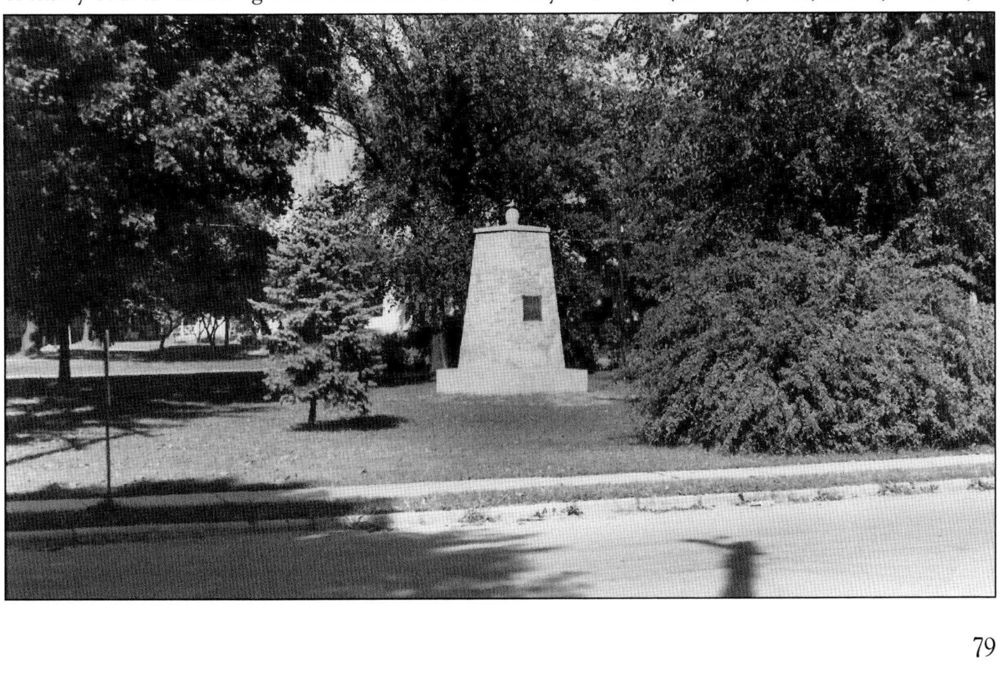

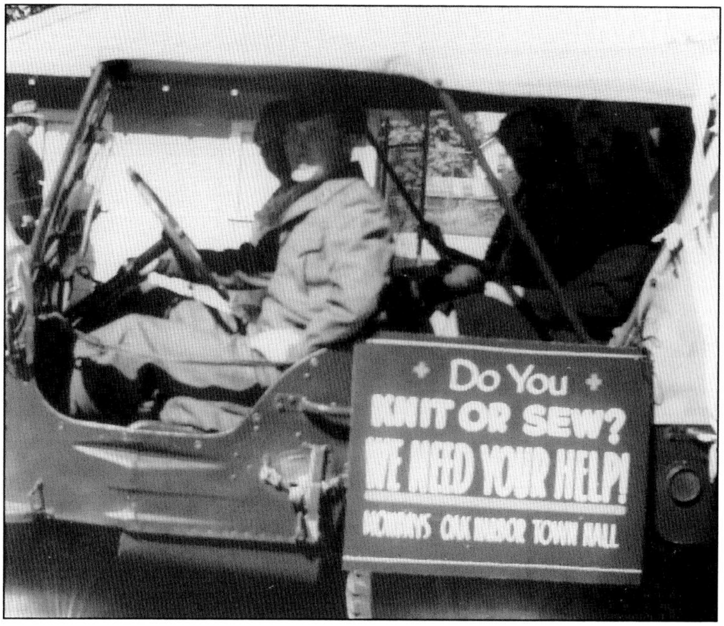

Following World War II, sewing assistance was requested to address the many needs of returning soldiers, Camp Perry prisoners, and war brides. This photograph was likely taken in 1946, prior to the Fall Fair parade, since there were no parades during the later war years. The location is Walnut Street near the entrance to the old high school athletic field. (Martin.)

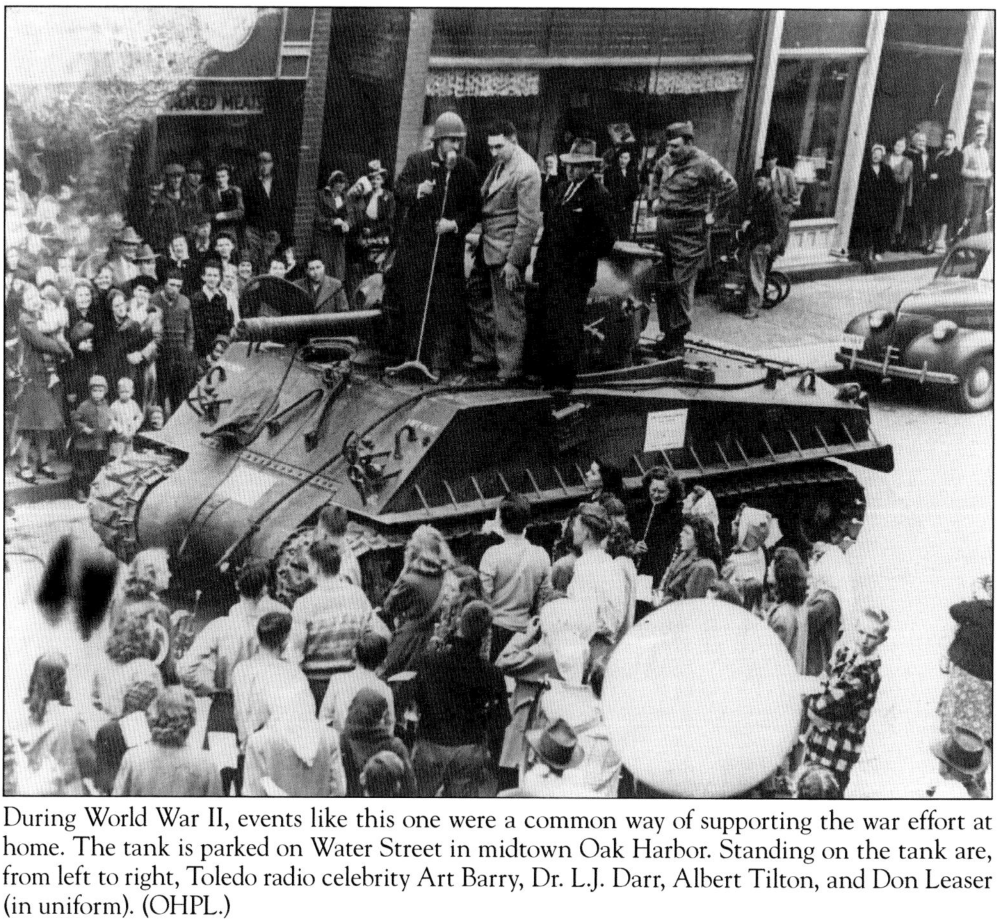

During World War II, events like this one were a common way of supporting the war effort at home. The tank is parked on Water Street in midtown Oak Harbor. Standing on the tank are, from left to right, Toledo radio celebrity Art Barry, Dr. L.J. Darr, Albert Tilton, and Don Leaser (in uniform). (OHPL.)

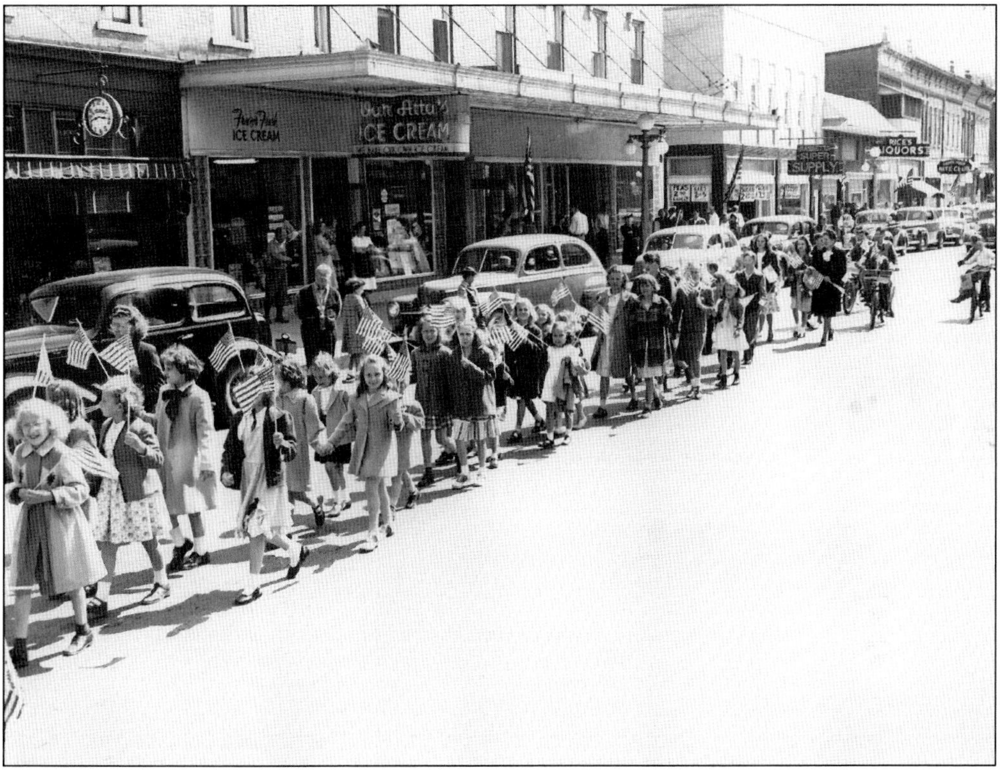

Girls Scouts and other children march in a typical Memorial Day parade in downtown Oak Harbor in the 1940s. In the background can be seen the popular VanAtta's ice cream store and Tschumy Jewelers. (Liske.)

German settlers formed the St. Paul Evangelical Church in 1879. The church was later known as St. Paul Evangelical and Reformed. The congregation purchased this existing frame church on the corner of Toussaint and Ottawa Streets, and it was used until a brick church was constructed in 1887–1888. (Liske.)

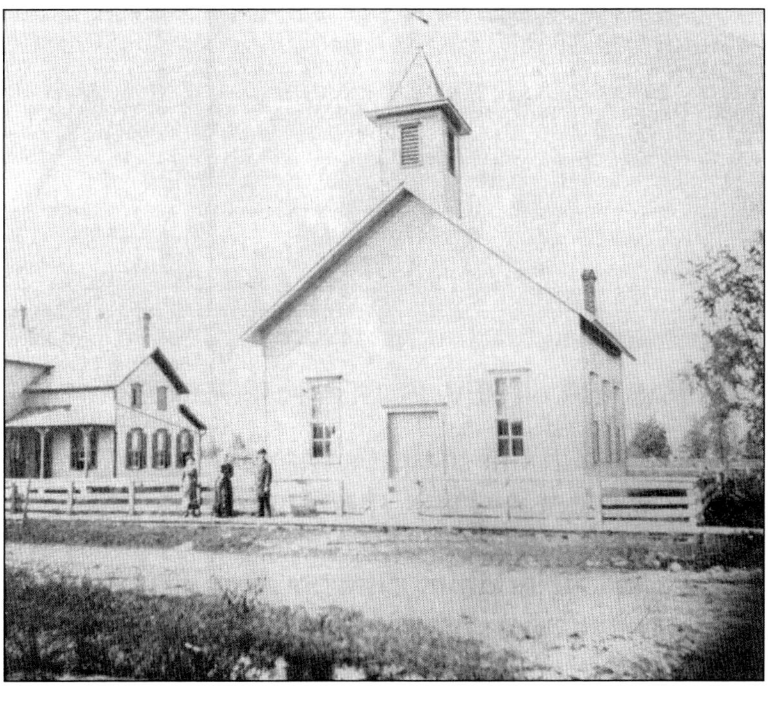

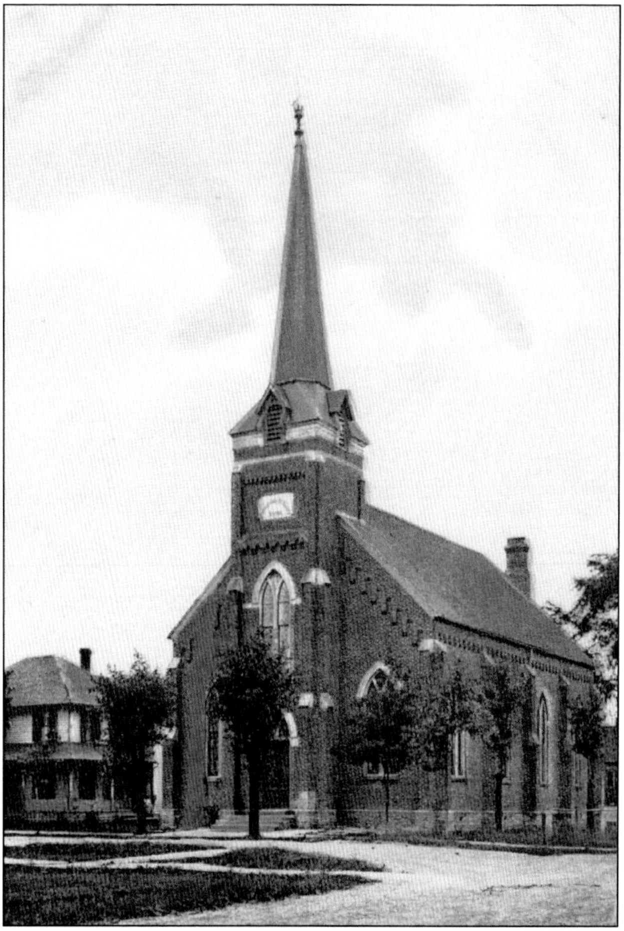

In 1887, the St. Paul Evangelical and Reformed congregation started construction of this church at the site of its frame building on the corner of Toussaint and Ottawa Streets. Dedication ceremonies were held on February 26, 1888. The photograph below shows the ornate interior of the 1888 church, which was used until the current church was constructed in 1930. The gold-and-white pulpit, lectern, and altar were moved from the 1888 church to the current building and are still in use today. St Paul Evangelical and Reformed Church is now called St. Paul United Church of Christ. (Both, Liske.)

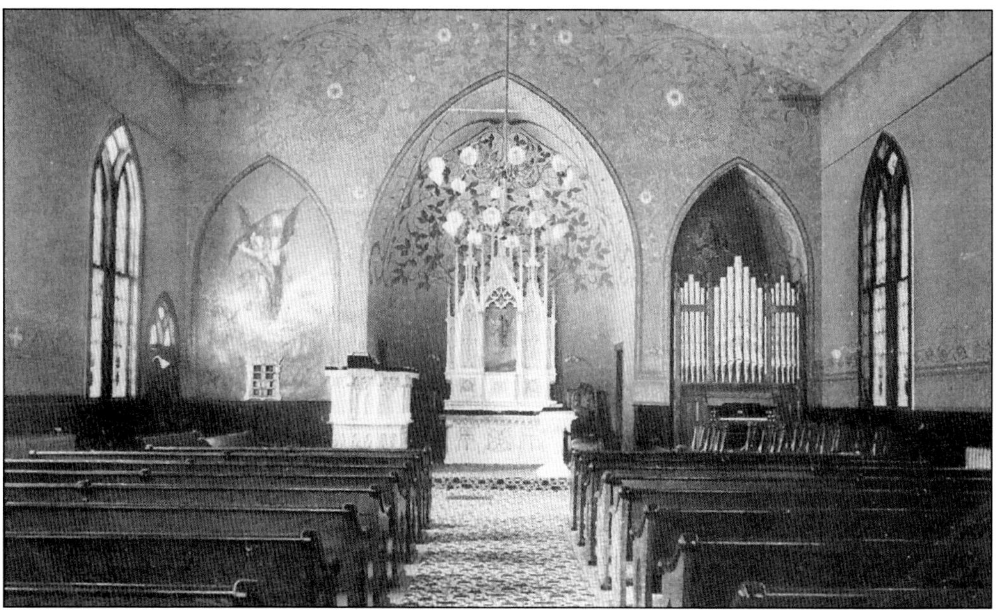

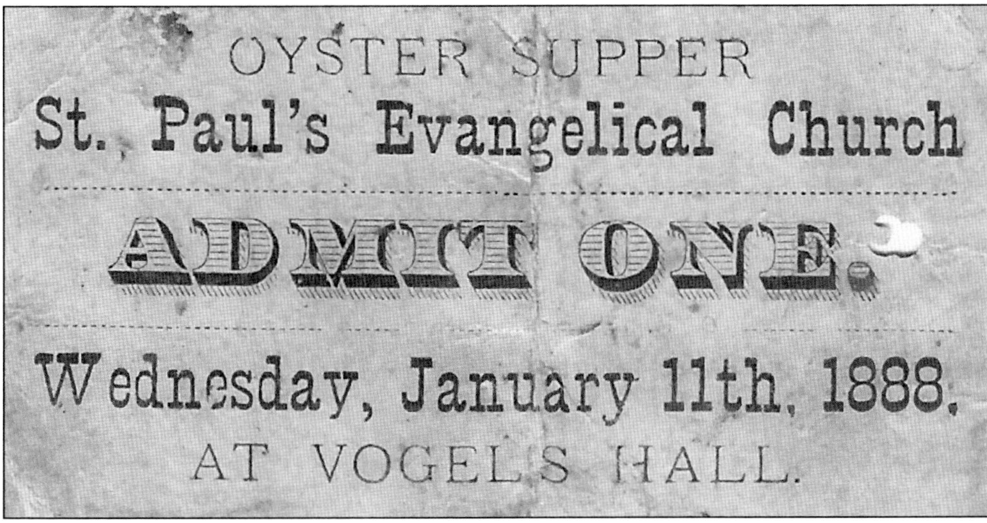

This oyster supper ticket was for a fundraiser for the construction of the 1888 church. Oyster suppers were popular winter events at the turn of the century. The dinner was held at Vogel's Hall, above Vogel and Bredbeck Hardware at 173 West Water Street, now the site of Oak Harbor Hardware. The inscription for Vogel's Hall can still be seen on the cornice of the building. (Martin.)

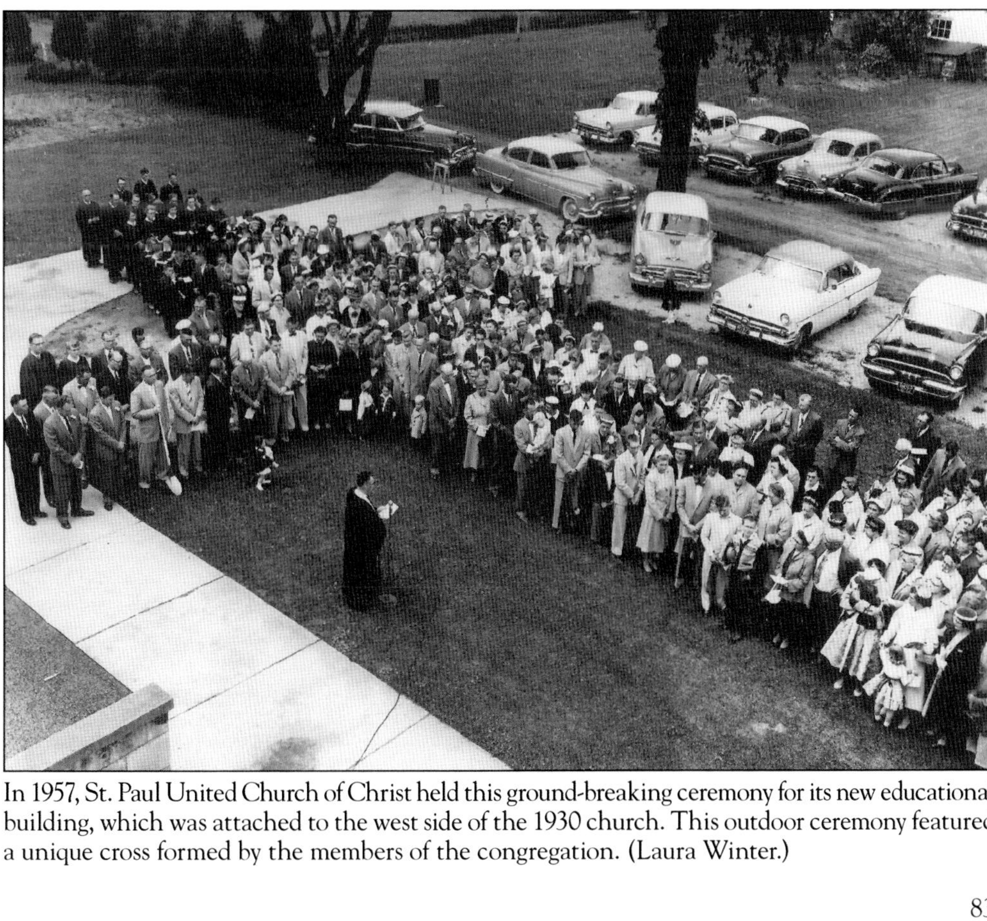

In 1957, St. Paul United Church of Christ held this ground-breaking ceremony for its new educational building, which was attached to the west side of the 1930 church. This outdoor ceremony featured a unique cross formed by the members of the congregation. (Laura Winter.)

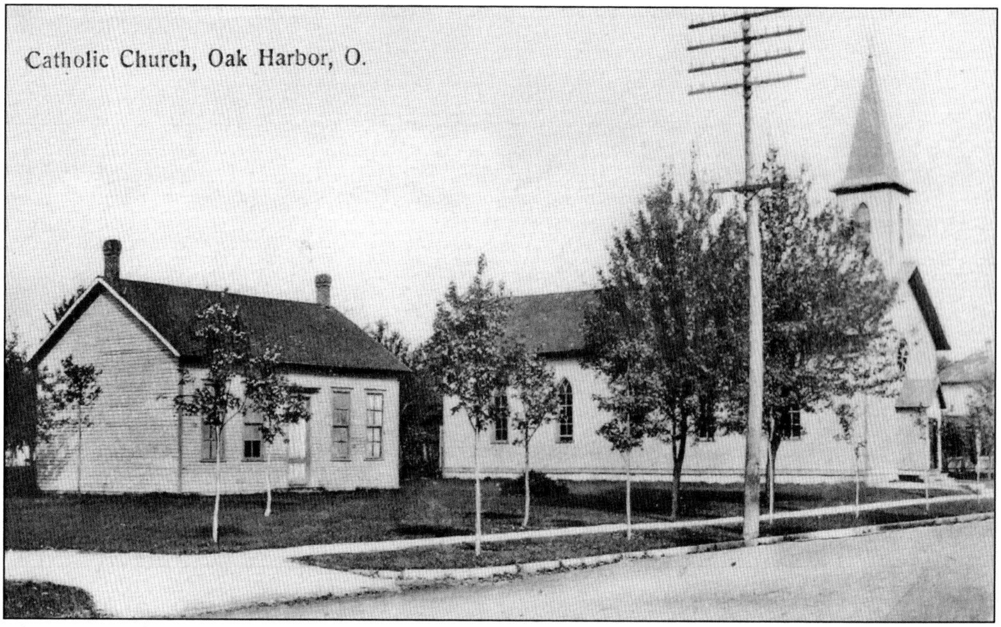

The St. Boniface Roman Catholic parishioners built this church in 1871–1872 on Church Street, the site of the current church. A rectory was added in 1880 on Oak Street, and was moved to Church Street around 1915 when a new brick church, the present St. Boniface, was built. In 1966, a new parochial school was added to the west side of the church. (Liske.)

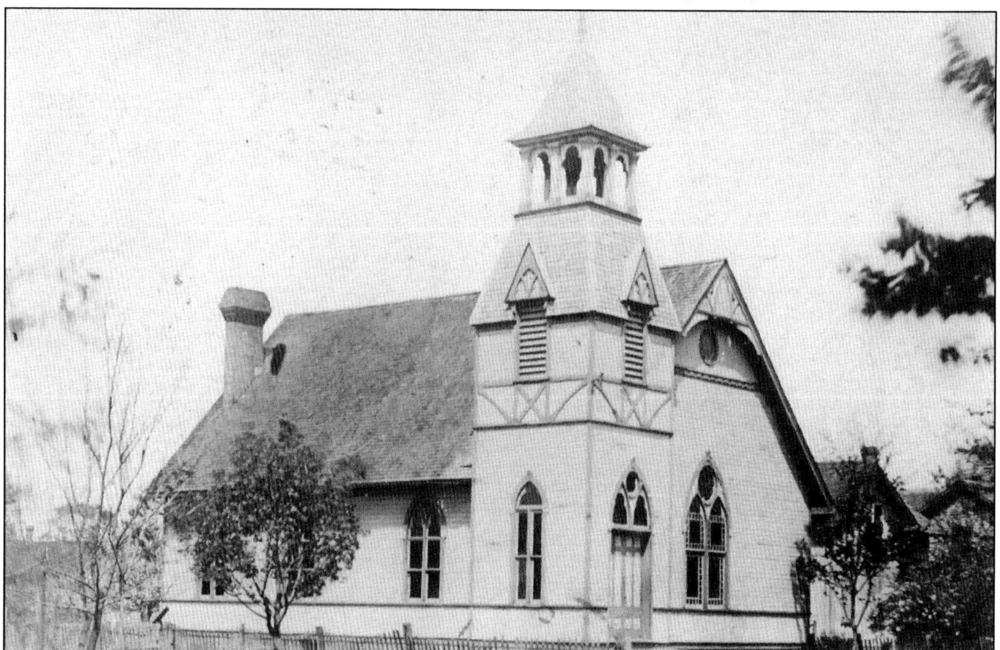

The Christian Church of Disciples of Christ was built about 1879–1880 and was abandoned in 1921. The building, located at 108 West Ottawa, has seen many uses, including being the home of the American Legion and the Knights of Columbus. The tower was removed about 1935 when it was struck by lightning. The building still exists as a private residence. (Liske.)

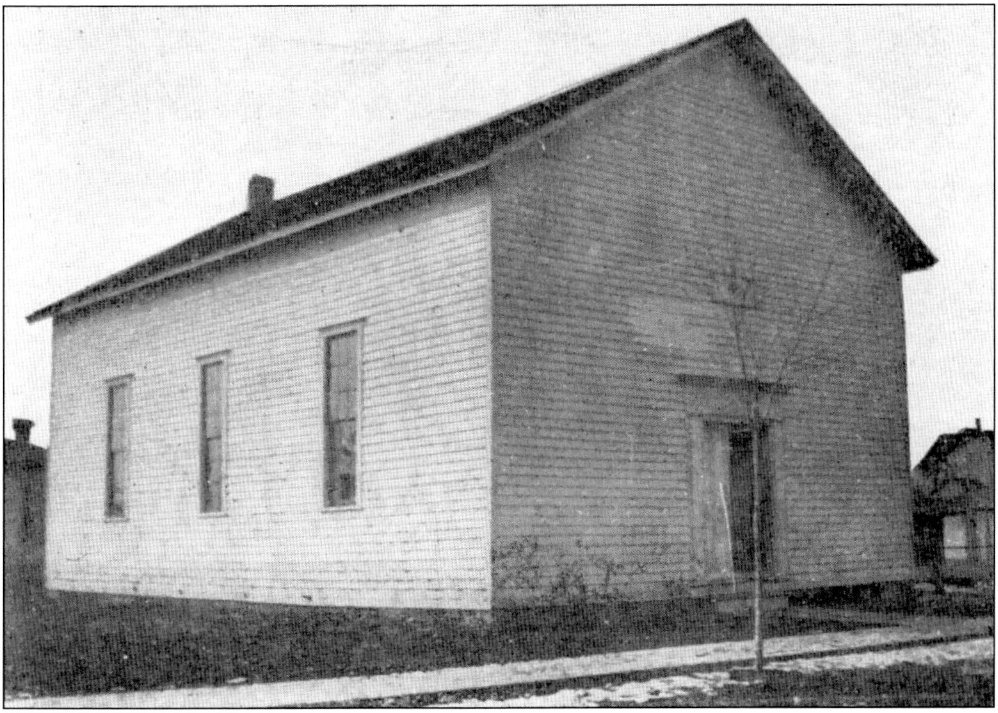

St. John's Evangelical Lutheran Church conducted its first services in 1860 in Hartford and Roose schoolhouses. This frame structure, constructed in 1867 at the corner of Church and Ottawa Streets, was its first church building. It was later used as a Lutheran school. (OHPL.)

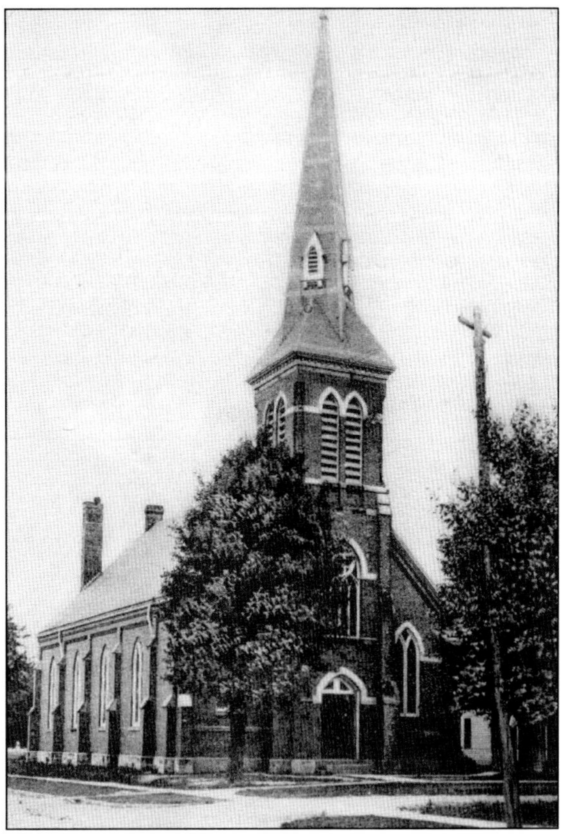

St. John's Evangelical Lutheran Church erected its second church, a brick edifice, in 1882. Located at the northeast corner of Church and Ottawa Streets, the church was used by the congregation until 1926, when the building was razed. A Lutheran school was also built in 1912 (see page 102), and a brick parsonage was added in 1933. (Liske.)

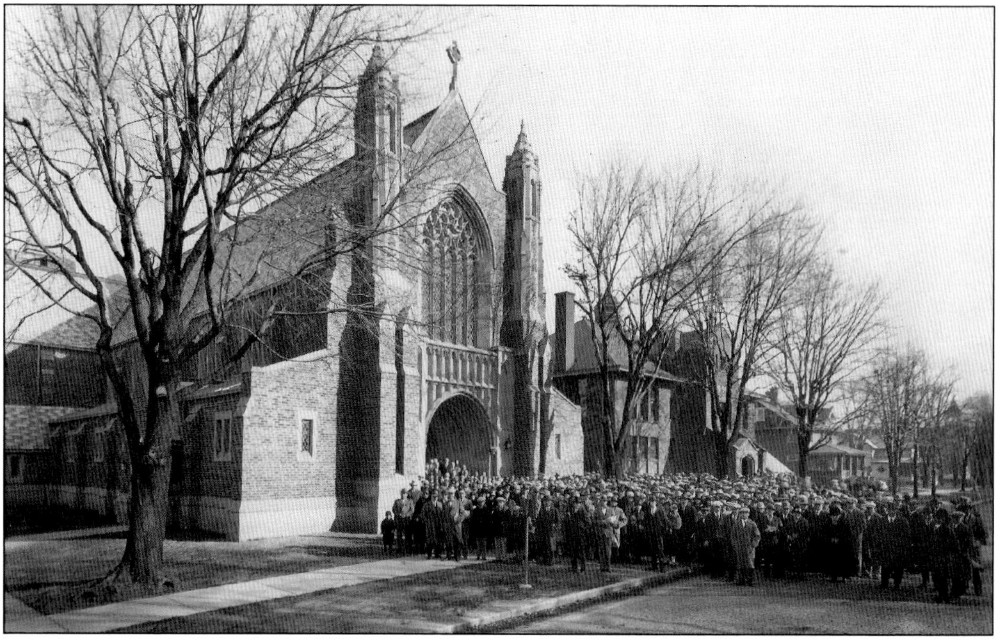

The present St. John's Evangelical Lutheran Church was dedicated at this ceremony on November 6, 1927. A new educational building was added in 1959, replacing the 1912 school. (Helen Pfeiffer.)

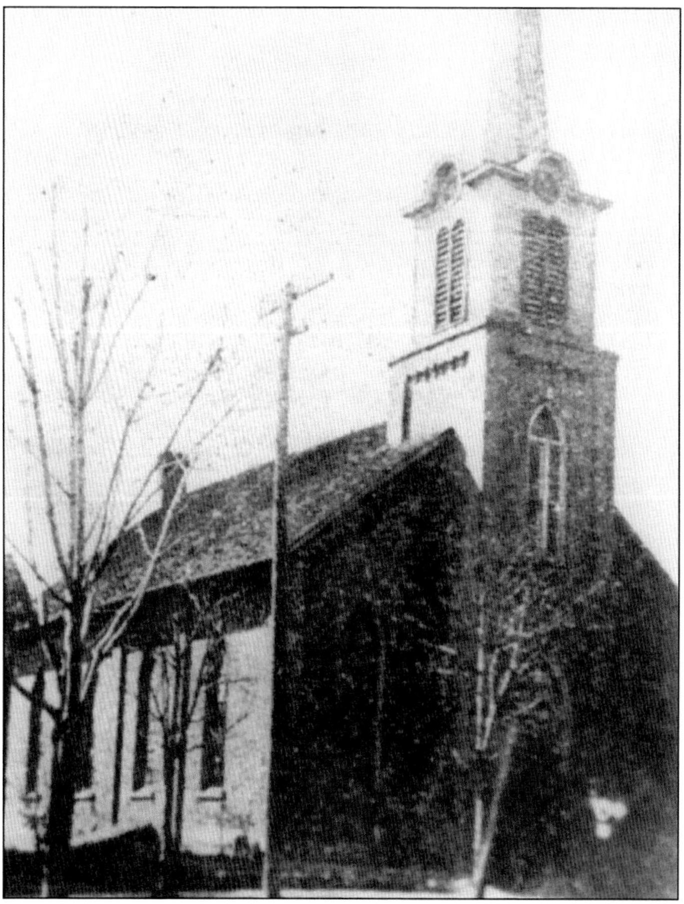

The Oak Harbor Methodist Episcopal Church was constructed around 1875 at the southwest corner of Church and Ottawa Streets. The church was extensively remodeled in 1902, with the removal of the steeple and the redesigning of the roofline. In 1962, the Methodist church moved to its new location on East Ottawa Street. (Liske.)

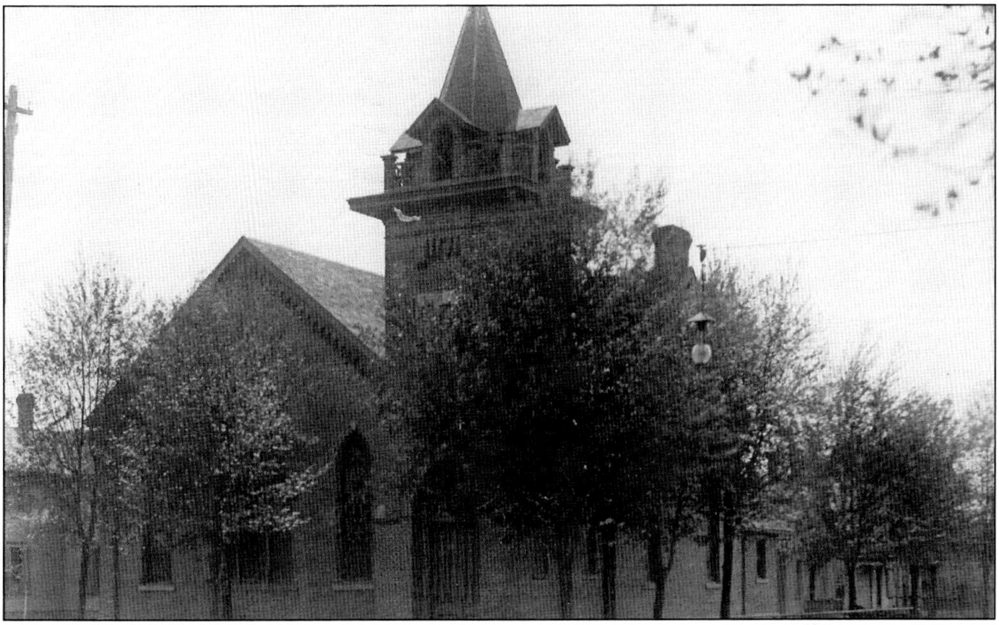

This is a photograph of the Methodist church after the extensive remodeling in 1902. While it is the same building as in the previous picture, the center steeple has been removed and a new, smaller steeple built above a new side entrance. After the Methodists moved to their new church in 1962, this church was used by various congregations. It remains today as a privately owned structure. (Liske.)

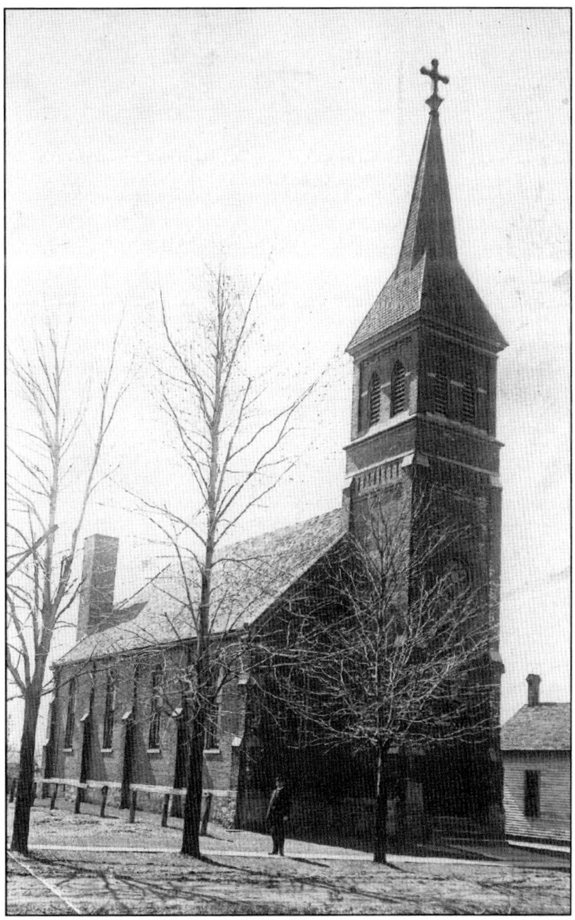

St. John's Lutheran Church in Rocky Ridge was dedicated in 1889, replacing a building destroyed by fire. Like many churches, it had a hand-pumped organ. The church was used until 1967, when the congregation built a new church on the south end of Rocky Ridge. The building still exists, although it is in very poor condition. (Liske.)

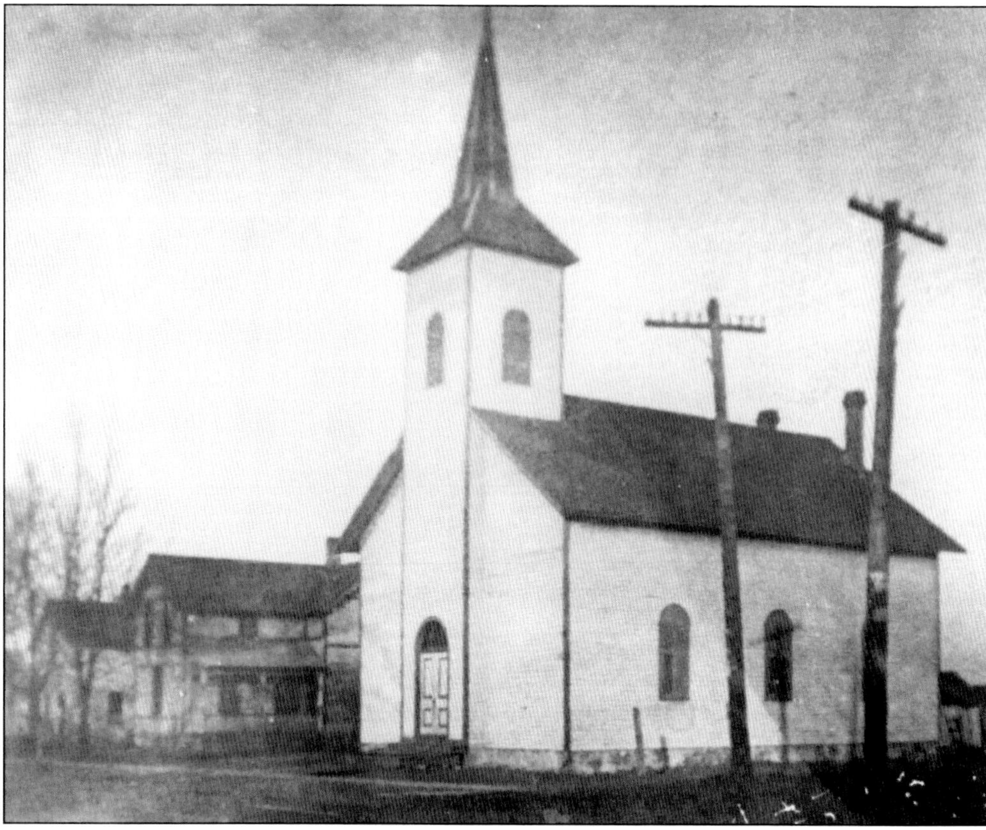

The Rocky Ridge Evangelical Church was erected in 1877 on the east side of Main Street, north of the railroad in Rocky Ridge. The organ had a pair of foot pedals that had to be pumped when the organ was played. The congregation disbanded in 1957. The photograph below was taken a few years ago, before the building was razed. (Above, OHPL; below, Liske.)

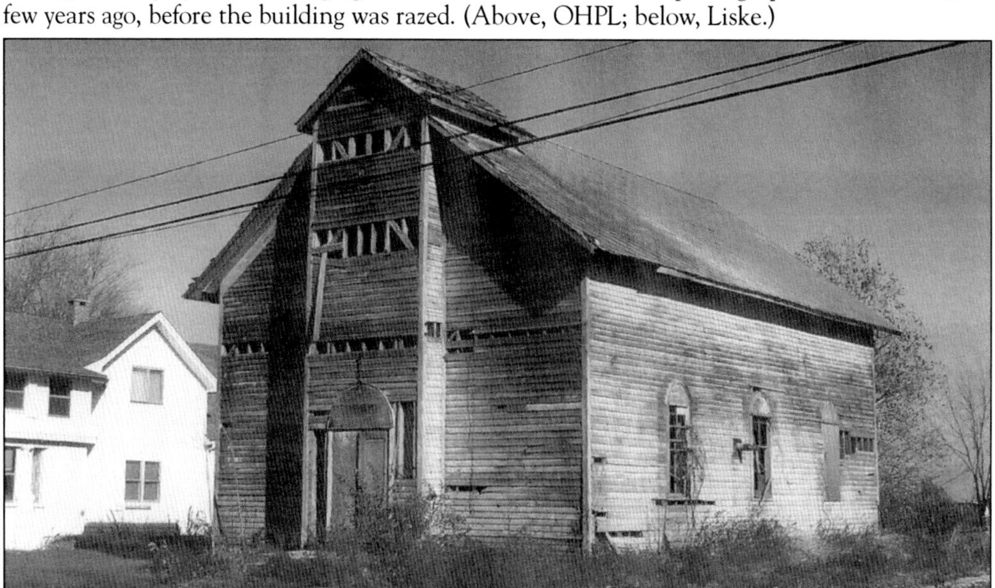

The picturesque St. Paul's Lutheran Church is located in the midst of lush farms on County Road 17, southeast of Oak Harbor in Salem Township. The first services were held in 1858 in local one-room schools. The frame structure that serves as the present church was built in 1872. A new parsonage was built in 1948 to replace one that had burned down. (Gluth.)

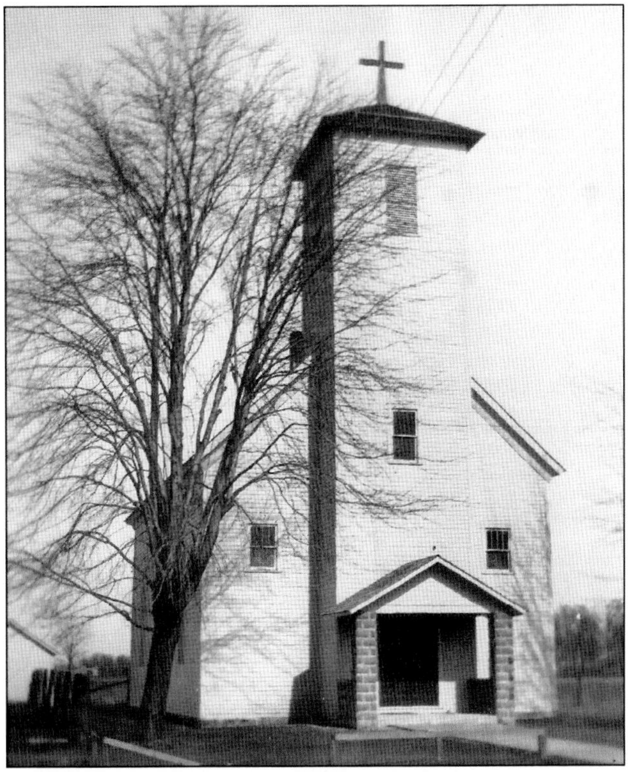

Members of the choir of St. Paul's Lutheran Church, seen here around 1900, are, from left to right, (first row) Augusta Roose, Katharine Lilje, and Bertha Noble; (second row) Fred Gratop, William Diedrich, Henry Meyer, Charles Noble, Laura Diedrich, Marie Lilje, Ernest Roose, and Charles Krieger. (Dolores Buhrow.)

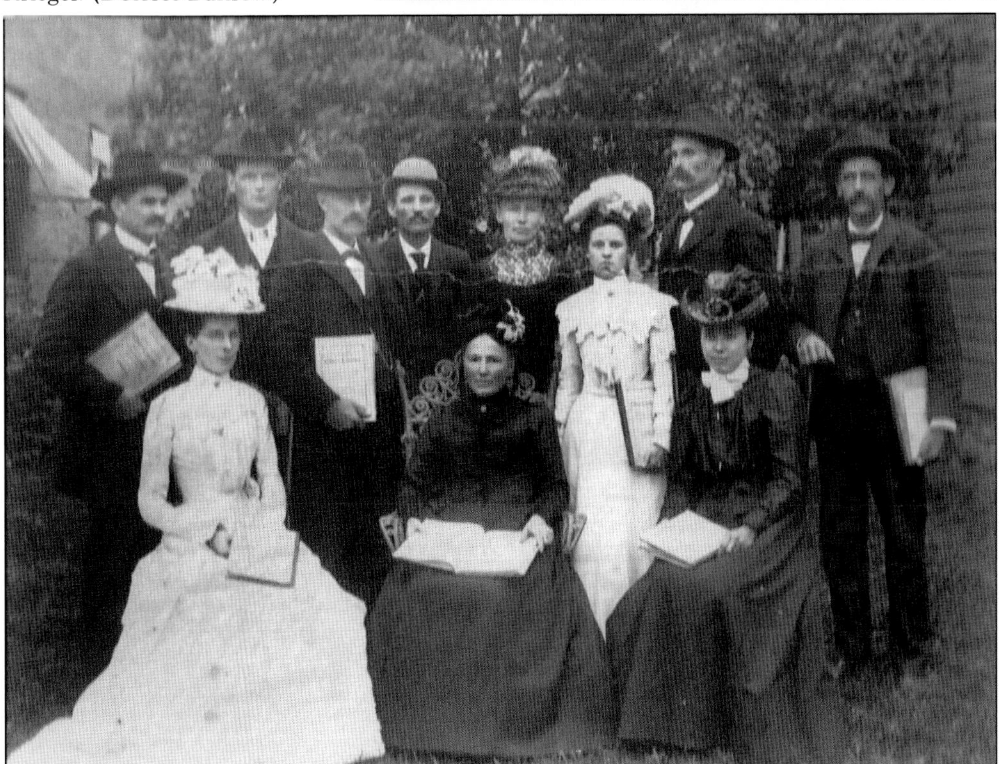

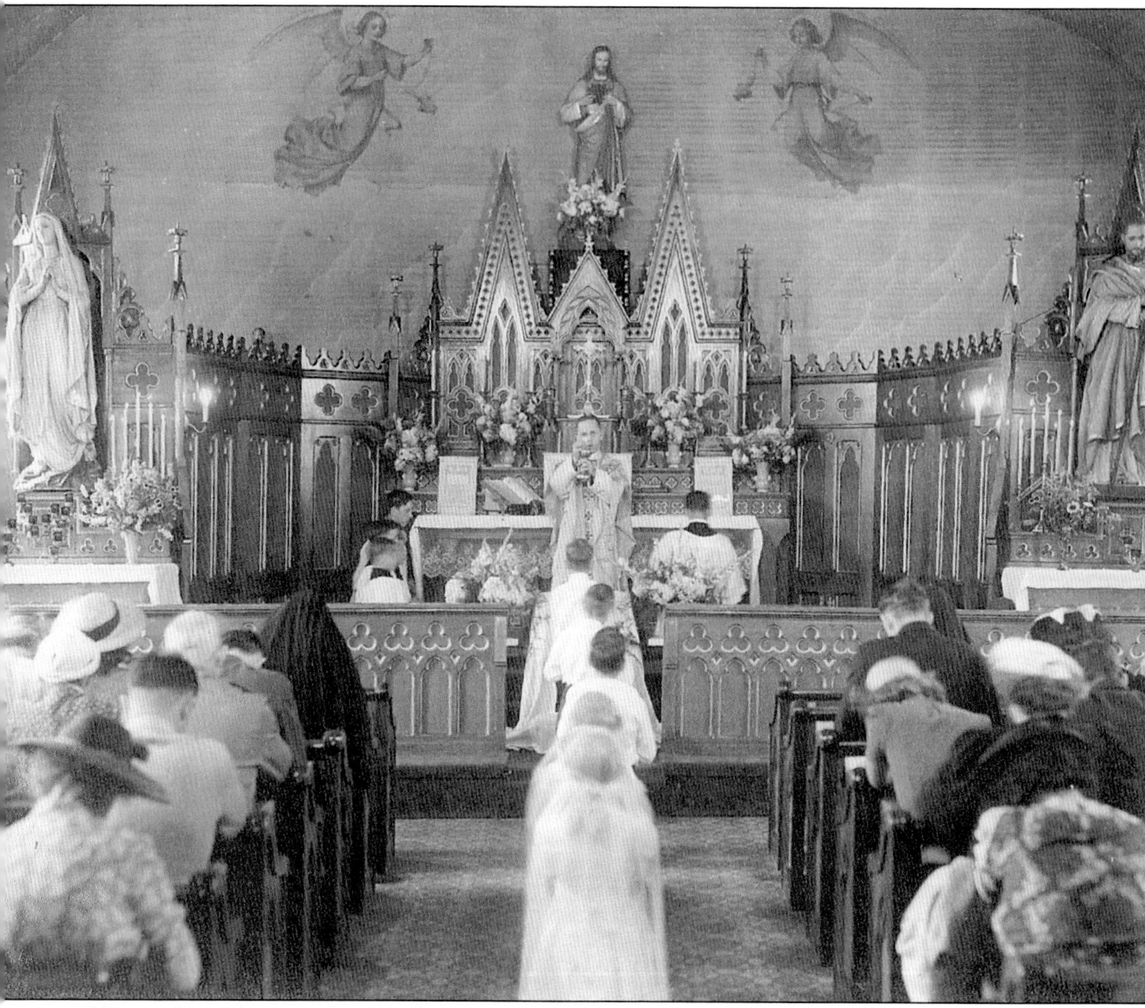

This striking photograph was taken in the former St. Joseph Roman Catholic Church on Duff-Washa Road in Carroll Township. The church was established in 1842 as a mission by early French settlers in an area known as Frenchtown. Mass was held in private homes until 1845, when a log church was built. The frame church shown here was built in 1861. The church was closed in 1942 and razed in 1944. A cemetery and former rectory remain. Many early Carroll Township settlers of French descent are buried in the cemetery. (CTHC.)

Seven

School Days

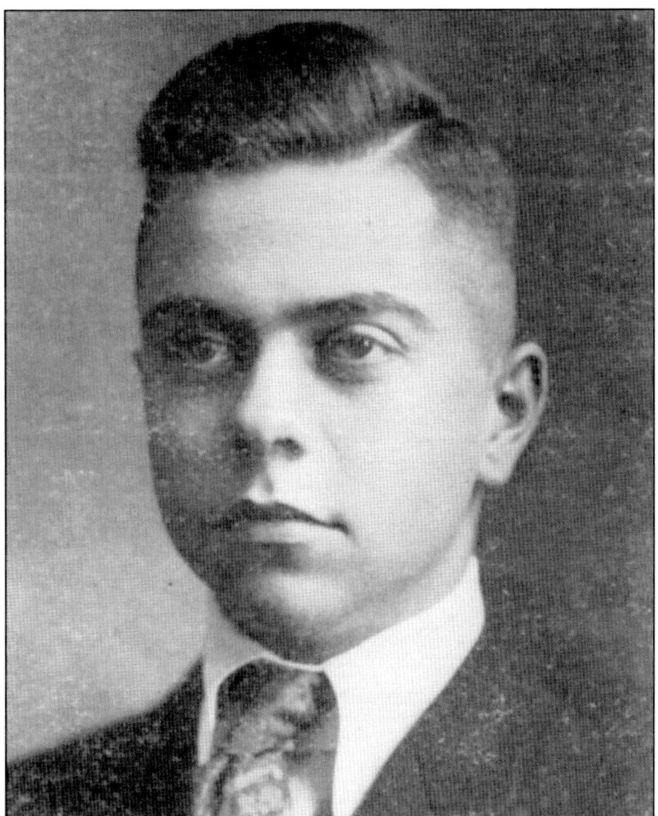

What better way to start a chapter on schools than with a portrait of a young Ralph C. Waters? Waters served as superintendent of Oak Harbor Schools from 1921 until 1962, almost 42 years. Very few, if any, school superintendents can match that record. Upon his retirement, Oak Harbor's new elementary school was dedicated as the R.C. Waters Elementary School. (Liske.)

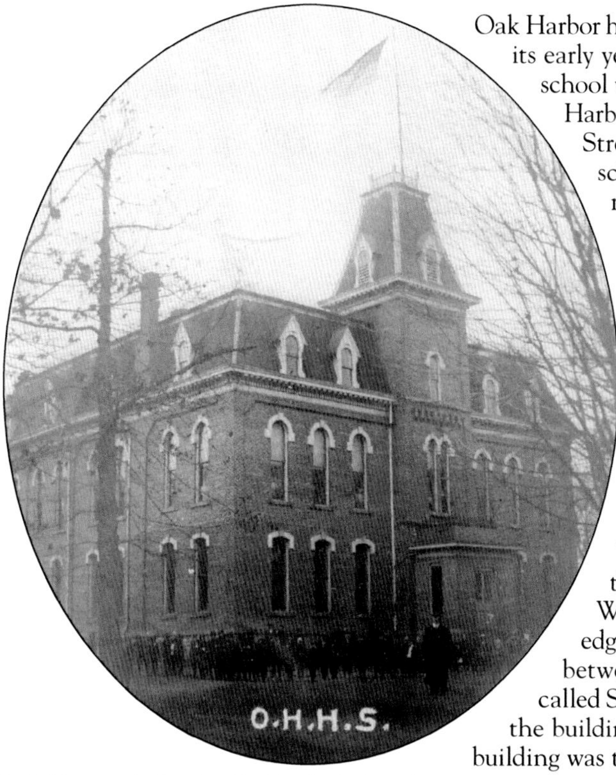

Oak Harbor had several small, one-room schools in its early years. The first multiple-room, graded school was built in 1875 by J. Wilson of Oak Harbor for $9,749. It was located on Church Street, at the site of the present middle school. Initially, the school had eight rooms, but an addition was made in 1889 to the west side to accommodate more students. (Liske.)

When the school was built in 1875, the southwest corner of Church and Walnut Streets was considered on the edge of town in a desolate area. The area between the school and Park Street was called School House Park. The third floor of the building was condemned in 1908, and the building was torn down in 1911. (OHPL.)

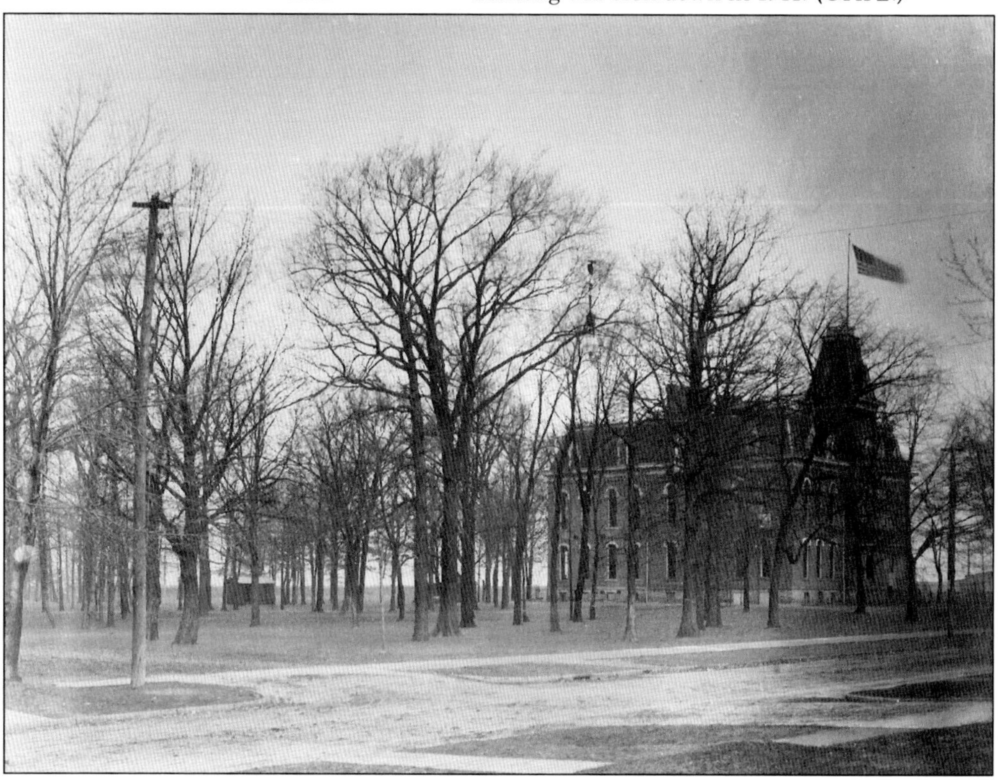

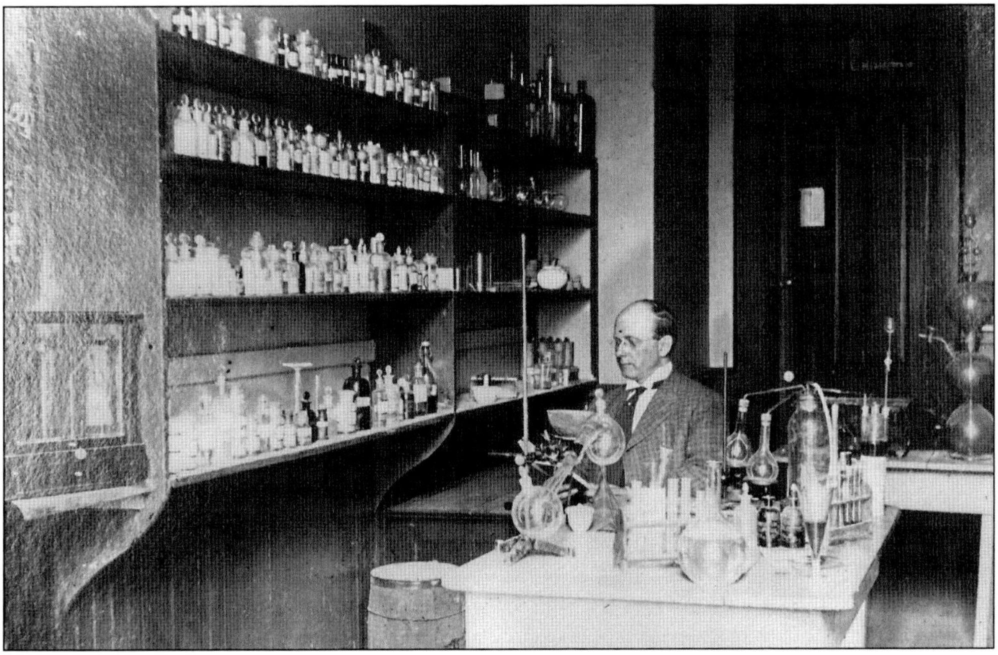

Professor H.H. Hoffman was superintendent of Oak Harbor School from 1902 to 1909, at a salary of $90 per month. He is seen here in the science lab of the 1875 school building. Hoffman is credited with starting the school band, interscholastic football, the first school yearbook, and the high school literary societies. (Liske.)

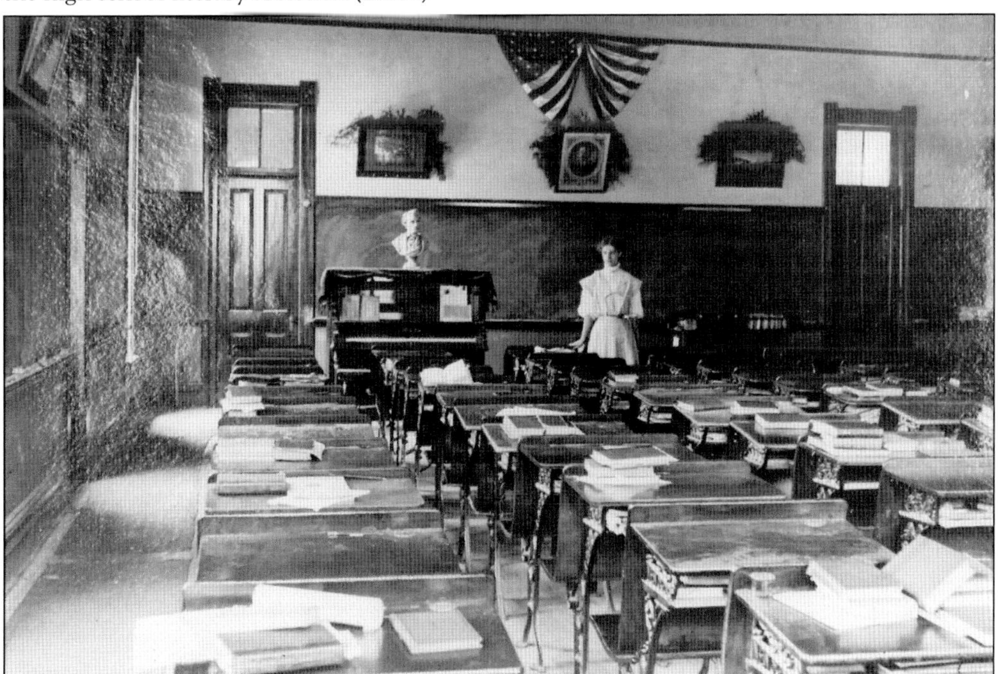

This interesting photograph, taken in the 1875 school building, shows Dora B. Moore, who served as assistant principal in 1908–1909. Note the wooden desks with inkwells and folding seats, wooden floors, and transoms above the doors for ventilation. (Liske.)

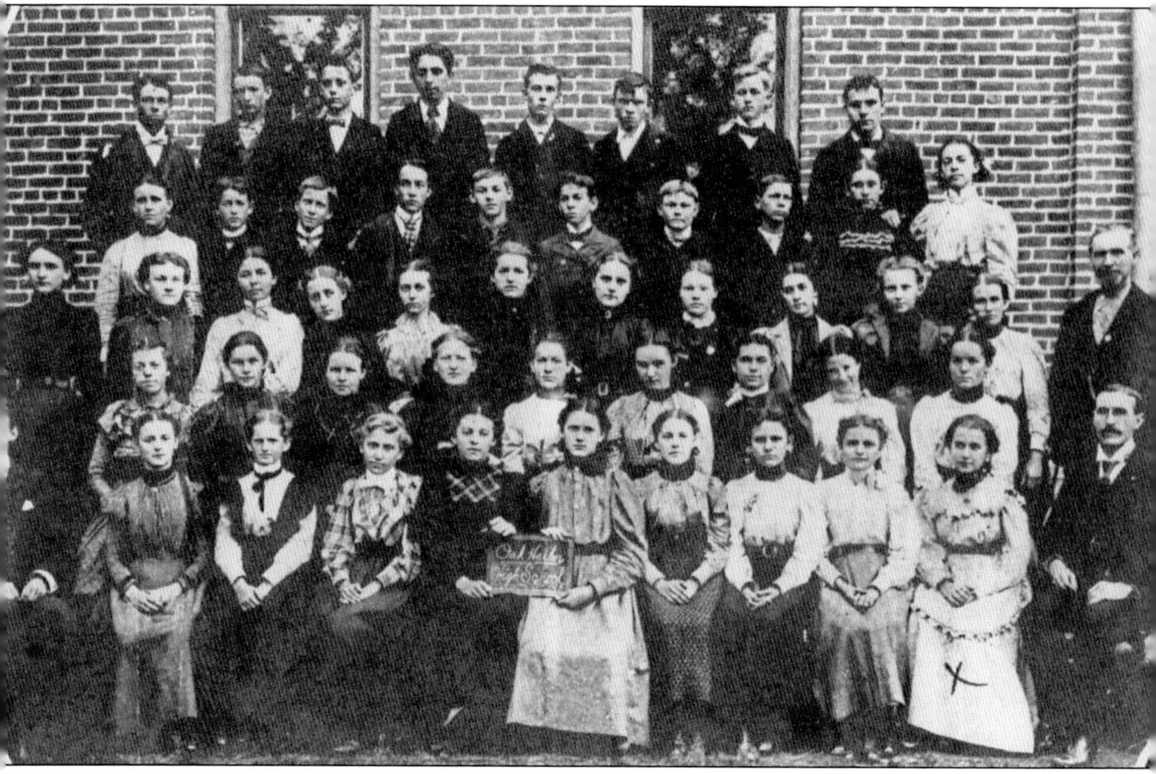

The first class to graduate from Oak Harbor High School, in 1887, consisted of three students: Sue Harrison, Gertrude Metzger, and George Guth. By 1898, the high school had expanded significantly. Shown in this 1898 photograph made at Oak Harbor High School in 1898 are, from left to right, (first row) Roy Turner (principal), Marguerite Favro, Mabel Maul, Emma Keener, Marie Cavalier, Julia Bauch, Iva Graner, Zula Binkley, Alma Sabiers, Mildred Thierwechter, and John Carson (teacher); (second row) Laura Sealing, Donna Bleckner, Bertha Brown, Phena Rahm, Pauline Bolgeroski, Lillian Brady, Luetta Meinke, Georgia Fetterly, and Ella Kraemer; (third row) Sophia Denk, Alta Gordon, Rose Miller, Kate Buck, Edith Anspach, Pearl Mylander, Lulu Bleckner, Christina Segard, Maude Vogel, Emma Hansen, Maude Thompson, and C.J. Biery (superintendent); (fourth row) Minnie Schroeder, unidentified, Adah Graner, Vern Vogel, Christ Jessen, unidentified, Otto Lilje, William Fleckner, Lena Joseph, and Elsie Meyer; (fifth row) Eugene Schroeder, Oscar Leutz, August Pomeranke, John Petersen, Ernest Echoff, Vincent Hennesey, George Vogel, and Henry Kramb. (Gluth.)

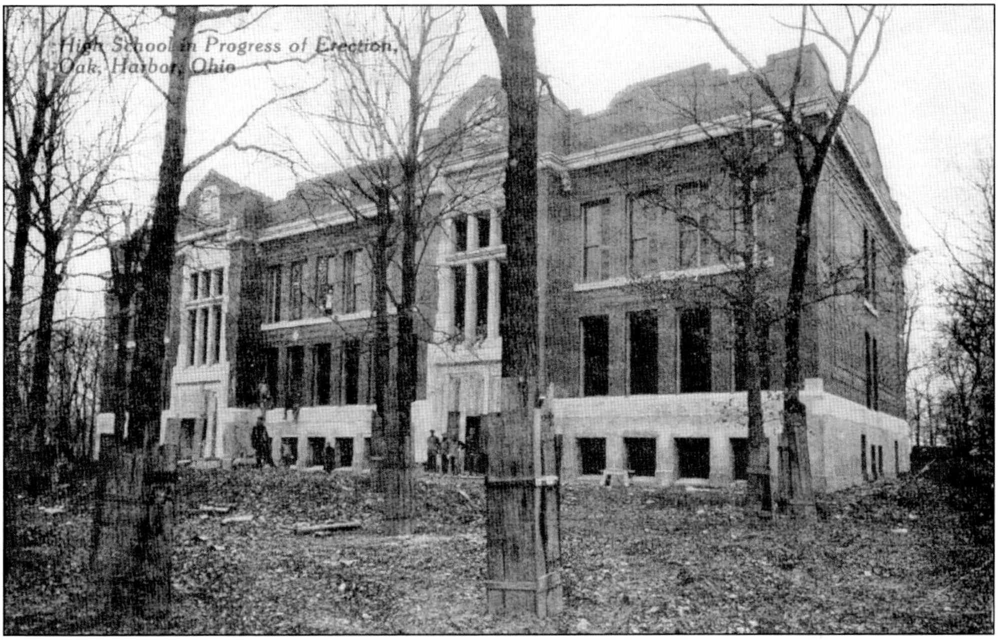

When the 1875 building was torn down in 1911, a new school was constructed on the same site. The above photograph shows this new building under construction. Note the wood barriers around the trees, placed to keep horses from chewing on the bark. This 1911 building still serves the students of Oak Harbor's Benton-Carroll-Salem Local School District over 100 years later, now as a middle school. The below photograph shows the 1937 addition, which included an auditorium/gymnasium and additional classrooms. The building today looks much as it did when this photograph was taken in the 1950s. (Both, Liske.)

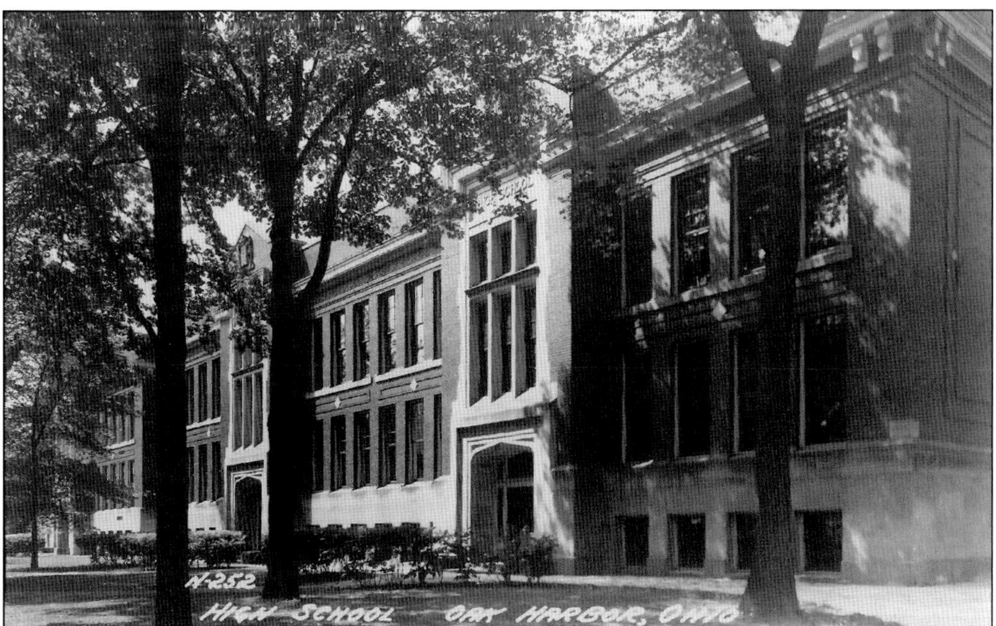

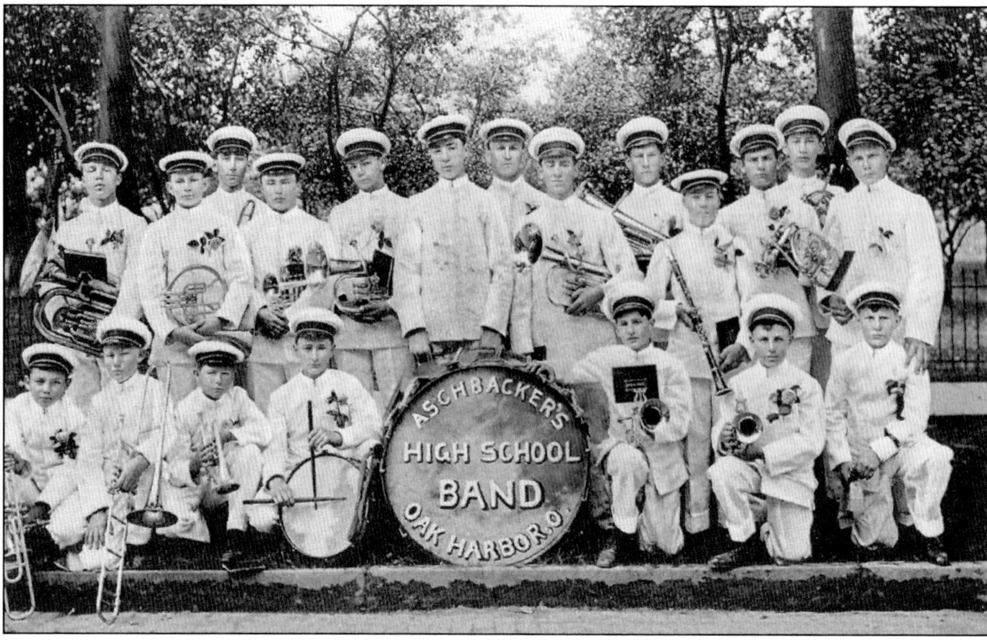

Music became an important part of the school curriculum in the early 1900s. At the time, George F. Aschbacher was assistant principal and music instructor at Oak Harbor High School. He organized this band in November 1906. The photograph was taken by George D. Smith on May 30, 1907, the band's first public appearance in uniform. (Liske.)

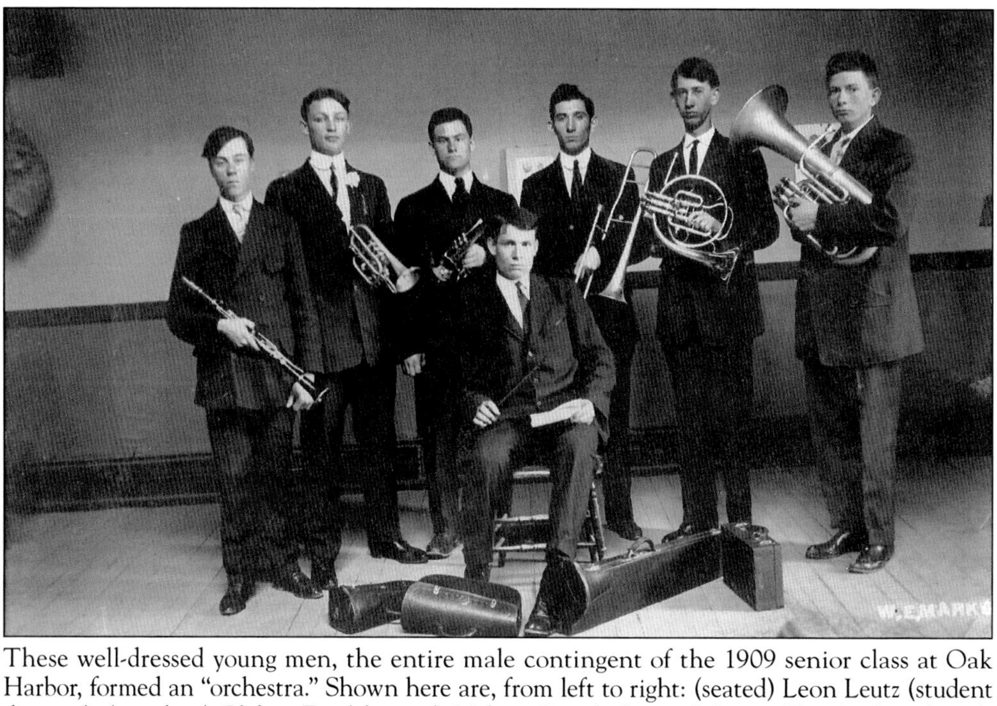

These well-dressed young men, the entire male contingent of the 1909 senior class at Oak Harbor, formed an "orchestra." Shown here are, from left to right: (seated) Leon Leutz (student director); (standing) Clifton Fry (clarinet), Nelson Davids (cornet), Lester Fought (trombone), Wesley Bredbeck (alto horn), and George Thierwechter (baritone horn). One can only imagine what they sounded like. (OHPL.)

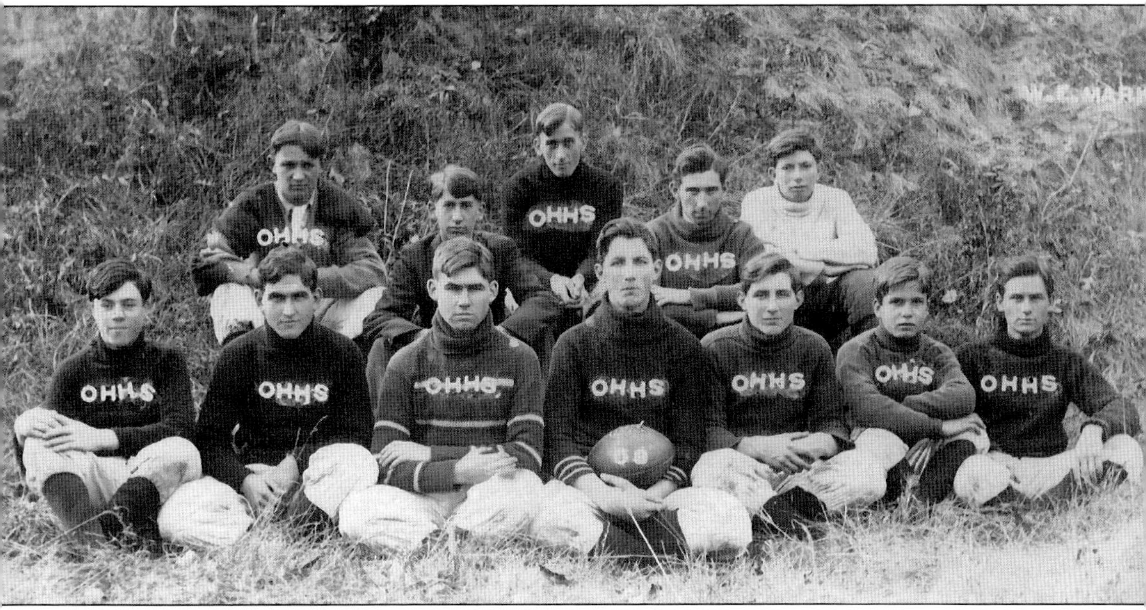

Oak Harbor High School football dates back to at least the 1908 team pictured here. The coach was Wesley Bredbeck, and the captain was Lester Fought. The team apparently practiced in the middle of Church Street just north of Water Street. Games may have been played at Yeisley Field, an undeveloped area somewhere north of East Water Street and west of Finke Road. Members of the team include, from left to right, (first row) Clifton Frye, Marvin King, Leroy Herring, Walter Balduf, John Balduf, Bliss Bowman, and William Marks; (second row) Nelson Davids, Wesley Bredbeck, Carl Berly, Lester Fought, and George Thierwechter. The team reportedly lost every game, including a 61-0 route by Fremont. However, the newspaper reported that the loss to Fremont was a minor matter, as the important part of the day was the delicious oyster stew that the team enjoyed following the game. The teams must have improved, because a 1914 news article tells of an 86-0 win over Port Clinton. (OHPL.)

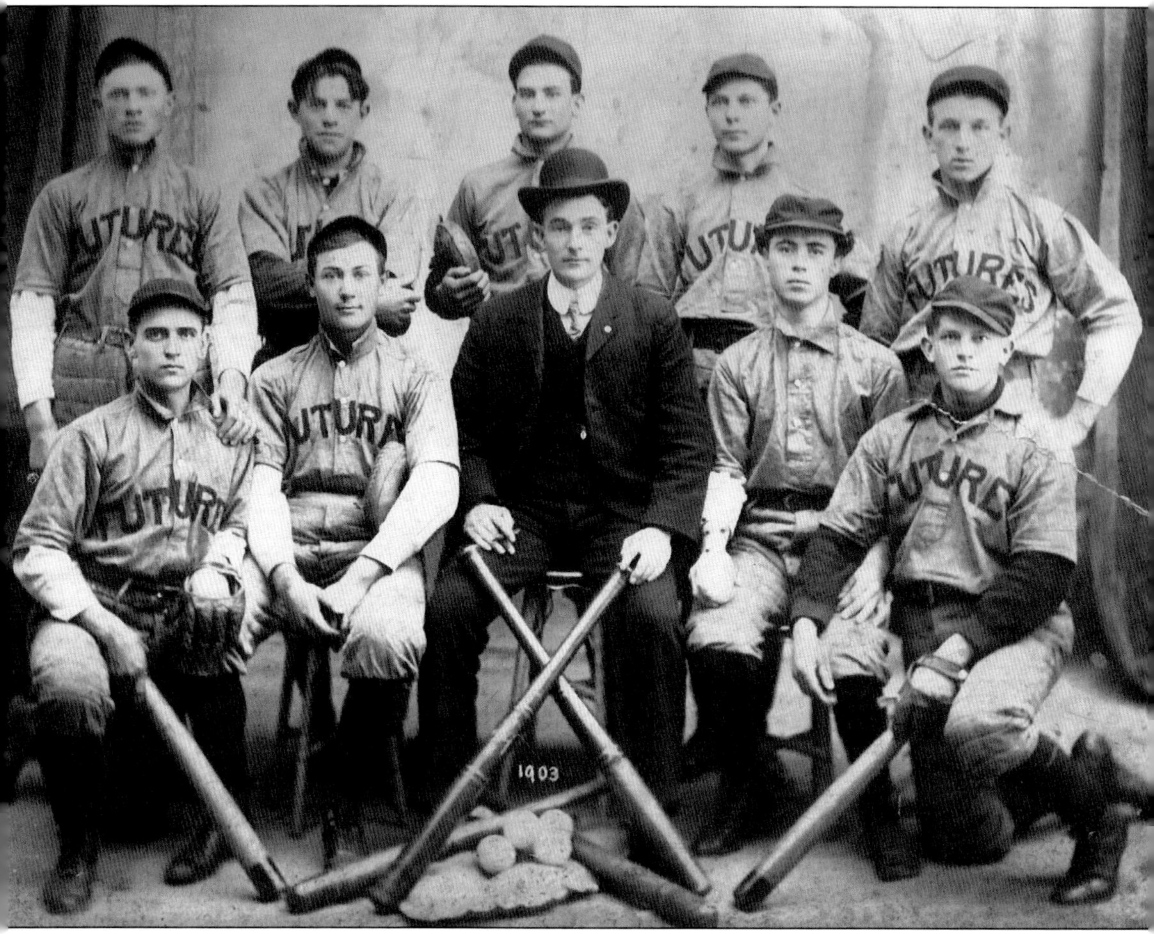

Baseball was a major pastime among young men in early Oak Harbor, both at the school and in the wider community. Many baseball games were held with teams from neighboring towns. The Futures was a team made up of community members, and included, from left to right, (first row) Wesley Zehner, Otto Hinderlich, Dr. Horace S. Woodward, Virgil Fry, and Bill Rahm; (second row) Bill Gluth, George Foreman, Otto Rose, Bill Fleckner, and Henry Guntsch. The team was sponsored by local grocery store owner Nahmy Bassett. (OHPL.)

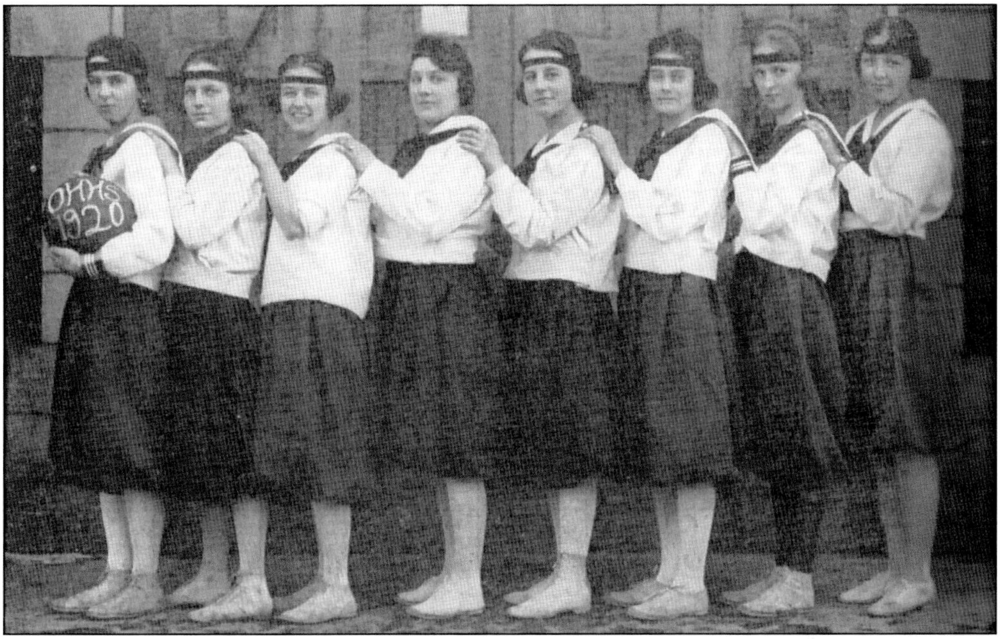

Since a gymnasium was not built at Oak Harbor High School until 1937, both boys' and girls' basketball teams played their home games in the armory on Water Street. The 1920 girls' basketball team poses in front of the armory doors. Shown are, from left to right, Helene Schimansky, Lila Metzgar, Pearl Price, Martha Peters, Velma Wolf, Grace Velliquette, Ruth Linder, and Marguerite Lantz. (Gluth.)

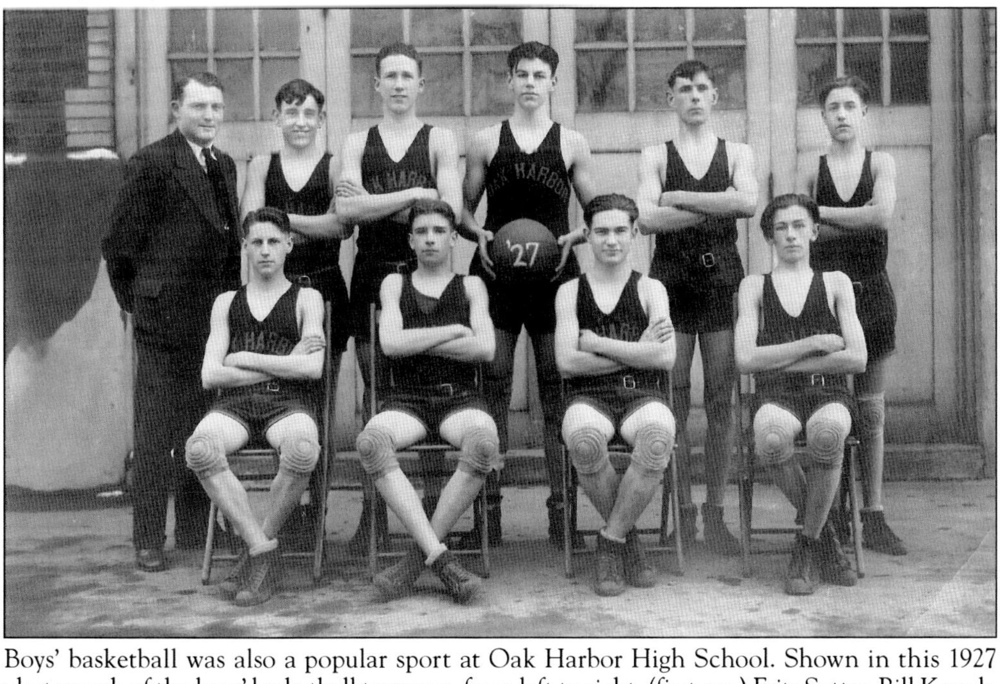

Boys' basketball was also a popular sport at Oak Harbor High School. Shown in this 1927 photograph of the boys' basketball team are, from left to right, (first row) Fritz Sutter, Bill Kramb, Emmett Balduf, and Howard Zimmerman; (second row) coach C.Y. Stubblefield, Fritz Pluckhorn, Bob Kilmer, Ed Zipfel, Fran Whittmore, and Norm Hetrick. (Gluth.)

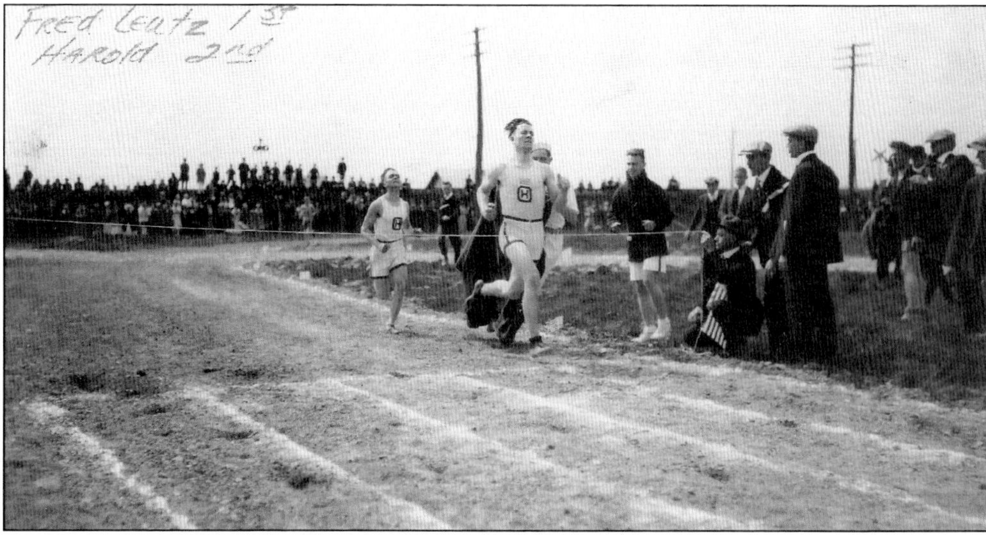

Two Oak Harbor High School runners, led by Fred Leutz, get ready to break the tape at a c. 1917 track meet. It appears from the railroad track in the background that the event was taking place in the field north of the high school. Note how the spectators are sitting along the railroad embankment. (Elizabeth Milbrodt.)

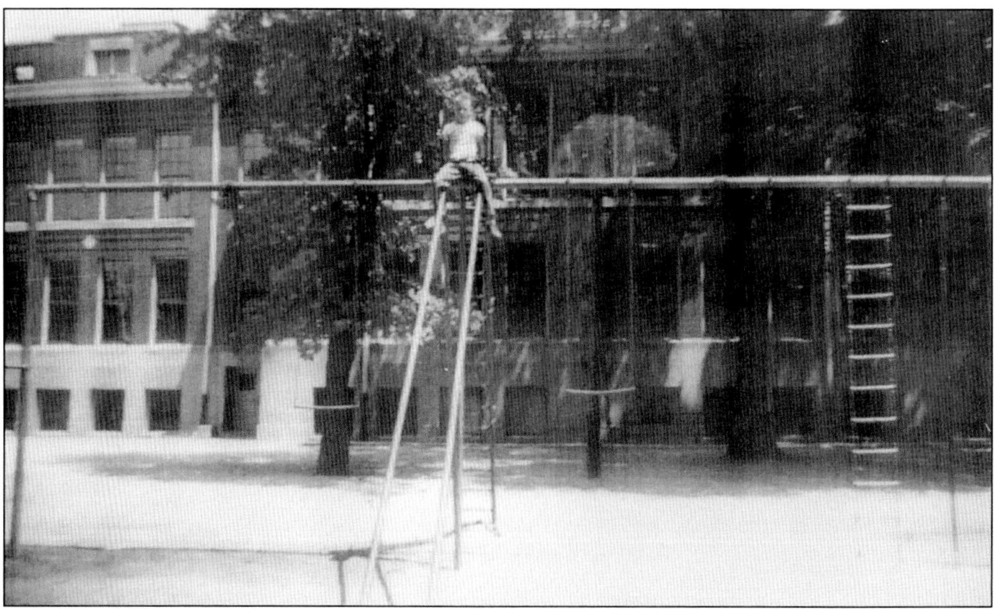

The playground behind the Church Street school had this unusual two-pipe slide from the 1930s through the 1950s. In this photograph from the late 1930s, Bill Duff starts down the slide by wrapping his legs around the pipes and letting go. Probably not safe by today's playground standards, the slide was finally removed in the late 1950s. (Gluth.)

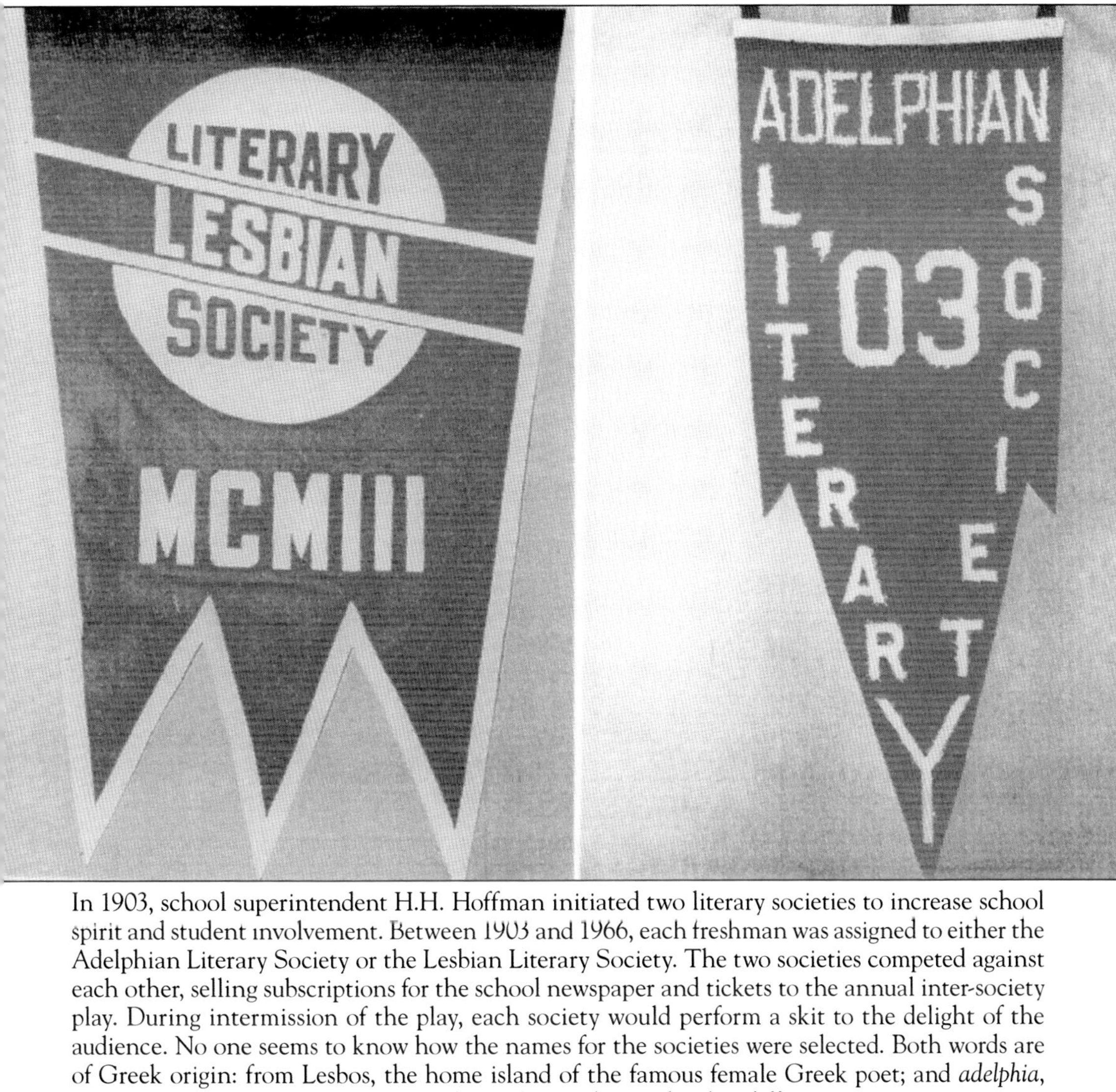

In 1903, school superintendent H.H. Hoffman initiated two literary societies to increase school spirit and student involvement. Between 1903 and 1966, each freshman was assigned to either the Adelphian Literary Society or the Lesbian Literary Society. The two societies competed against each other, selling subscriptions for the school newspaper and tickets to the annual inter-society play. During intermission of the play, each society would perform a skit to the delight of the audience. No one seems to know how the names for the societies were selected. Both words are of Greek origin: from Lesbos, the home island of the famous female Greek poet; and *adelphia*, the Greek word for "brotherhood." Obviously, words can develop different meanings over time. However, if any graduate of that era is asked which society he or she belonged to, an answer will be proudly provided. (OHPL.)

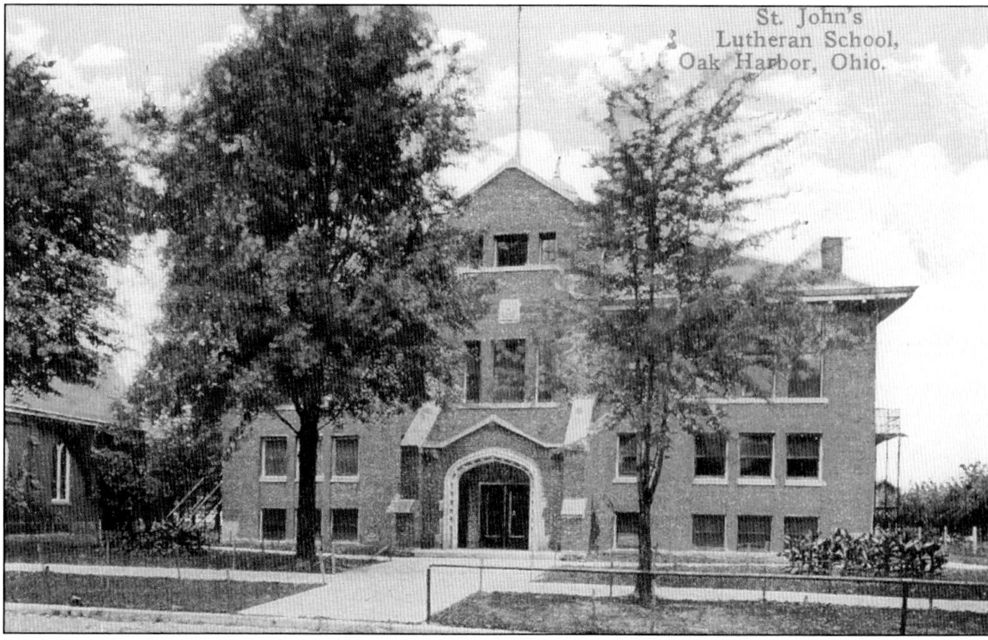

St. John's Lutheran Church on Ottawa Street had a parochial school from 1897 to 1929. The original wood-frame structure was replaced by the school shown above in 1912, for $22,000. This building was used by the students of St. John's and provided overflow classrooms for the public schools until 1959, when it was torn down for the new St. John's educational building. In the photograph below, taken on September 15, 1910, in the old frame building, J.J. Ballmer, teacher and head of the school from 1908 to 1929, poses with students. Ballmer was the father of Josephine Ballmer, longtime Oak Harbor schoolteacher and principal of R.C. Waters Elementary School. (Both, Liske.)

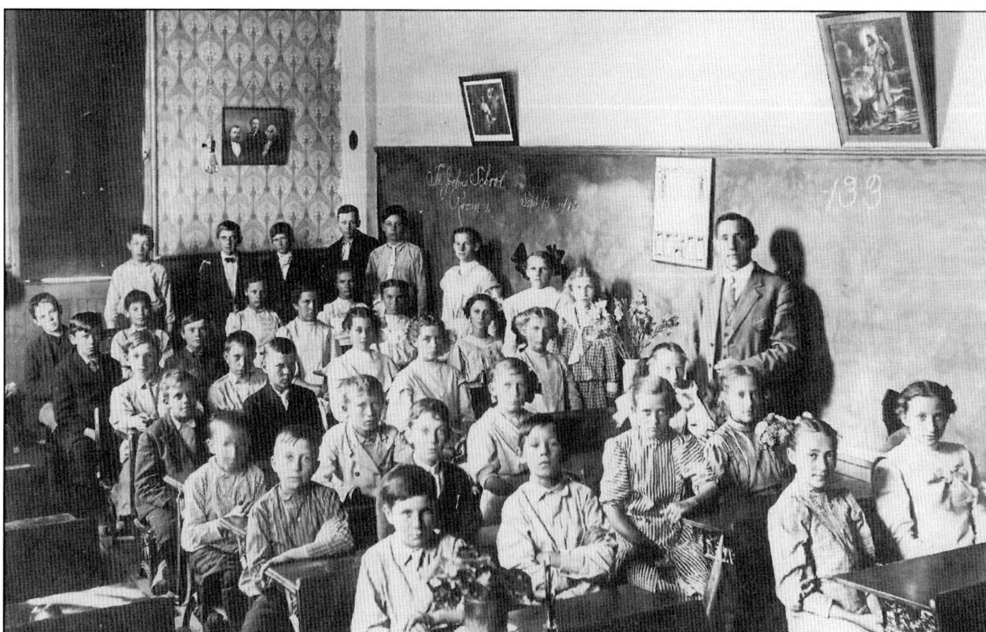

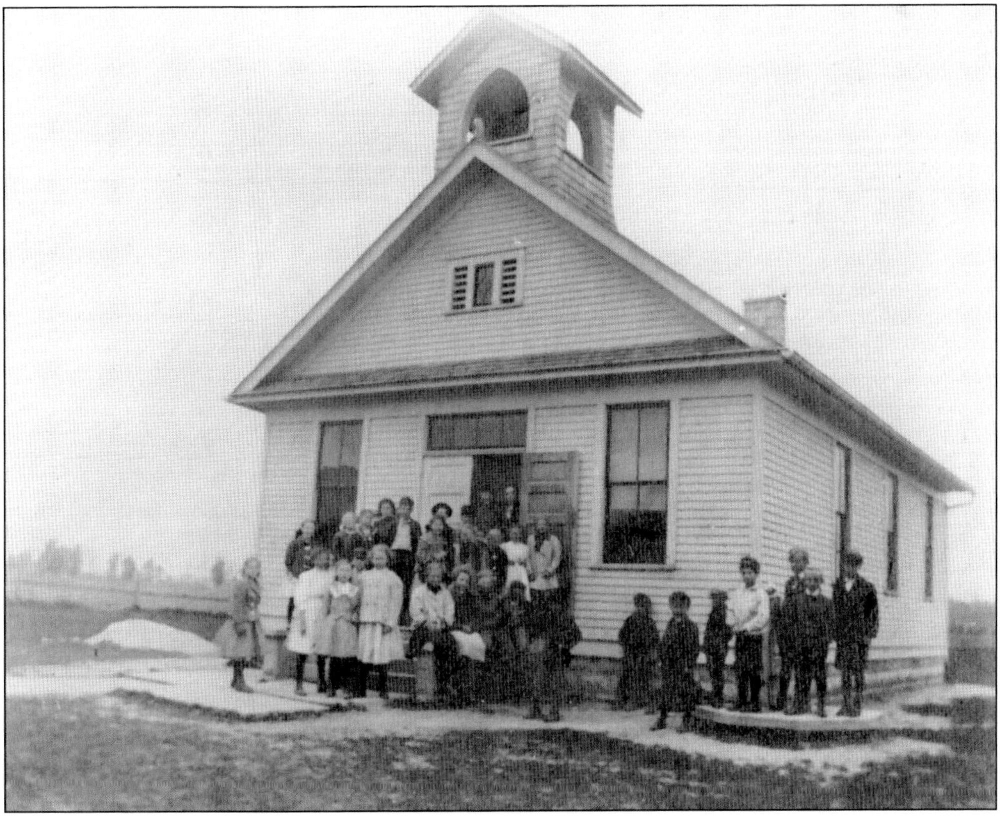

Although the village of Oak Harbor had a multiple-classroom school, the surrounding townships of Salem, Benton, and Carroll primarily relied on one- or two-room schoolhouses until the 1930s. Students at Lincoln School, located on Bier Road between Behlman and Leutz Road, were part of the Carroll Township School District. (CTHC.)

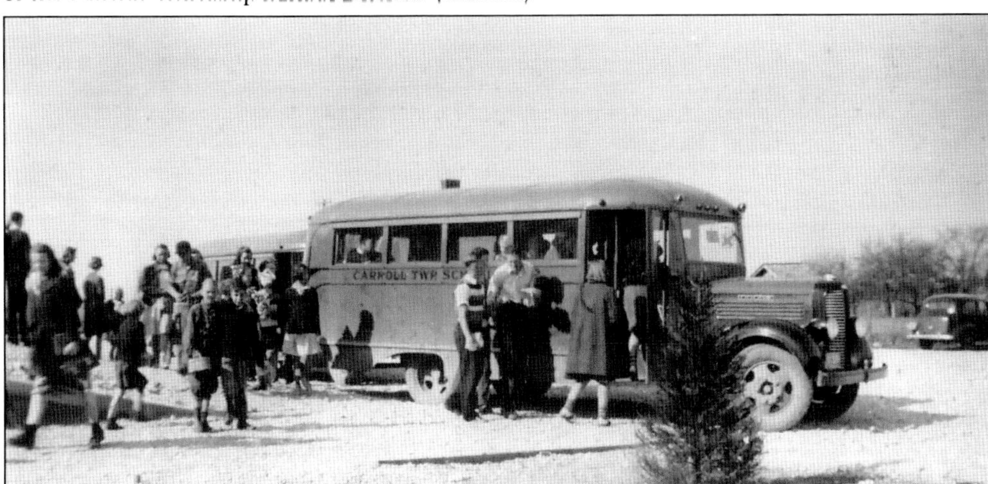

In 1939, Carroll Township closed its one-room schools and built a new school at the corner of State Route 19 and Toussaint East Road. Since students were now being transported to one location, school buses were needed. The Carroll school became part of the Benton-Carroll-Salem District in 1967. The 1939 building was closed in 2012. (Martin.)

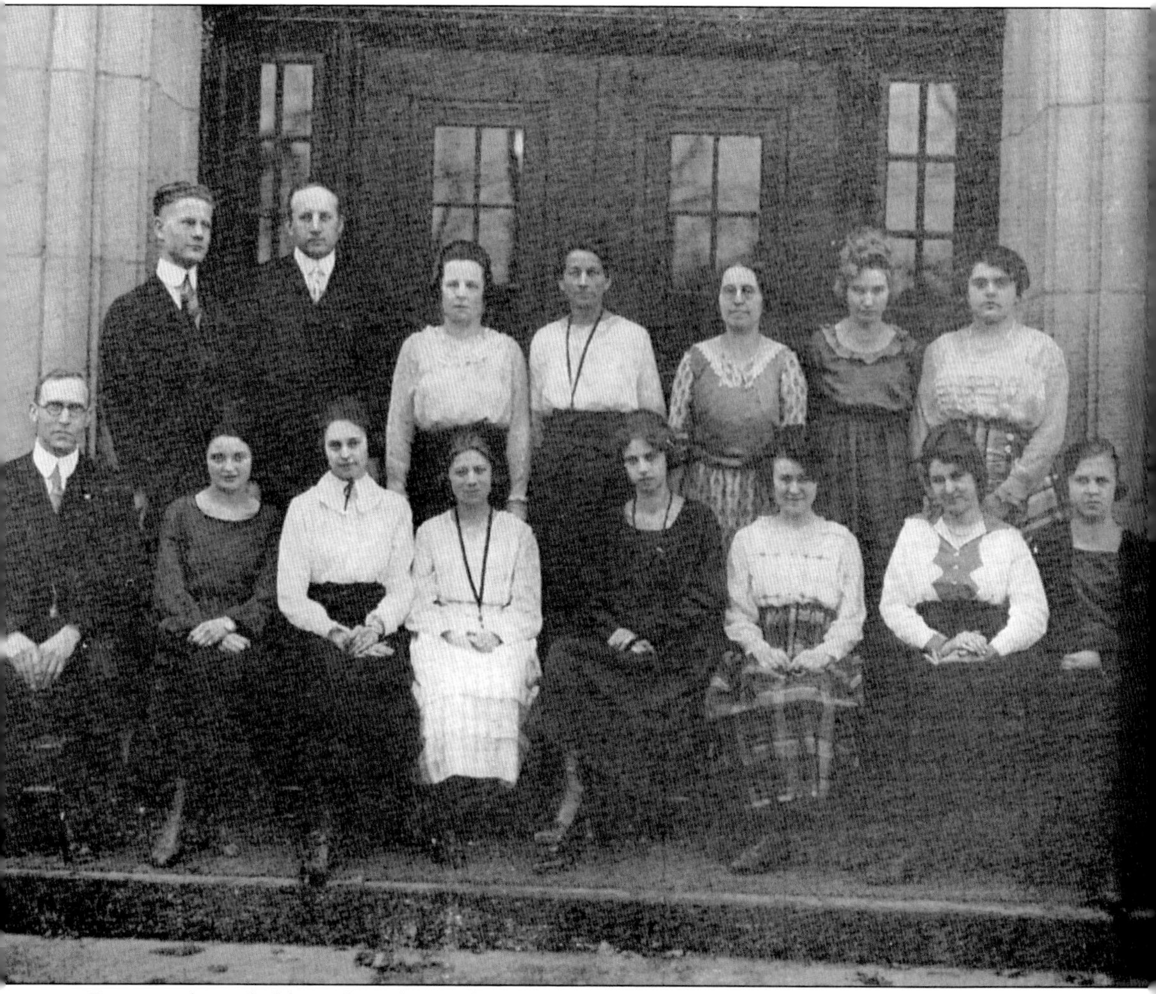

Few people probably realize that Oak Harbor once had a normal school, or teacher training college. The Ottawa County Normal School was housed in the basement classrooms of Oak Harbor High School from 1914 to 1926. Graduates from the two-year normal school often became teachers in area one-room schoolhouses. Students and faculty in the 1920 class are, from left to right, (first row) Carl G. Pemberton (superintendent), Mae Murphy, Grace Hoeltze, Marie Kinsel, Enola Schnoor, Irene Hellwig, Esther Ganske, and Harriet Bredbeck; (second row) Kenneth Reed, A.O. Dehn (county school superintendent), Florence Applegate, Hattie Fields, Erma Ferguson (director), Orlena Meinke, and Leta Wainwright. The school closed in 1926 when classes became available at Bowling Green State University and other colleges. (Liske.)

Eight

Having Fun

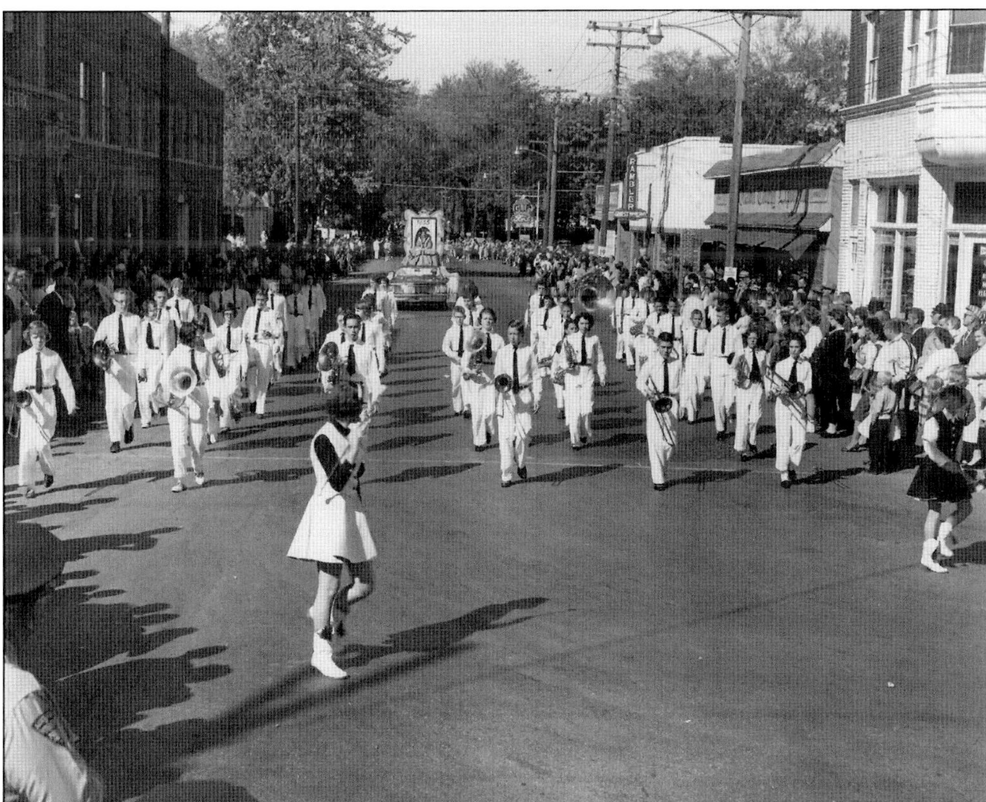

The Cadet Band consisting of seventh and eighth graders from Oak Harbor Junior High School march down Locust Street during the 1960 Oak Harbor Fall Fair. John Freytag was the director of the bands at Oak Harbor School at that time. (Martin.)

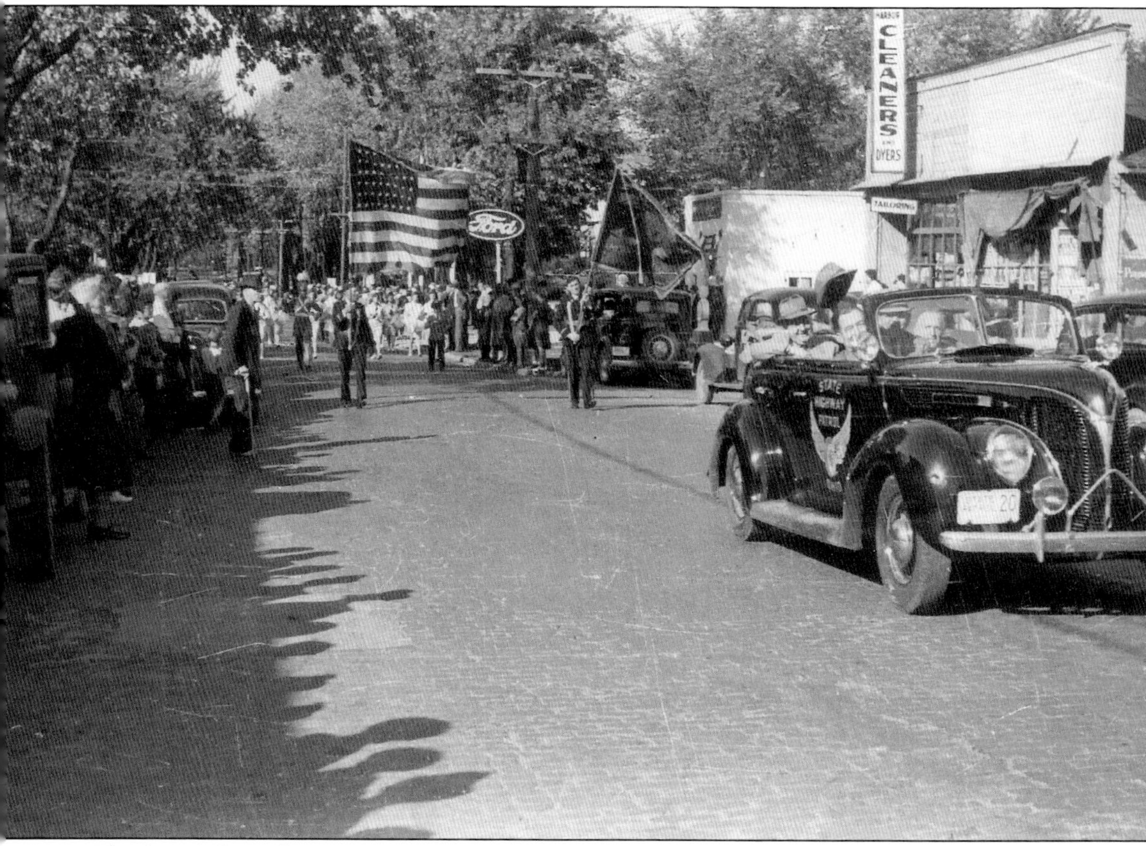

The first Oak Harbor Fall Fair was held in 1932 as a way to build community spirit during the depths of the Depression. The fair continued through 1962, with a three-year hiatus in 1943–1945. The fair was primarily sponsored by the Oak Harbor Businessmen's Association, with support from many community groups. The event effectively ended after the 1962 fair, when a local businessman objected to the blocking of Water Street. Several shortened events were held in 1963 and 1964. Then, in 1965, the first Ottawa County Fair was held at Veterans Park. The following year, it was held at the new fairgrounds east of Oak Harbor. Today, the Oak Harbor Apple Festival, held downtown, is reminiscent of the old Fall Fair. Shown here is of one of the early Fall Fair parades, with an unusual convertible patrol car leading the parade. (OCHM.)

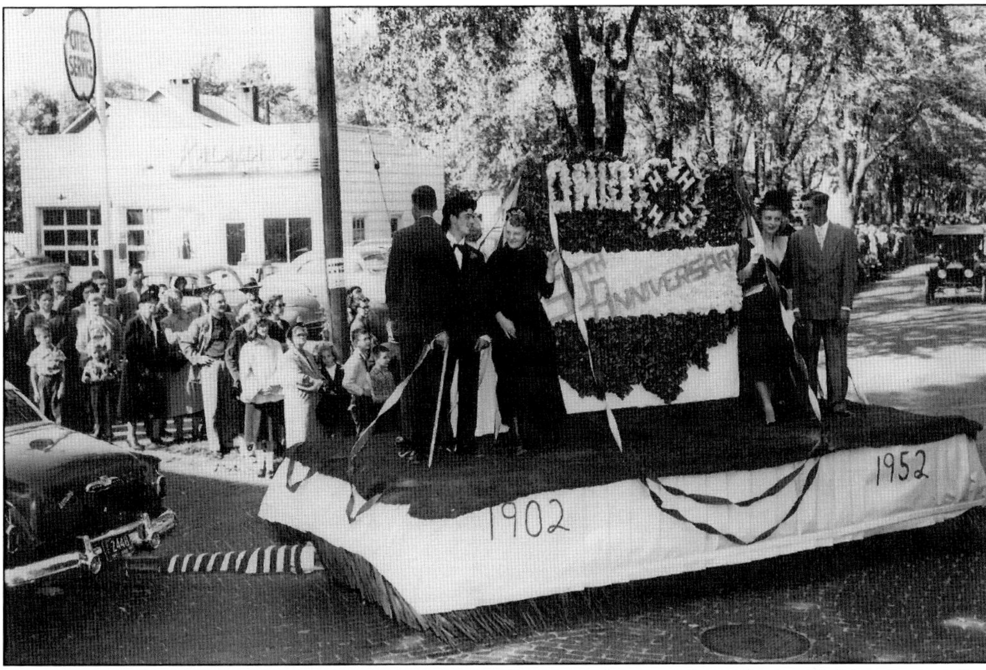

Since Ottawa County did not have a traditional county fair until 1965, the Fall Fair served as Ottawa County's Junior Fair for 4-H and Future Farmers of America members. Seen above is a 4-H float from the 1952 fair, as 4-H celebrated its 50th anniversary. The parade was always one of the fair's major events. The Ottawa County Junior Fair Queen was also crowned during the fair. Below, queen candidates are on the stage at the 1962 fair. They are, from left to right, Linda Risch, Janet Schimming, Connie Sandrock, and Joan Brough. Schimming was selected as the queen. (Above, OHPL; below, Linda Dehring.)

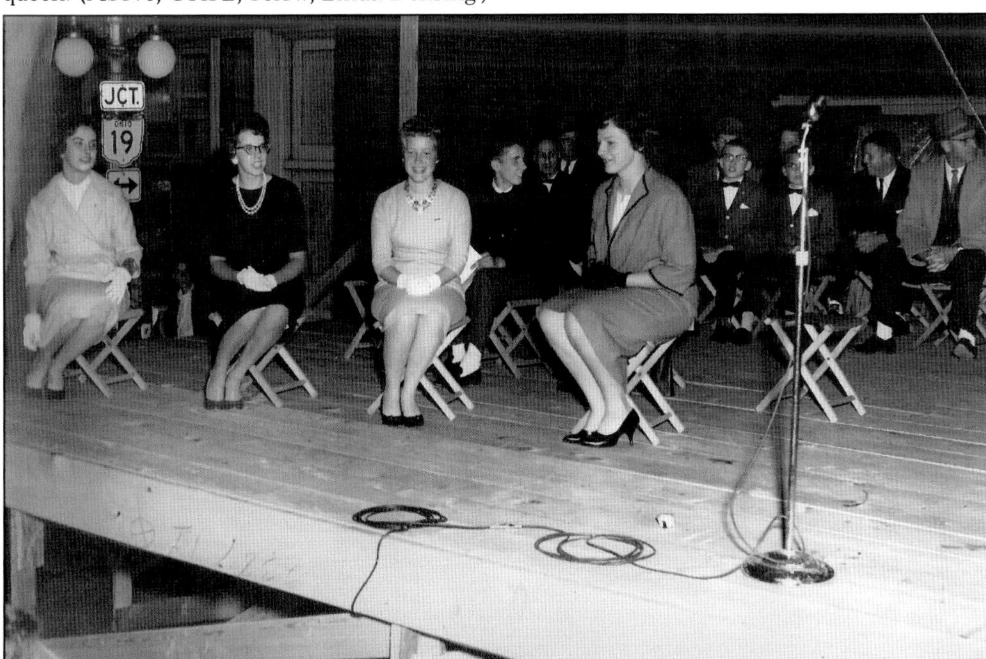

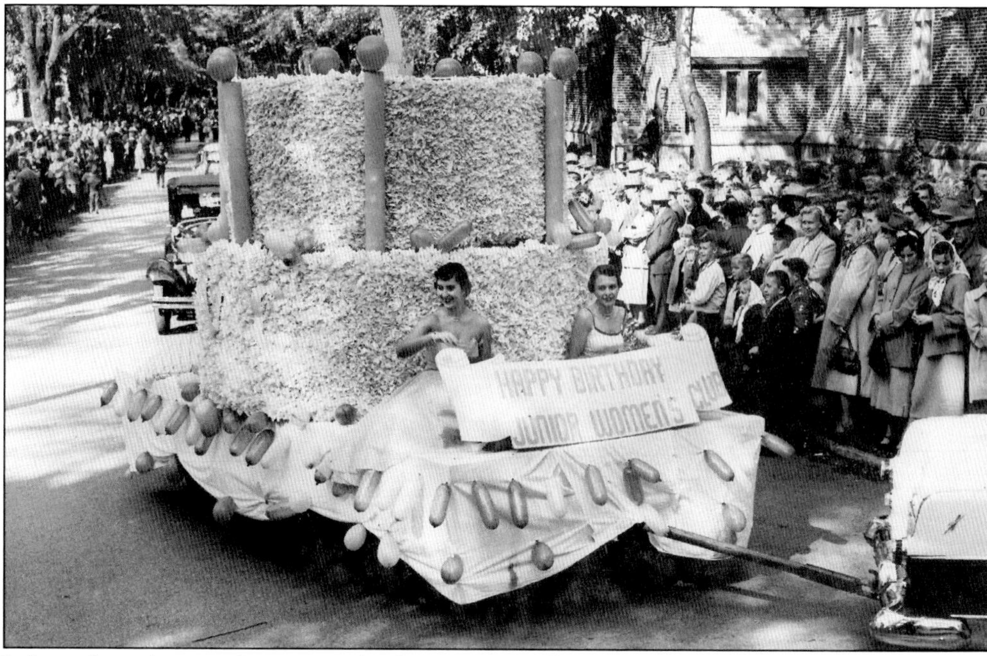

Judging from the coats being worn by the spectators along the parade route, the two young ladies from the Junior Women's Club riding this float must have been quite chilly. This photograph, along with hundreds of other photographs of Oak Harbor events from the 1940s through the 1970s, was taken by Oak Harbor photographer Clint Fehlhaber. (OHPL.)

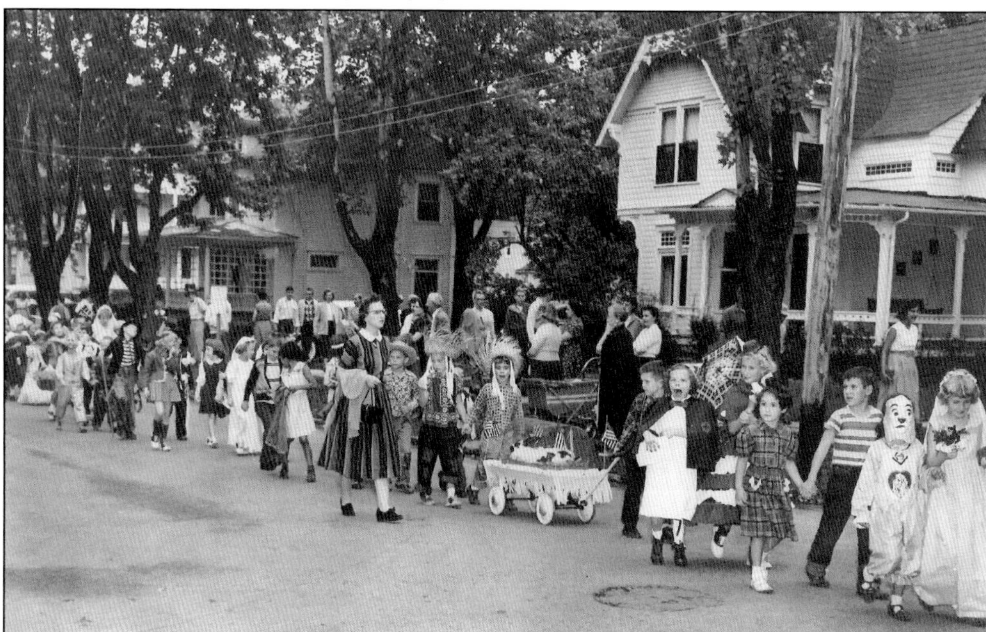

On the opening day of the fair, schoolchildren were let out early to march in a Kiddies Parade from the schoolhouse to downtown. Some children dressed in costumes, others decorated their bikes or brought their pets. Here, Gladys Milbrodt and her second-grade class march in the 1955 parade. (Martin.)

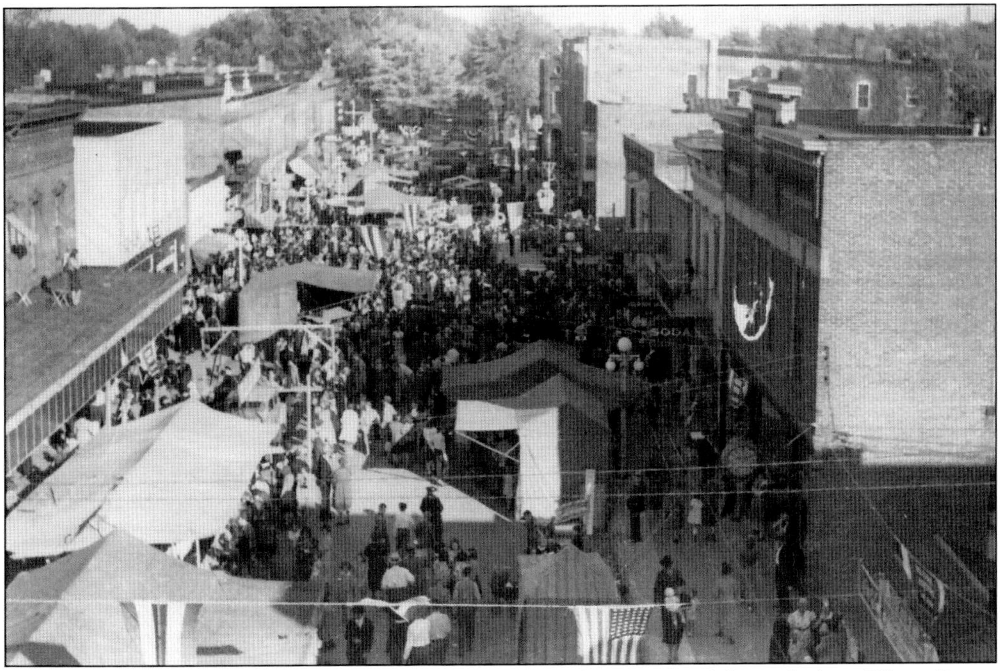

This c. 1938 photograph of Water Street is looking east during one of the early fairs. Water Street was closed to vehicular traffic as the crowds took part in the fair activities. People are seated on the roof of the area covering the sidewalk over the Family Food store. (OCHM.)

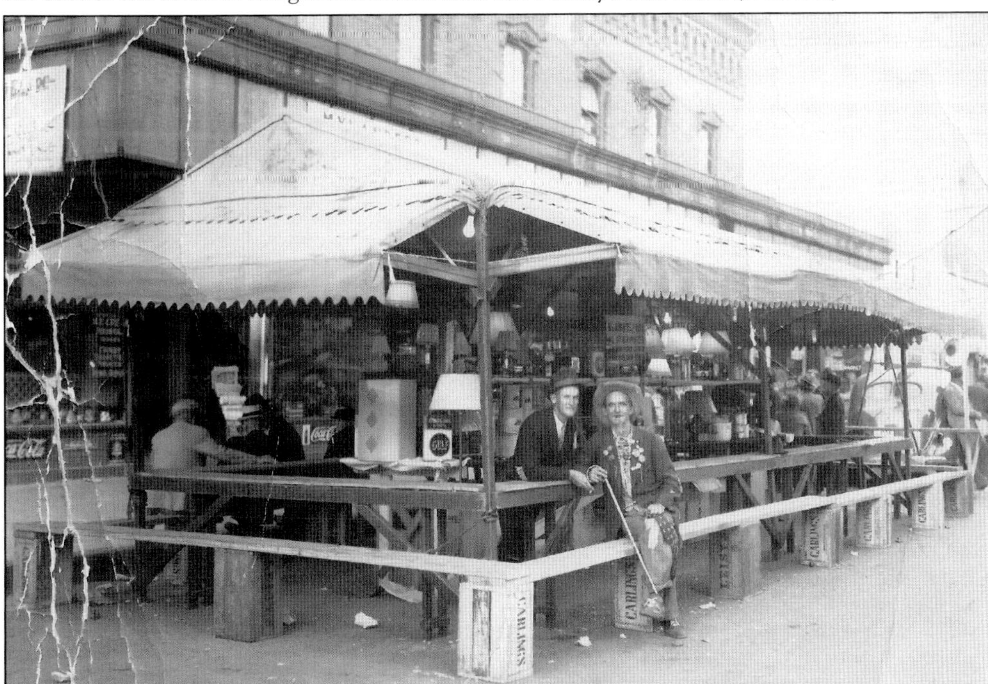

At the 1937 or 1938 fair, this crudely constructed bingo tent provided entertainment for fairgoers. Harold Probel was in charge of the tent. Note the beer boxes and wood planks used as seats. The new Dodge sedan in the background was raffled off on the last night of the fair. (Mary Paulsen.)

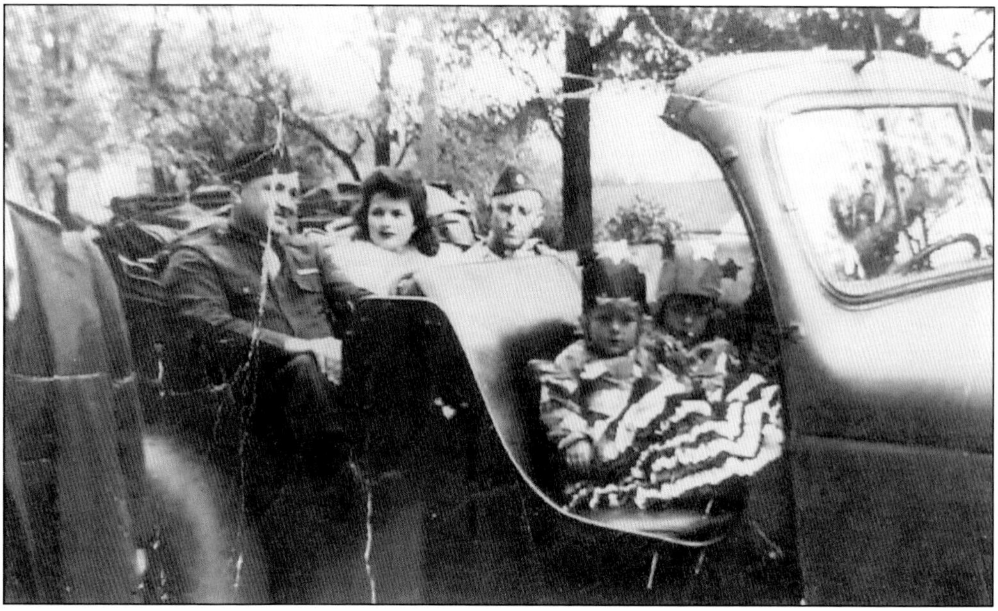

Miss America, Jo Carroll Dennison, visited the Oak Harbor Fall Fair in 1942. She is seen in the above photograph riding in a military-type car in the parade. In the front seat are Lonnie (Gluth) St. Clair (left), age 5, and Darleen (Cluckey) Van Der Geiseen, age 6. In the photograph below, hundreds of people crowd the stage on Water Street to catch a glimpse of Miss America. The stage was erected in front of a house built by H.H. Mylander in 1861, which still stands on Water Street. The frame building to the right of the stage was one of Mylander's early stores, also built in 1861. It was moved when the Kinsel Building was erected about 1950. (Above, Gluth; below, Martin.)

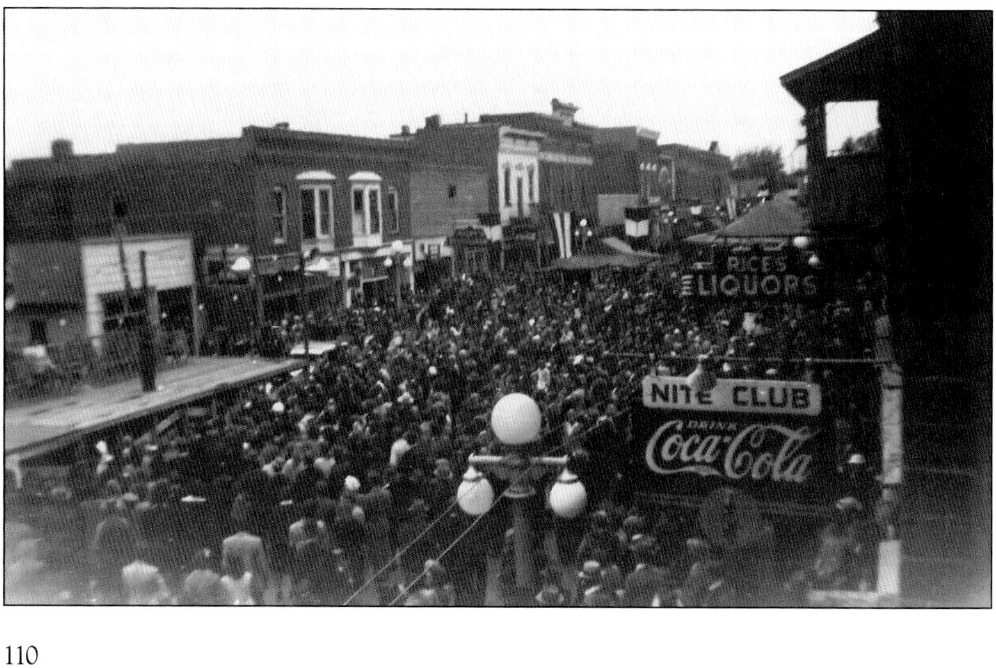

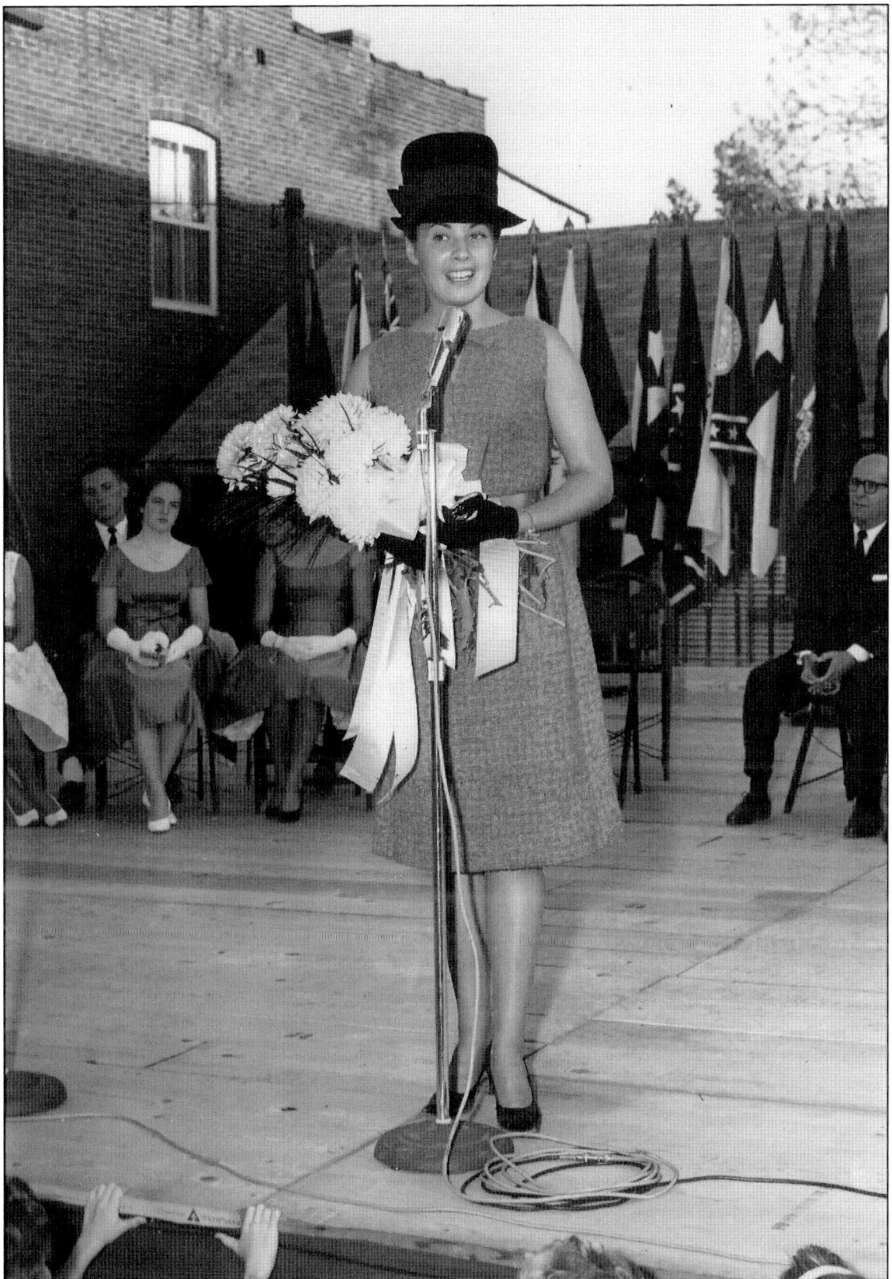

Miss America for 1963, Jackie Mayer, of Sandusky, Ohio, is seen onstage at the 1963 abbreviated fair. The fair was shortened to a single-day event due to legal issues involved with closing the state highway (Water Street) for the entire fair. But the disappointment of an abbreviated fair was negated somewhat by a visit from Miss America. Actually, Mayer was the past Miss America, this being one of her first public appearances since turning her crown over to the 1964 Miss America a few weeks prior. As painful as it was for many to see the Fall Fair end, its demise probably helped to create two new events that are enjoyed by many: the Ottawa County Fair and the Oak Harbor Apple Festival. (Linda Dehring.)

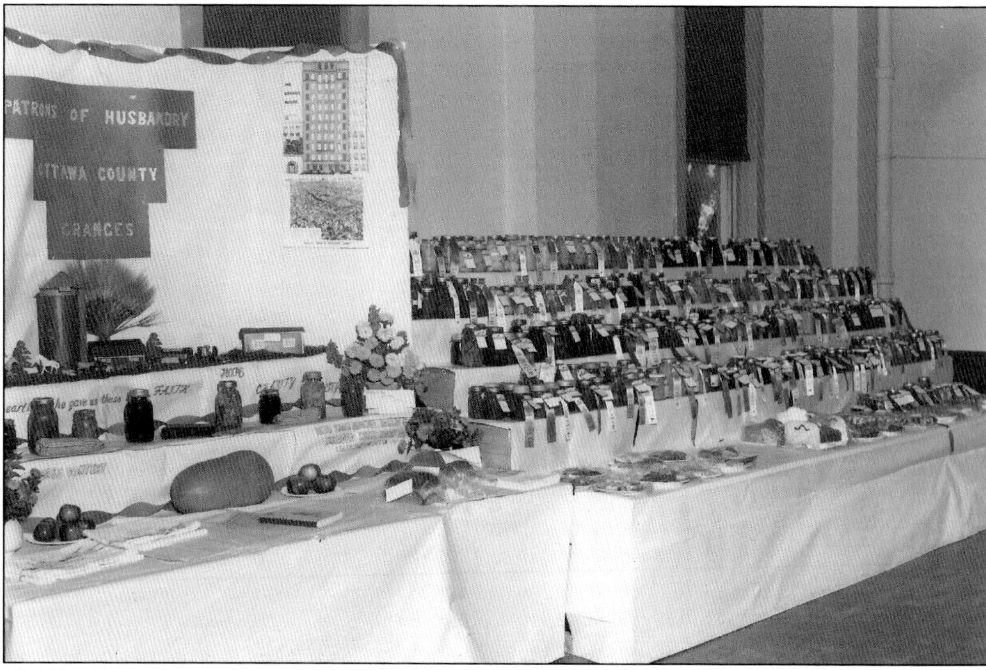

The Fall Fair offered opportunities for homemakers, 4-H youth, and others to show off their skills. This canning exhibit was in the town hall's main floor meeting room. On the left is a Grange display. Other displays were located in the armory and in vacant storefronts in the community. (Linda Dehring.)

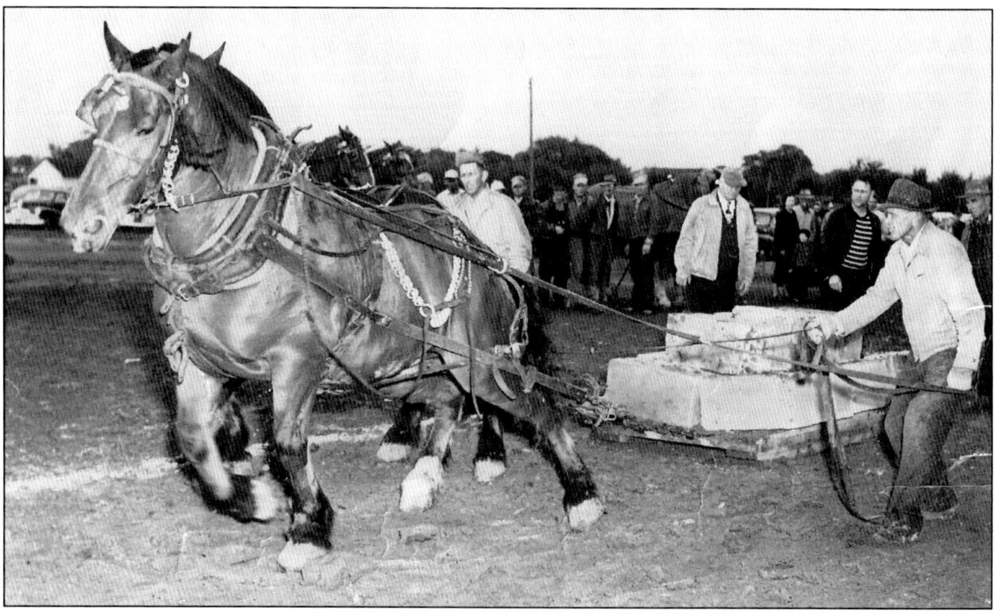

Another event of many Fall Fairs was the horse pull. In this photograph, William Hofacker and his horse pull a sled of cement blocks. This horse pull was held on the high school athletic field off of Walnut Street. The committee for early horse pulls included LeRoy Herring, Carl Bittner (county extension agent), Cy Frank, and Robert Thayer (vocational agricultural teacher). (Gaylyn and Robert Hofacker.)

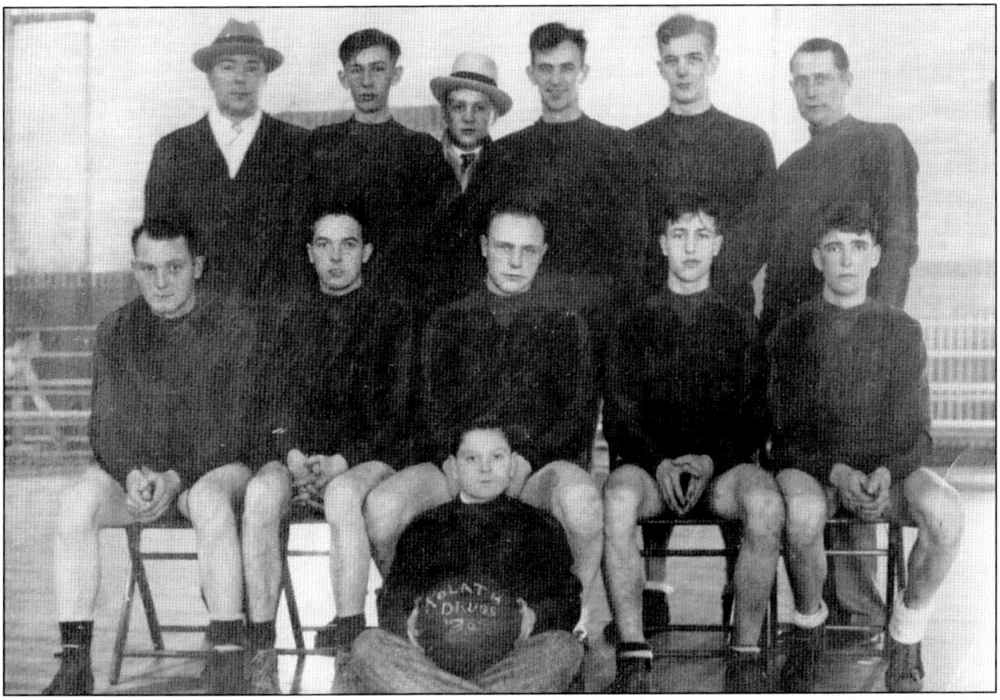

Sports participation often continued beyond high school with semipro teams, such as this 1930 Kolath Drug Store team. Team members include, in no set order, Edgar Kolath (sponsor), Howard Zimmerman, Grayson Gratop, Boozy Favro, Al Nissen, Rudy Fleckner, Red Stubblefield, Ray Forrester, Ronnie Keller, Norm Hetrick, Bill Kramb, and Skip Brindley (mascot). Games were played in the armory. (Mary Paulsen.)

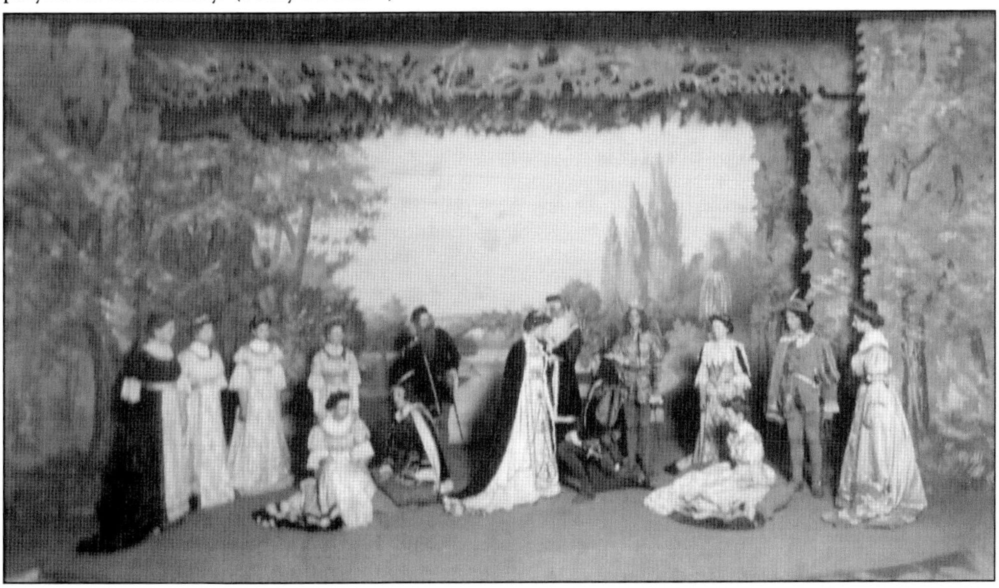

The second floor of the 1907 town hall contained a large auditorium with this stage. Many different organizations, including the Grange, Farmers' Institutes, schools, and churches put on plays, musicals, and orations for the community. High school graduations were also held here until 1938, when they were moved to the high school. (OHPL.)

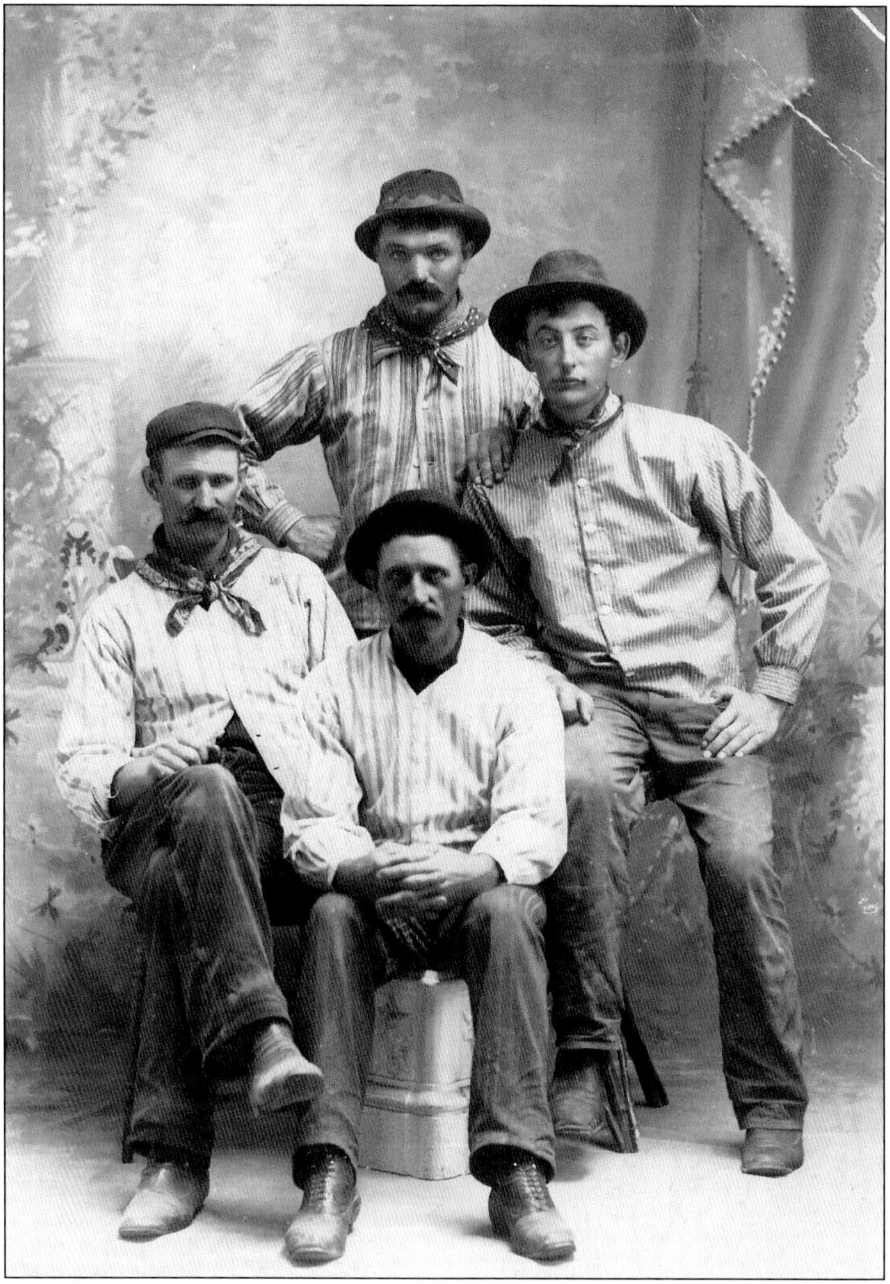

While life on the farm was hard work, it was not always dull for the community's young people. This photograph, entitled *Thresher Boys*, was taken about 1900 by Oak Harbor photographer George D. Smith. It shows four young men who apparently cleaned up after a dusty day threshing wheat and came to town to have their photograph taken. Perhaps they went to one of Oak Harbor's many saloons after the portrait for a cold adult beverage or two. The local newspaper at the turn of the century often listed a column called Lodges, Parties, and Doings, which told of the many sleighing parties, card games, and dances that the younger folks attended. It appears today's citizens' ancestors were a very social group. The men shown here are, clockwise from the top, John Link, Ballin Mylander, John Masonbrink, and William Smith. (Martin.)

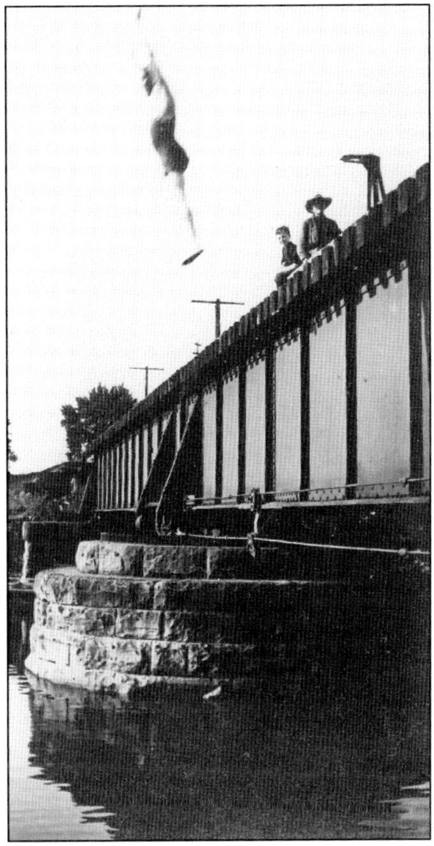

Living along the Portage provided entertainment for Oak Harbor's youth. Although definitely not allowed today, jumping off the railroad bridge in downtown Oak Harbor was a great way to beat the heat of a summer day. In 1880, the village passed an ordinance outlawing naked swimming after sunrise and before sunset. Does that mean it was allowed after dark? Is that ordinance still on the books? Below, three skaters enjoy the iced-over Portage on a winter day. When the ice was thick enough, young people took sleigh rides up and down the river. (Both, OHPL.)

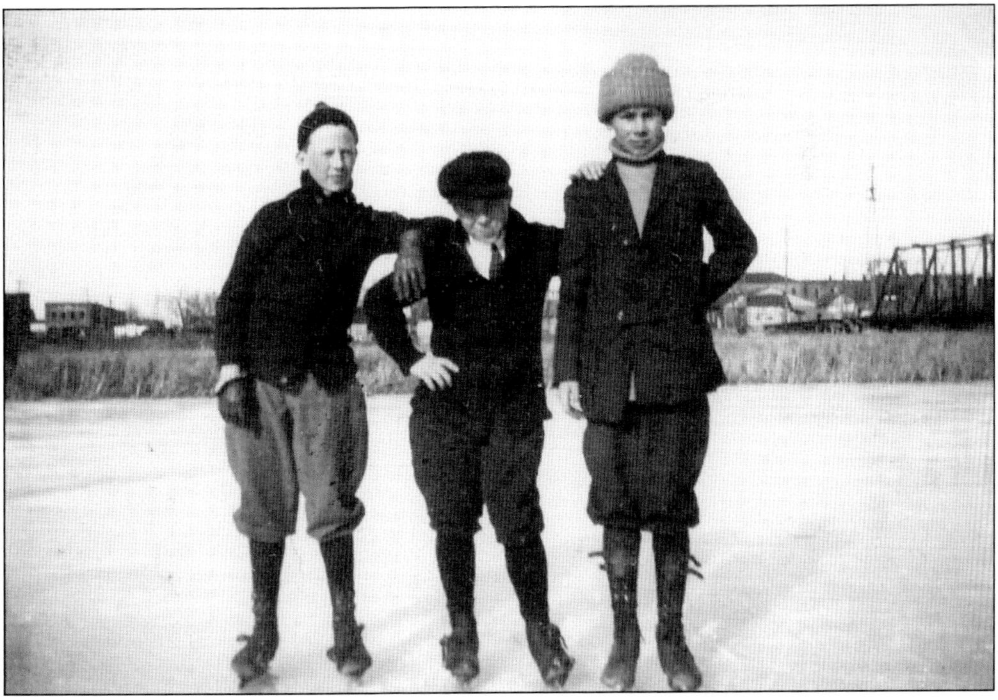

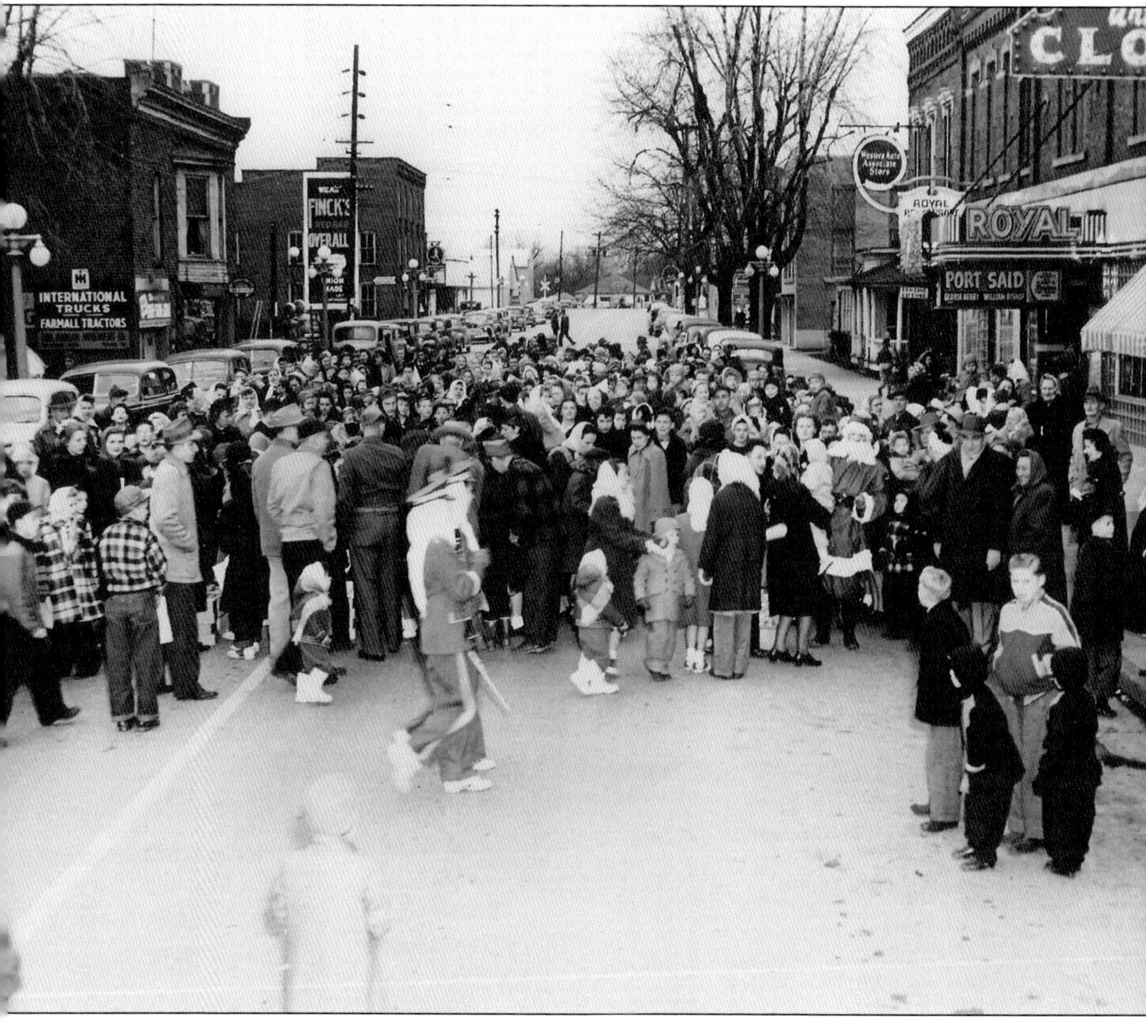

Hundreds of schoolchildren await Santa's arrival in front of the Royal Theater on Water Street in 1948. Children were given admission to a free cartoon show in the theater and an orange or some candy. In the 1950s, Oak Harbor school bus drivers treated their riders to a movie at the same theater on the way home from the last day of school before Christmas vacation. The three-story building on the left advertising Finck's overalls was the L.D. Link Blacksmith & Wagon Works, built after the 1894 fire. None of the buildings on the left side of the street remain today. (Liske.)

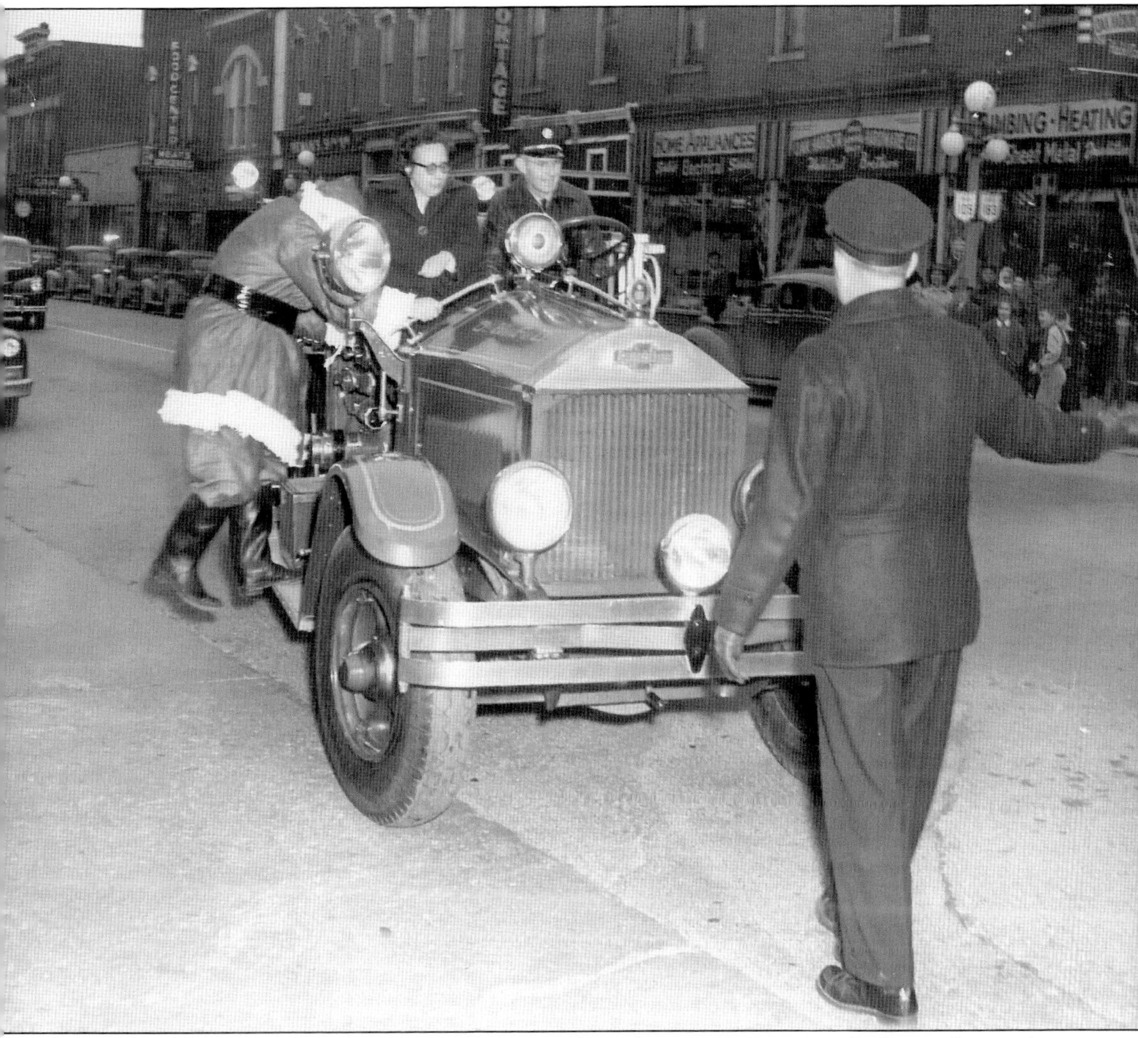

In this late-1940s photograph, Santa arrives on Oak Harbor's 1928 American LaFrance fire truck at the corner of Church and Water Streets. Shown here are, from left to right, Santa (unidentified), Margaret Kramb (clerk of Oak Harbor Board of Public Utilities), and Jack Pinson (fire chief). Police Chief Al Brown has his back to the camera. Note the children waiting in anticipation for Santa's arrival and the names of the businesses on the south side of Water Street. (Liske.)

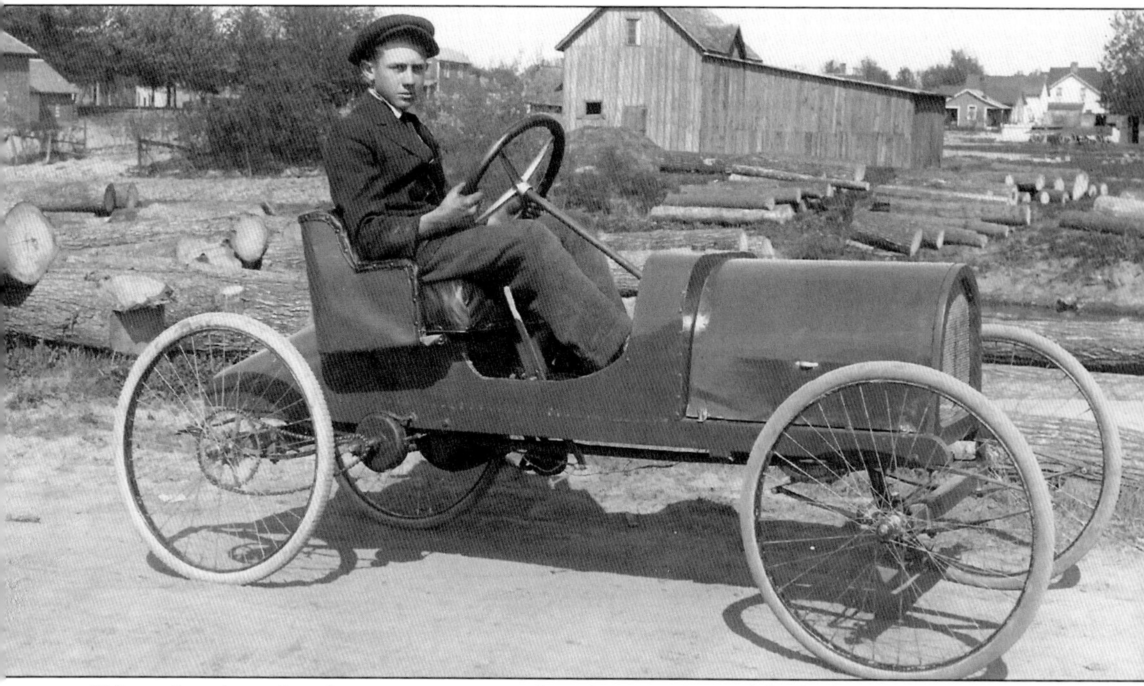

Talented students found interesting ways to keep busy. Ira Hetrick built this homemade car while a student in the manual training program at Oak Harbor High School in 1918. He won first prize for his efforts. The car was powered by a motorcycle engine from the Shea Motor Company in Toledo. The wheels on the car were bicycle wheels that were changed later for more rugged motorcycle wheels. Hetrick made several trips to Fremont in the car, which had only one light. He did not need a license to operate the car, but Oak Harbor's policeman, Smoky Kahler, warned him not to run with only one light at night. The logs in the background were for use by the basket factory. (Elizabeth Milbrodt.)

Nine

Our Neighbors

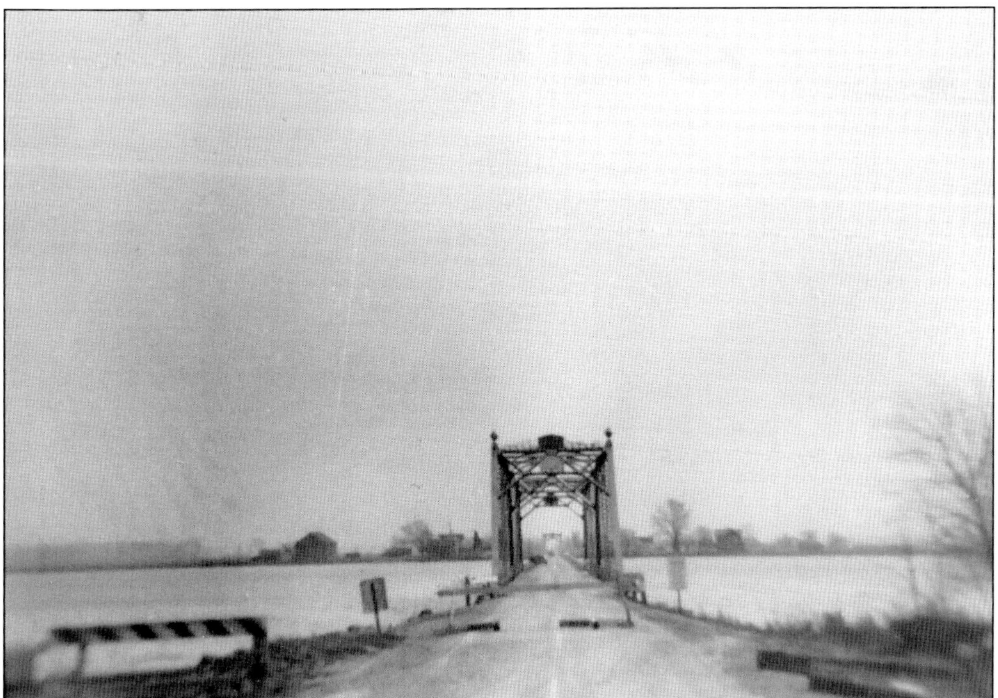

This bridge was actually a pair of bridges across the Toussaint River on State Route 19 north of Oak Harbor in Carroll Township. *Toussaint* is the French name for All Saints' Day. The river was reportedly named by Etienne Brulé, a French explorer/trapper who discovered and named the river on November 1, 1615. Locally, Toussaint is pronounced "Too'sang." (CTHC.)

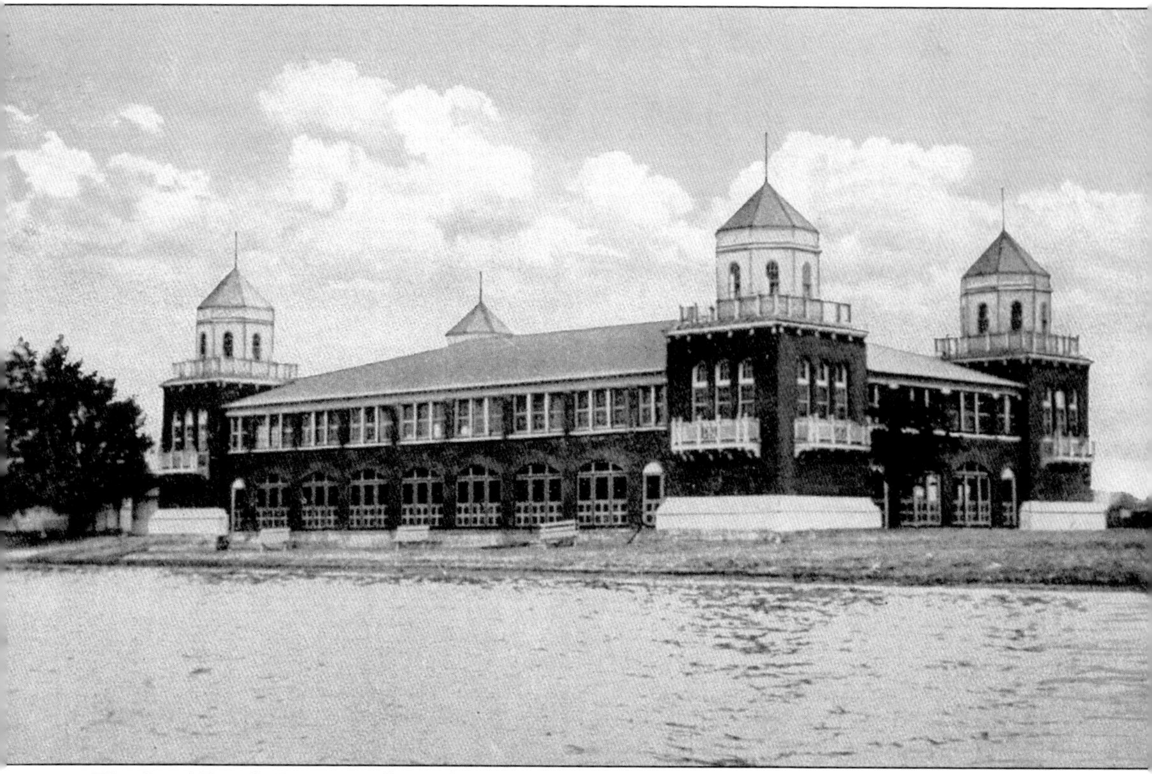

The Sand Beach Dance Hall Pavilion was located on Sand Beach in Carroll Township along Lake Erie. Construction began in 1924 and cost $100,000. The edifice was once the largest dance hall in the area. The magnificent two-story brick structure had a large dance floor that extended over the entire second floor. Refreshments were served on the first floor. During World War II, antiaircraft guns were mounted on the beach, naval personnel were quartered in the pavilion, and the guns were used to teach aerial gunnery. The building caught fire in the summer of 1944, when ammunition stored in the pavilion ignited, resulting in destruction of the second-floor dance hall and roof. The lower floor foundation remained for many years, but any evidence of this magnificent dance hall has long since vanished. (Liske.)

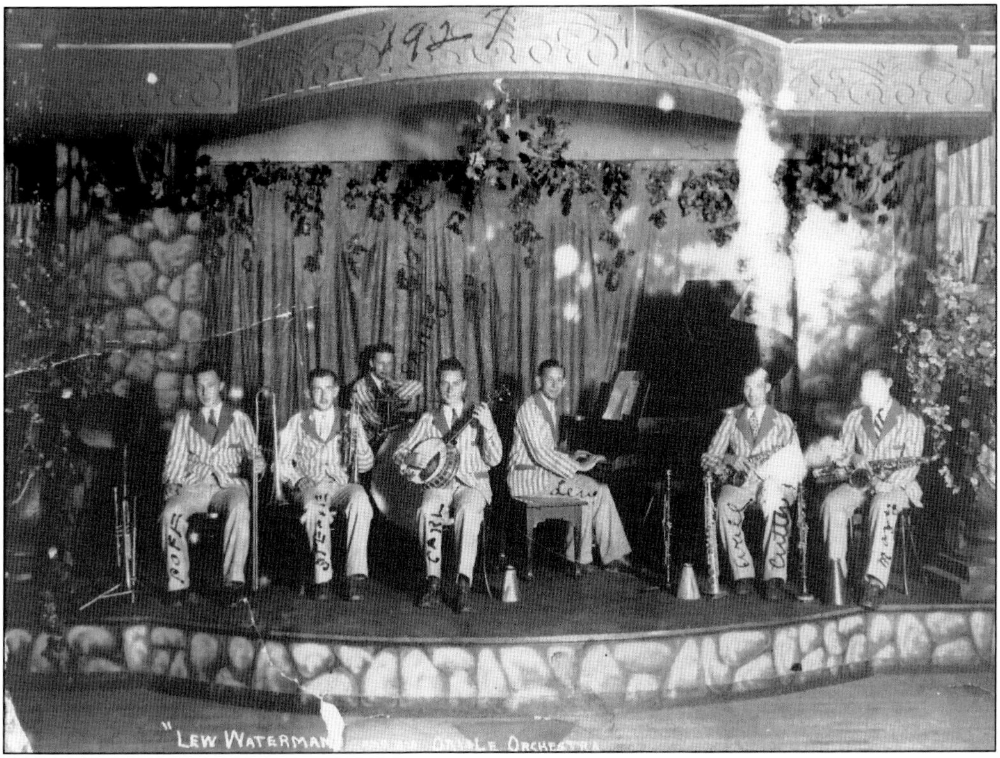

The Sand Beach Pavilion was popular during the Big Band era, and the roster of prominent acts that played there would fill a book. From this bandstand, orchestras such as Lew Waterman and His Oriole Band entertained massive crowds, which filled the hall on Saturday evenings. Admission was 75¢. (CTHC.)

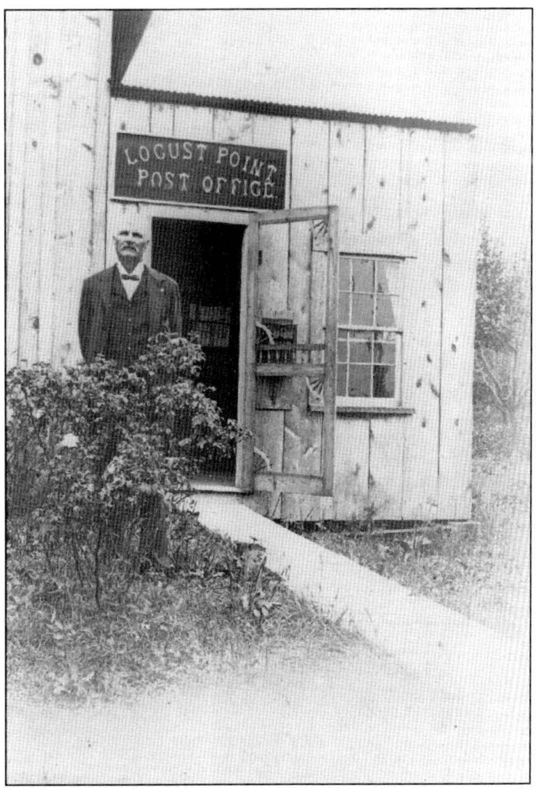

James Saddoris stands in front of the Locust Point Post Office, which was established on March 20, 1858. This structure, built in 1884–1885, was on the north bank of the Toussaint River. Half of the first floor was a post office and general store. The other portion of the building provided living quarters. The post office was decommissioned on December 12, 1903. (CTHC.)

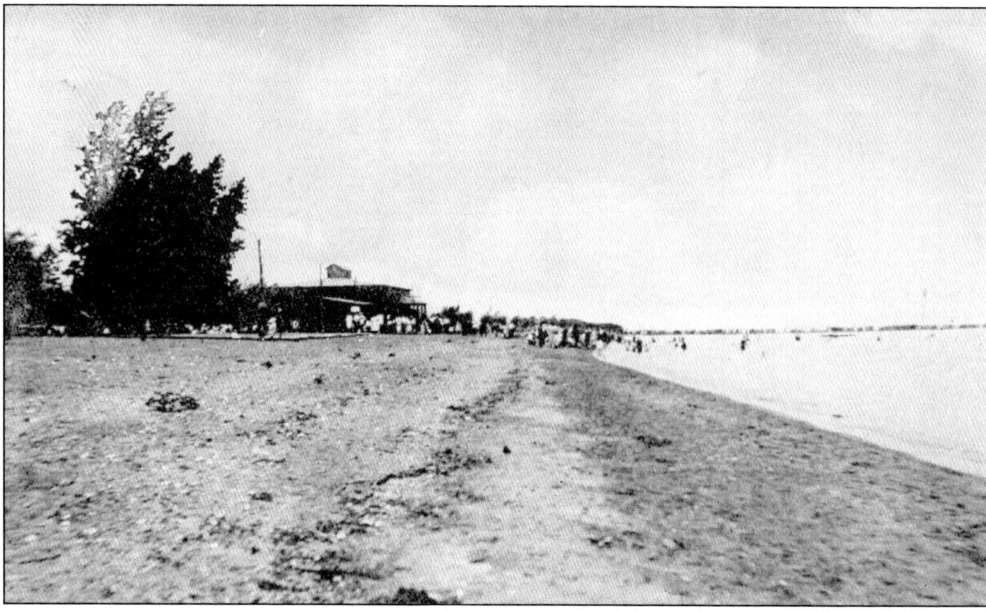

The beach at Locust Point became a mecca for swimmers and sunbathers. Many Toledo residents bought property and erected small summer cottages in the 1930s and 1940s. In the early part of the 20th century, Locust Point was home to an amusement park with a merry-go-round, skating rink, and other attractions. (Liske.)

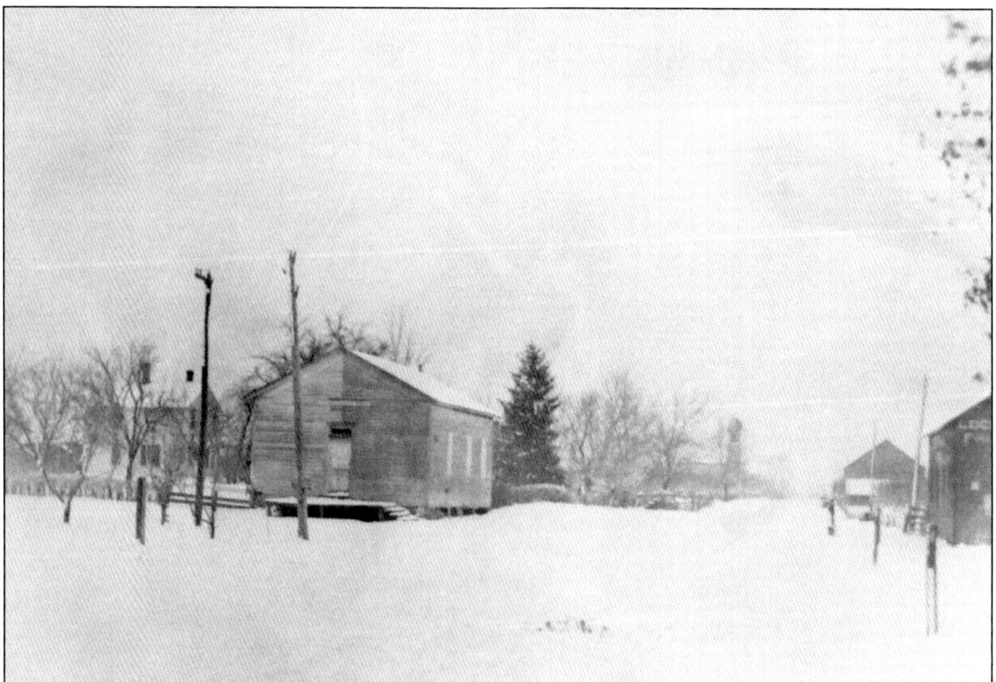

Winter comes to Nina, Ohio, a small area at the intersection of Toussaint South and Toussaint East Roads in Carroll Township. Enos Williams served as postmaster. The town derived its name from Williams's daughter, Nina. The Nina Post Office was authorized on December 23, 1858, and operated until October 31, 1903. (CTHC.)

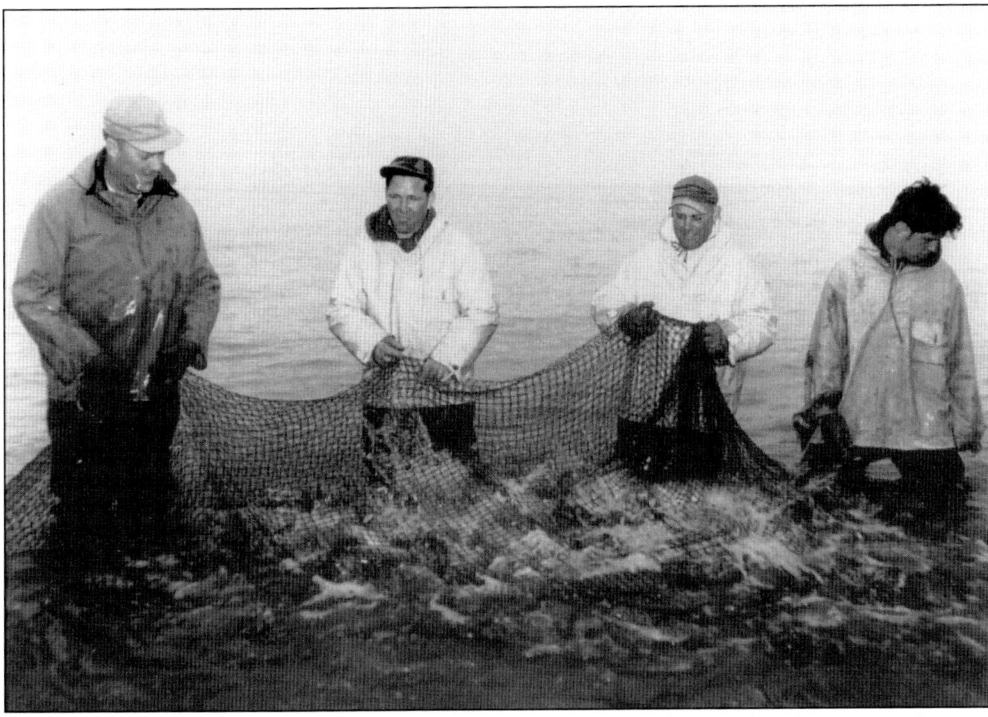

Some commercial fishing still continues on Lake Erie at Carroll Township, but it is no longer a main source of income. The area is thriving, however, with marinas and charter boats catering to today's sport fishermen. (CTHC.)

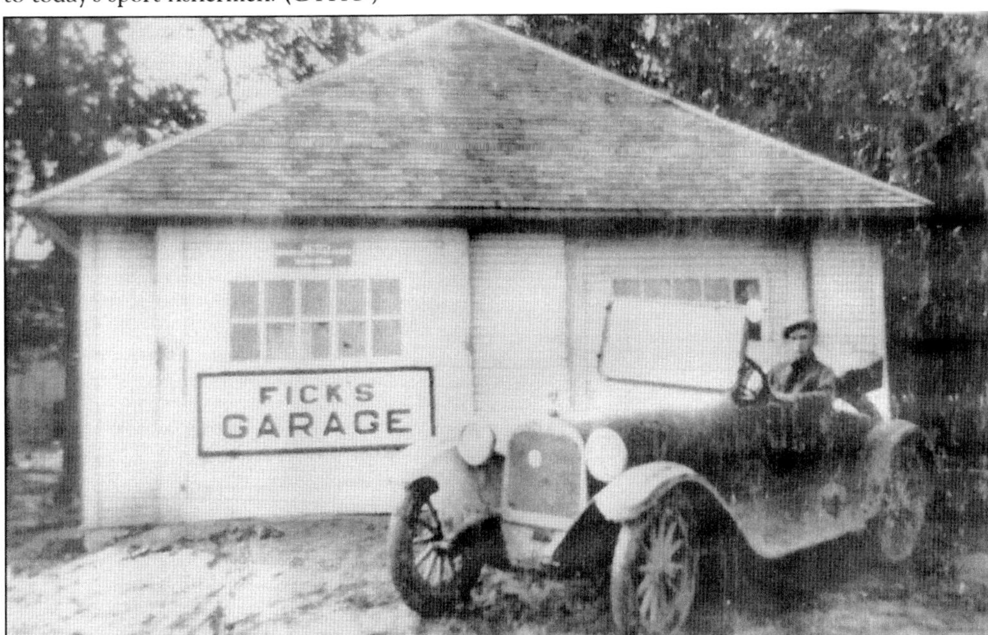

Small auto repair shops were common around the area. Fick's Garage, owned by mechanic Walter Fick, was in operation until the mid-1950s. The building, at 2770 Leutz Road in Carroll Township, still exists as a garage. (CTHC.)

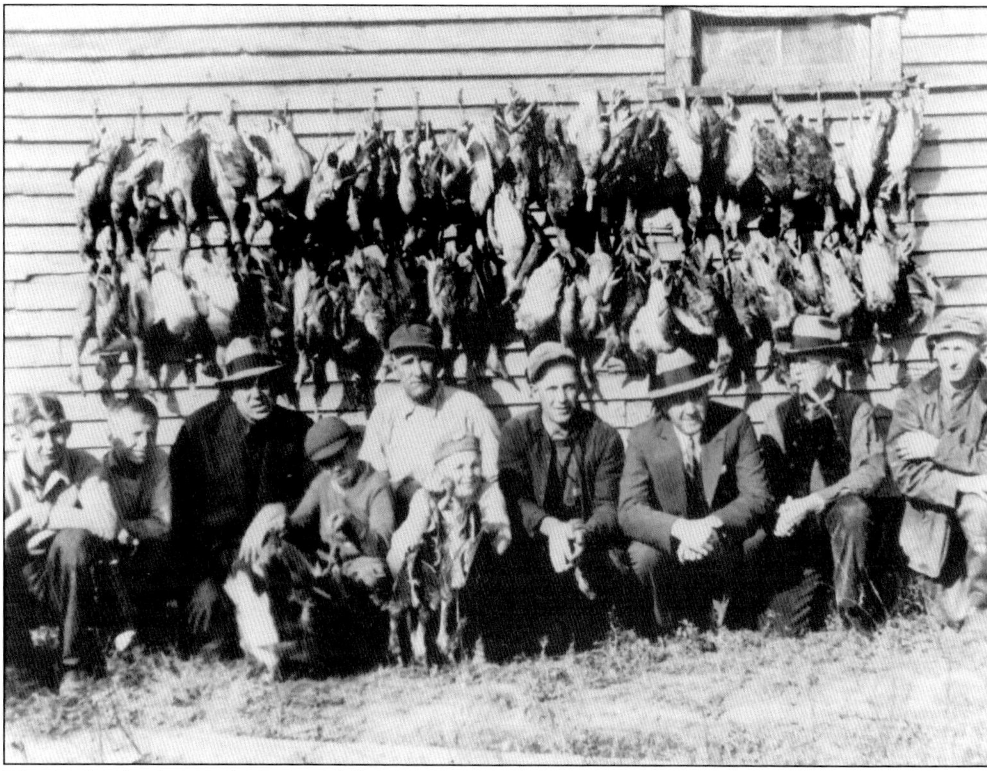

The lowlands along Lake Erie and the Toussaint River were favorite hunting grounds for sportsmen from all over the country. In the above photograph, hunters pose with their bounty. The area was so popular that Pres. Dwight D. Eisenhower visited on a hunting trip in 1958. Shown below are, from left to right, President Eisenhower, Virgil Priesman, Don Sinon, and Doris Mominee. (Both, CTHC.)

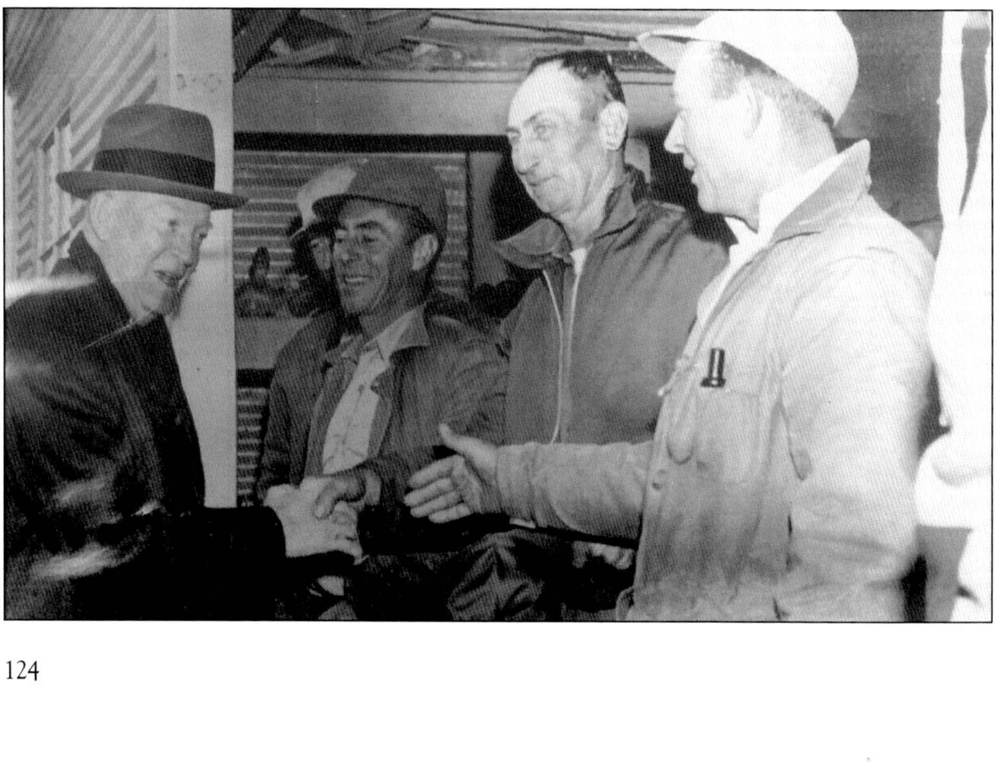

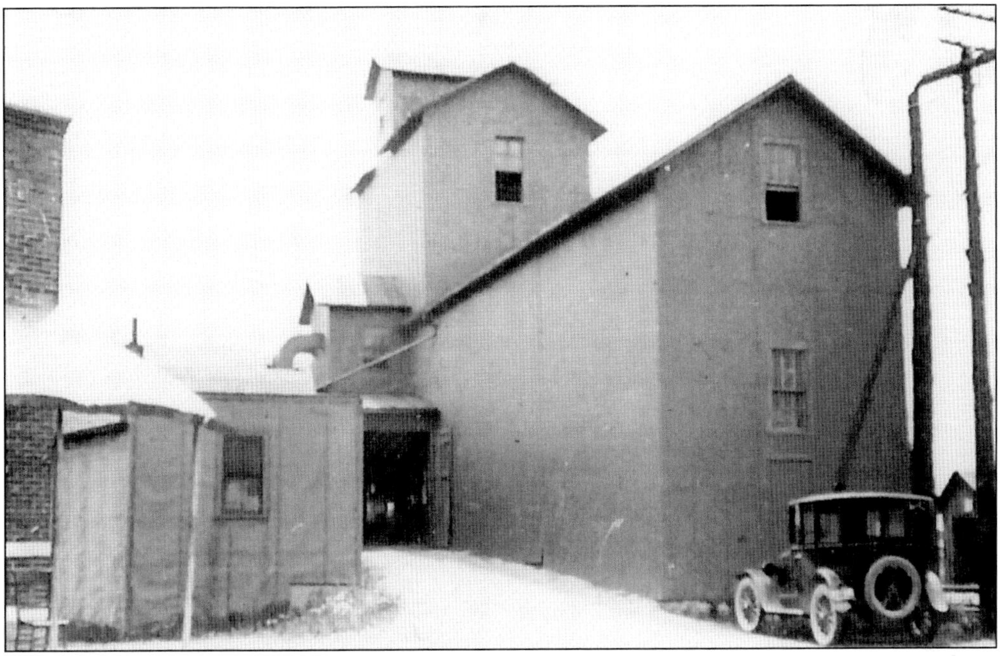

This grain elevator, located in the small community of Trowbridge in Benton Township, was a familiar symbol to the area's farming industry. Elevators like these dotted the landscape in nearly every small town. With major farming operations and large grain trucks, grain is now shipped to larger elevators, and these small facilities have all but disappeared. (Gluth.)

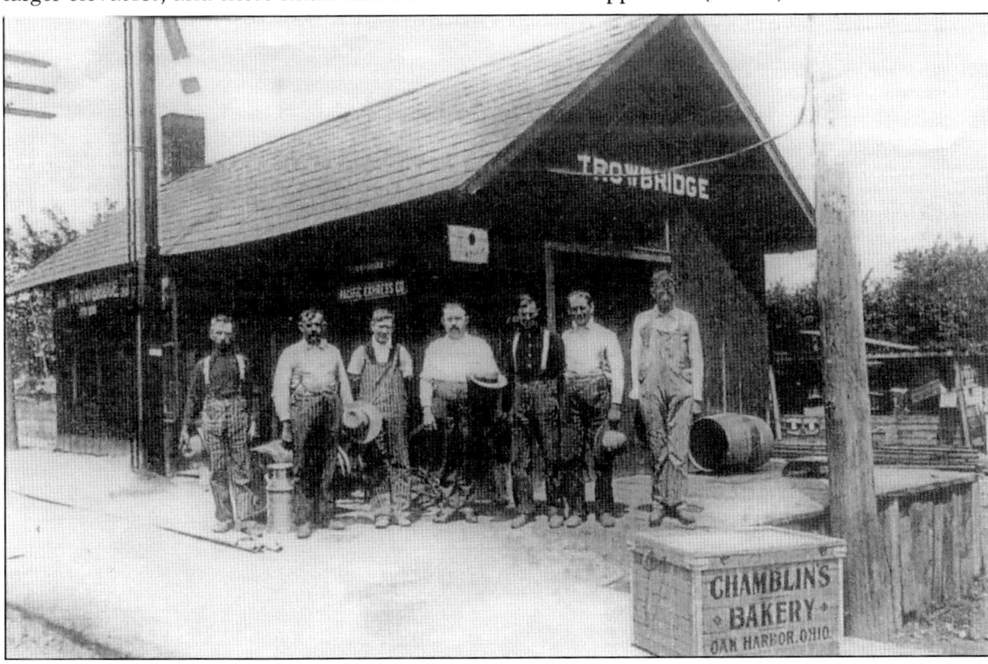

The Trowbridge depot on the Wheeling & Lake Erie Railway symbolized the connection between local residents and the larger world. Even in small towns, trains regularly stopped for passengers and freight. A victim of the automobile, most small-town rail stations in the area no longer exist. (Gluth.)

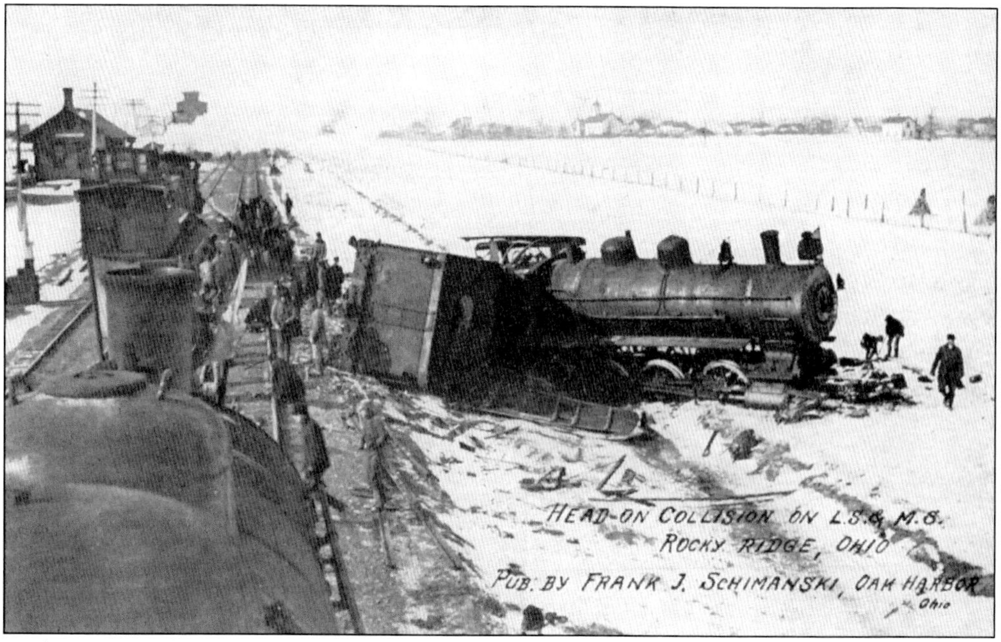

In the winter of 1906–1907, a head-on collision occurred in front of the Rocky Ridge depot. Two trains of the Lake Shore & Michigan Southern Railway collided. There were no fatalities, although, initially, it was feared that both the engineer and fireman of one engine would not live. They later recovered from their injuries. (OHPL.)

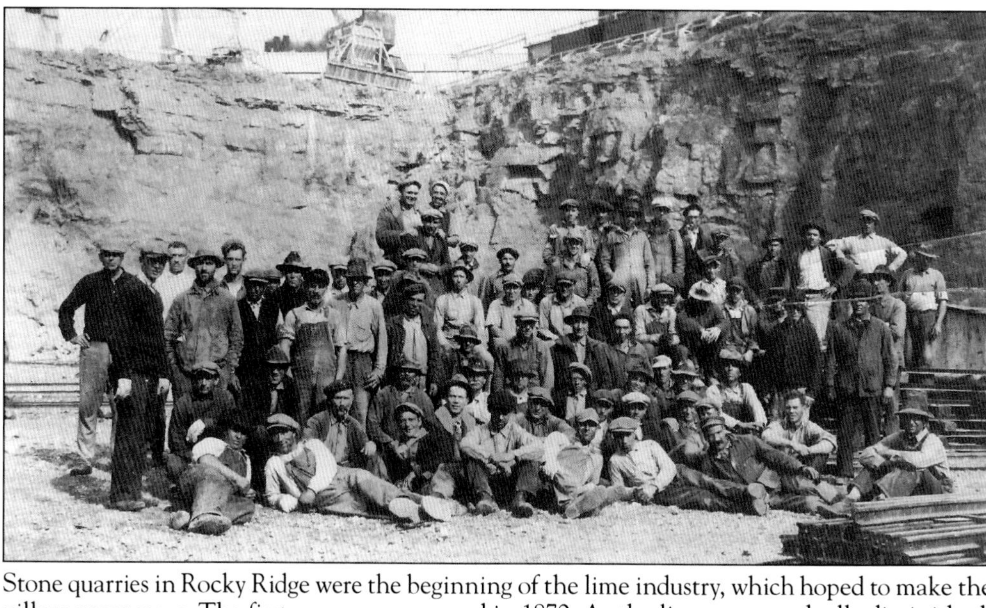

Stone quarries in Rocky Ridge were the beginning of the lime industry, which hoped to make the village prosperous. The first quarry was opened in 1870. As the limestone gradually diminished, the quarries were abandoned and eventually filled with water. One of the quarries was left intact, with rails and small railcars at the bottom. They can still be seen from the air. One of the quarry crews is shown here. (OHPL.)

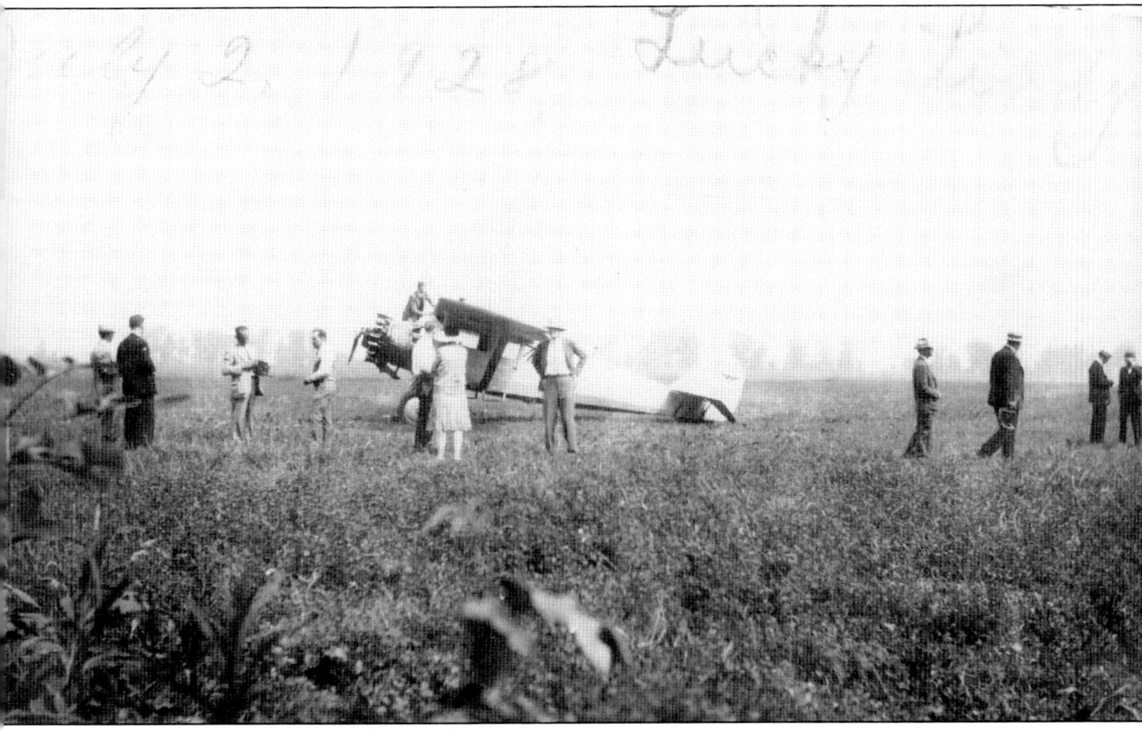

World-renowned aviator Col. Charles Lindbergh paid Ottawa County an unannounced visit on July 2, 1928, just over a year after his famous New York–Paris flight. Lindbergh and his party were making a nonstop flight in two planes from New York to Detroit when the Lindbergh plane ran out of fuel. An emergency landing was made in a Carroll Township field near Sand Beach. Gasoline from the second plane was used to refuel Lindbergh's plane. Lindbergh's mechanic, Emilo Carranza, stayed with the second plane while Lindbergh and his men took off for Detroit. With a guard from Sand Beach to watch over the plane, Carranza attended a dance at the Sand Beach Pavilion. The young ladies who danced with the mechanic spoke highly of his skill as a dancer. Carranza, the grandson of a former president of Mexico, was tragically killed in a plane crash less than two weeks later. (Larry Lickert.)

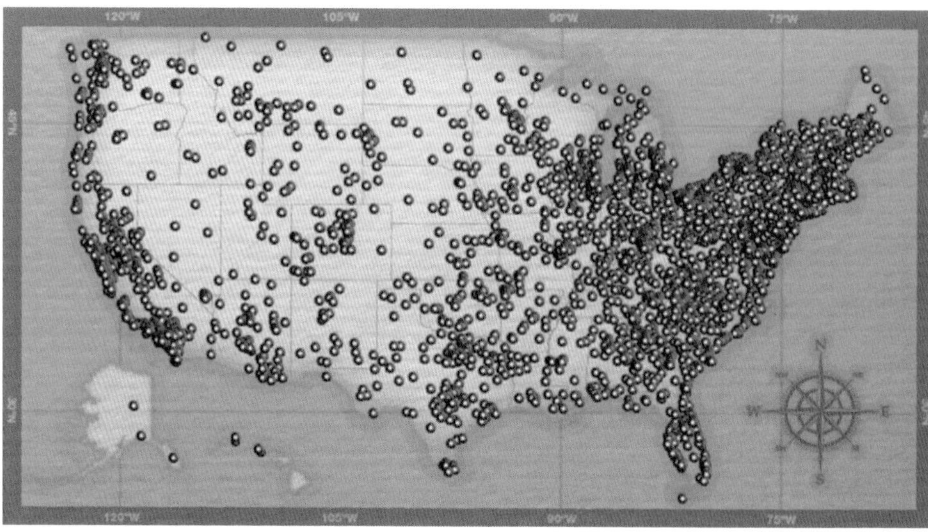